# THE
# INVISIBLE HAND

# THE INVISIBLE HAND

by
## Victor Dunstan

MEGIDDO PRESS LTD.
CARDIFF, S.WALES
1984

*Published 1984 by*
*Megiddo Press Ltd,*
*Grosvenor House,*
*20 St. Andrews Crescent,*
*CARDIFF, S.Glamorgan. U.K.*

*ISBN 0 946922 00 4*

# Contents

# 1.
# The Invisible Hand - The Silent Voice

Most of us enjoy reading our horoscopes in the morning papers though, I suspect, few of us give them much credence.

The possibility of there being someone who can foretell future events, though it fills us with a certain foreboding, also fascinates us. That's why almost every publication in the Western world carries a 'What the Stars Foretell' column and why the casters and publishers of horoscopes are so numerous.

Now I want you to imagine that one morning you open your morning paper, read your horoscope and, during the day, find that it has come to pass in the minutest detail. Imagine further that many of the prognostications were most unlikely to happen but did: How would you feel about the foretelling business then?

Well, if you are as incredulous of these things as I, you would attribute the whole thing to coincidence but certainly you would read your horoscope in the same paper the following day.

Let us assume that each day's horoscope predicted something quite involved, unlikely but specific. Not the proverbial 'You will meet a tall dark stranger' but rather 'You will meet a complete stranger. He will have red hair, be driving a large American car painted red, green and purple, be of Irish birth but have been brought up in Hawaii and have a wart in the middle of his forehead.' If every word of that came to pass what would your feelings be then?

Perhaps, if you are as cynical as I, you would be impressed, surprised, and would regard it as a very good after-dinner story. You wouldn't, of course, expect people to believe you but, just maybe, you yourself would have the beginnings of an eerie feeling deep inside you. You may begin to feel that there was something more to this thing than chance. That predictions so unlikely and so specific came to pass would no doubt make you feel that to attribute their fulfilment to chance was to stretch the admittedly long arm of coincidence to it's limits

Let us assume that predictions similarly detailed, and just as unlikely, came to pass the next day, and the day after that, and the following day again. Would you then, be you the most ardent cynic, not have to give the most serious consideration to the phenomena? It would be a foolish person indeed who in the face of such evidence would disregard the possibility of there being something supernormal or at least 'beyond our ken' about the fulfilment of such predictions.

I have asked you to imagine. You may well think what I have asked you to imagine is very unlikely to take place and yet, as we shall see in the following pages, there are many ancient writings of prediction which are detailed, specific and were, at the time of writing, very unlikely to come to pass, but which have been fulfilled precisely. Such predictions have often dealt with events several thousand years future to the time in which the seer lived. Sometimes the prognostications seemed absolutely contradictory and the fulfilment impossible until events proved otherwise.

The question we will ask in this book is : Did those ancient seers have the ability to foresee and foretell future world events? If so, are there unfulfilled prophecies which are to be fulfilled in our day and age? Are their predictions of any value to us other than mere interest value? Perhaps the most fascinating question is: Is the world really under the control of mankind or is there an 'invisible hand' moving mankind toward an ultimate foreseen or predestined destination?

I will not suggest that all the answers to such questions are to be found in this book, nor do I profess to know all the answers. The question, however, is of undoubted importance — who ultimately controls this planet Earth? There are a whole range of possibilities; that the world plunges hither and thither, it's history dictated by the mental aberrations of a minority of it's inhabitants, a Hitler here or a Stalin there; that mankind will continue until some crazed specimen is produced who will be insane enough to press the wrong button. But what if there is, after all, a power, a 'something out-there', an 'invisible hand' guiding the actions of men, fitting them into the jig-saw of some super-plan?

It is my hope that you will find this book both enjoyable and entertaining. If it broadens public debate about the future of our planet — so be it, and, if you, my reader, find the material convincing, that will be a bonus.

## THE ANCIENT SEERS

Many thousands of years ago there lived in the land of ancient Israel seers, men who claimed to be able to see into the distant future and predict the things which would come upon the earth many thousands of years after their time.

Their belief was that all earth's history is ordered by a 'supreme being' and that, far from following an eratic course, the affairs of men and of nations are guided by an 'invisible hand' and follow a pattern foreordained and foreseeable. They claimed to have a unique relationship with the great universal spirit — a being, incidentally, quite unlike the God of commercialised religion as depicted in icon, effigy and painting. Their claim was that this 'spirit' or influence 'spoke' to them and that they were able to 'speak' to him. Furthermore, they recorded in permanent form the messages of warning, guidance and prediction they claimed he communicated to them.

All this would be of only historic interest if it were not for the fact that they spoke of events taking place in a time they called 'the end time' and 'the last days'. They gave dates which many believe have relevance to our time.

They predict, these ancient seers, events both horrific and hopeful for all mankind. They foresee that last great battle of earth's history, Armageddon, and their words are both majestic and horrific:

*For I will gather all nations against Jerusalem to battle; and the city shall be taken, the houses rifled and the women ravished... Then shall the Lord go forth and fight against those nations, as when He fought in the day of battle ... and this shall be the plague with which the Lord will smite all the peoples who have fought against Jerusalem: their flesh shall consume away while they stand upon their feet, and their eyes shall consume away in their holes, and their tongue shall consume away in their mouth.*

The Book of Zechariah 14.

Another prophet predicting a massive invasion of Palestine in the 'last days' writes:

*And the word of the Lord came unto me, saying, Son of man, set thy face against Gog, of the land of Magog, the chief prince of Meshech and Tubal, and prophesy against hem,*
*And say, Thus saith the Lord God: Behold, I am against thee, O Gog, the chief prince of Meshech and Tubal,*
*After many days thou shalt be visited; in the latter years thou shalt come into the land that is brought back from the sword, and is gathered out of many peoples, against the mountains of Israel, which have been always waste; but it is brought forth out of the nations, and they shall dwell safely, all of them.*
*Thou shalt ascend and come like a storm; thou shalt be like a cloud to cover the land, thou, and all thy hordes, and many peoples with thee ... And thou shalt come up against my people of Israel, like a cloud to cover the land; it shall be in the latter days, and I will bring thee against my land, that the nations may know me, when I shall be sanctified in thee, O Gog, before their eyes.*
Book of Ezekiel Chapter 38. V. 1,2,3,8,9, & 16.

Some of the national names used by the prophet were the names of the nations at the time he prophesied: It is most interesting to see who occupies those territories today. Which major nation on earth today occupies the territory of 'Gog'? The answer is inclined to make one view world events in a very different light.

## MYSTERIOUS PREDICTIONS

Though many of the ancient seers did not meet and did not have access to each others writings, and though some of them lived many hundreds of years apart, they all agreed on the events which were yet future to their time.

We shall see how they predicted the coming of 'The Most Mysterious Man Who Ever Lived', foretelling the date of his birth, the number of years he would live and exactly, in detail, the kind of death he would die. We shall see, too, how astronomy has brought what many people regarded as a myth 'in from the cold'.

Examining the writings of one ancient seer, we shall see how he foretold five hundred years of human history from the time of Cyrus to the time of Tiberius Caesar. He wrote of Cleopatra 450 years before she was born. Similarly we will read of the prophet who gave not only the details of the destruction of a great city but gave the NAME of the commander of the forces that destroyed it 175 years BEFORE that commander was born.

There is, too, in these pages, mention of the ancient seer who

4

pre-empted Charles Darwin and his theory of evolution by three thousand years and how science today is finding that the ancient seer was RIGHT in those matters in which Darwin had disagreed with him.

We shall investigate fully the predictions of the two prophets who foretold the outcome of a battle in the First World War, almost 2,000 years before that war took place. Not only did the ancient seers tell of the battle and it's outcome but the location of the battle, the year of the battle and the exact DAY of the battle.

What did the ancient seers say about the end of the world? Did they give a date for 'The end of the world'? Why does the year 1992 loom so large in their predictions?

In 1948 David Bengurion proclaimed the Jewish State of Israel in the Land of Palestine. We shall see that the prophet writing 2,500 years before the event foretold in which year the Jewish State of Israel would be set up. How did the ancient seers know that the exact name would be "The JEWISH State of Israel" and not simply "The State of Israel"?

We shall see how the ancient seers foretold the events taking place in our generation; what they said about the peace movements, the League of Nations, the United Nations Organisation and the 'Ban the Bomb' people.

Adolf Hitler, Mussolini, Marx and Stalin were all socialists — what else did they have in common?

The ancient seers had a lot to say about a revival of Islam which is due to take place in the next few years, a revival which goes far beyond anything we have seen in Iran, and about the rise of Islam as a mighty military and economic power — but only for a short time.

Britain, the Commonwealth and the United States of America are to become one nation according to the prophets. How and why is a fascinating story which began over 3,900 years ago in Mesopotamia.

Will there be a Third World War? If so, where will it be fought and who will be the protagonists? What will be the outcome? The ancient seers answer all those questions!

Is there a prophetic clock by which we can 'tell the time' at which we live in earth's history? If so, are we living at a-minute-to-midnight? What are the secrets of telling the time by the prophetic clock?

The ancient seers foretell that the greatest economic and financial disaster ever to afflict the world is about to take place. The ancient seers predict when, why and how.

The prophets all foretold that Jerusalem would be the focal point of national unrest at 'the end of the age' and the cause of a world-wide conflagration. They describe, too, an event which was not possible in their time and which did not become possible until 1945 when the first nuclear weapon was unleashed on Japan:

*The day of the Lord will come as a thief in the night, in which the*
*heavens shall pass away with a great noise, and the elements shall*

*melt with a fervent heat ... seeing then that all these things shall be dissolved, what manner of people ought you to be ... looking for and hasting unto the coming day of God, in which the heavens, being on fire shall be dissolved, and the elements shall melt with a fervent heat? Nevertheless we, according to his promise, look for new heavens and a new earth ...*

Second Book of Peter. Parts of Chapter 3.

We shall later examine these prophecies at greater length and in greater detail. Meanwhile we may dwell on the words "melt with a fervent heat" and "all these things shall be dissolved" and ask ourselves if these phrases are not applicable to a nuclear explosion. But is not 2,000 years rather a long time ago to have anticipated atomic warfare? Why, my old science master, just before the Second World War, was teaching the impossibility of splitting the atom, and my Sunday school teacher used to explain how the heavens could NOT melt with a fervent heat, so, he said, Peter must have meant something quite different — surprising how ideas change, isn't it?

The seers were not always prophets of doom, however, they also give assurances of the survival of the planet Earth and tell of ultimate universal peace. Their prophetic vision pierced the shrouding mists of time, right through the darkening clouds of tribulation and the war, famine and pestilence which they foresaw afflicting the latter day man, to the time when the lion would lie down with the lamb, and men would beat their swords into ploughshares.

All the prophets agree with the last of the great Israelite seers when he writes:

*And I saw a new heaven and a new earth for the first heaven and the first earth were passed away... and there shall be no more death, neither sorrow, nor crying, neither shall there be any more pain; for the former things have passed away.*

The Apocalypse. Parts of Chapter 21.

The prophets paint a picture of a world going through the 'Valley of the Shadow of Death', of a time which they call 'The Great Tribulation' and they see it emerging at the other side of that dark valley, a glorious place to live.

Jerusalem and Palestine are the centre of the stage for this last drama though, if we interpret the prophets aright, Britain and America are to be recognised in their prophecies too, as is the Soviet Union.

Perhaps, when you have finished reading this book and you read your morning newspaper, you will feel that what we are witnessing is not just a random movement of nations and policies but rather a fitting together of a great jigsaw. Perhaps as good an explanation as any of the seemingly irrational behaviour of planet Earth's so-called civilized societies?

## NO NUCLEAR DESTRUCTION IN BRITAIN OR AMERICA

Much we will investigate will be sad and some of it frightening, but one consolation from the writings of the ancient seers will be that Britain and America need never fear mass destruction through nuclear war on their shores, nor need they fear ultimate defeat. There are indications, too, that we are almost at the end of history's dark tunnel and that the future is exceedingly bright.

The writings and predictions of many of the seers are preserved for us in the ancient Hebrew Scriptures, better known to us as 'The Old Testament' and many others are to be found in what we know today as 'The New Testament'.

Perhaps I should make it plain at the outset that, though I use the predictions of the seers of old as I find them recorded in the ancient scriptures, this is certainly not a book which will give comfort to organised religion. Though my source material is largely taken from the books upon which the church bases it's teachings, yet the difference of interpretation is such that many a 'religious' person may find his thinking turned upside-down.

With the greatest respect to those committed people of many faiths, I must say I regard their version of God — the God made in the image of man— as almost completely spurious. I further feel that no good can come of our investigations into the ancient writings and the predictions of the ancient seers if we do not shake off, for at least as long as it takes to read this book, the constraints of thought which have been put upon us by the interpretations of ancient writ by organised religion.

## THE MOST PROLIFIC BOOK OF PREDICTION IN THE WORLD

Much of superstition-ridden Christendom has altogether missed the sheer wonder of the book it has purported to extol. Had they read it thoroughly and with minds unfettered by generations of wholly unjustified tradition, they would see in ancient writ their own condemnation.

The 'Bible' is a Book of PREDICTION — how many churches will accept that? At the time the ancient scripts which now compose the Bible were written, two thirds of them were written to PREDICT FUTURE EVENTS. That makes the Bible the most prolific book of prediction in the world!

Perhaps as we examine the writings of the ancient seers, my readers will be surprised to see that their writings are both POLITICAL and NATIONALISTIC.

Certainly this book, which graced the homes of many of our ancestors as the family aspidistra stand, is the most MYSTERIOUS book in the world. Though it is comprised of 66 books — written by people of diverse backgrounds — shepherds, kings, rich men, poor men, men who lived in palatial surroundings, men who wandered the deserts clothed in rags and living in caves, and even a prisoner condemned to penal servitude in a marble quarry — there is a oneness, an uncanny oneness, about it as though it were dictated by one 'universal mind'. The first author was dead a thousand years or more before the last author was born, yet all the authors tell one story.

Mysterious, too, is the fact that though few of the authors met and fewer still were able to compare ideas or read each other's writings — they ALL foretell exactly the same events.

It is regarded almost as heresy among many to write the things I am about to write, that is the ancient writings were written to WARN US OF THINGS WHICH ARE TO HAPPEN IN THE NEXT FEW YEARS.

## THE UNUSUAL PATRIOTS

One thing all the ancient seers had in common was that they were all great patriots of their nation — Israel. It is therefore surprising that the constantly reccuring theme of their message is the decline of the nation of Israel. As one would expect, such a message made them very unpopular. Nevertheless they continued speaking their message, suffering often indescribable deprivation in the process.

It would seem the more natural thing for a patriot to exhort his nation to greatness. Hopeful visions of the future one could understand, but not their constant predictions of deportation, loss of national identity, persecution and tribulation, with the only rays of hope several thousand years in the future.

Yet they were convinced they spoke words given them by a 'being' they called the 'Lord'. Therefore, despite unpopularity, they persistently foretold the destruction of their people — and what they foretold came to pass, quite literally, in the way they said it would and at the time they said it would.

They foretold the subjugation of their land hundreds of years before it happened. They foretold the division of their nation into two parts — their nation did become divided into two parts! They foretold the destruction of the most holy place in their kingdom, the Temple — the Temple was destroyed! They foretold the cessation of the most sacred happening in their religion, the daily sacrifice — the daily sacrifice ceased!

The seers foretold the coming of the Messiah-God to die. A rather unusual concept of the ultimate deliverer?

In their predictions the major empires of the world are seen rising, and falling into oblivion. The rise, consolidation and decay of the world's economic, social and political systems are predicted from the corruption of ancient Babylon to the corruption of the Soviet Union today.

I will attempt to show in this book that the majority of the messages of the ancient seers concerned the twentieth century — THE DAYS IN WHICH WE LIVE.

"The time of the end" is a phrase much used by the prophets. We sha see that we live in this "time of the end" — the time when our world wil divide into three great and conflicting systems of thought and government the time when there will be a great gathering of the whole world to a Thirc World War, a time of tribulation followed by universal peace — FOREVER.

## THE DEATH OF PRESIDENT JOHN F. KENNEDY PREDICTED

On November 22nd, 1963, a young lady by the name of Jean Dixon told friends in Washington D.C. "My mind isn't at ease. I am afraid our President will suffer something terrible today." She was right — the world was stunned by the news of the assassination of President John F. Kennedy. Little wonder Jean Dixon has become one of the most famous predictors of future events in the United States of America.

Wonderful as her predictions are, they do not compare with the prophecies we shall consider. The ancient seers did not predict events which would happen the following day, or week, or year, but often events which were hundreds, even thousands of years hence.

A Dr. Grattan Guiness wrote a book in the year 1887 entitled "Light for the Last Days". He applied his mathematical skill to dates given, thousands of years previously, in the writings of the ancient seers. Working solely from their dates and neither applying nor claiming any psychic gifts of his own, he foretold that Jerusalem would be delivered from the Turks in the year 1917. This prediction was based purely upon mathematical deduction from the writings of men who had written THREE THOUSAND years before his time.

The deliverance of Jerusalem not only happened in the YEAR foretold, but on the exact DAY foretold all those thousands of years before. We'll examine that event, and much more, in depth in the following pages.

Is there an 'invisible hand' and has it written the horoscope of the nations? Are we after all, not the masters of our own destiny? Were the seers in tune in a very special way with some 'influence' outside of our sphere, which for the want of a better phrase we may call the "Great Universal Spirit"?

We know that a degree of telepathy can exist between human beings, thoughts can be transferred without sound being emitted, Is it not just possible that certain men in past ages had a sense which we appear not to have? Was this sense an ability to receive messages from that 'something' beyond our senses? Has this 'something' been desperately trying to trickle messages through to such people as are attuned to 'It's' wavelength?

Perhaps it is trying to bring our species back from the brink of self-made disaster. It would be a comforting thought if there were someone we could rely on for good advice, wouldn't it?

## THE ACID TEST

To claim contact with the Great Spirit of the universe is no ordinary claim, yet such is the claim these ancient seers made. They were not, of course, alone, in their day, in making such a claim, there were many who made pretentions to having what we would today call 'a hot line' to their gods.

The difference between the ancient seers we shall study and the others lies in the results of their prophesying. They themselves laid down the test to be passed by those who professed to speak the name of the Supreme Being; it carried with it the DEATH PENALTY for failure:

> *But the prophet who shall presume to speak a word in my name, which I have not commanded him to speak, or who shall speak in the name of other gods, even that prophet shall die. And if thou say in thine heart, How shall we know the word which the Lord hath not spoken? When a prophet speaketh in the name of the Lord, if the thing follow not, nor come to pass, that is the thing with the Lord hath not spoken, but the prophet hath spoken it presumptuously.*

Book of Deuteronomy. Chapter 18.

Faced with such a death penalty the foretelling of future events became a very precarious business indeed.

On the eve of the British General Election in 1970 the Public Opinion Polls almost unanimously predicted a Labour victory. The predictions were based upon well proven, scientific sampling methods, using samples that had been taken only a few hours earlier. Never before in a British General Election had such expertise been deployed and as much money spent in predicting the result of a poll. Yet, despite the sophisticated sampling methods, despite the use of the latest computers to sift the information received from the samples, the prediction was WRONG. The following day several newspapers used the word 'discredited' of the opinion polls.

Exactly the same happened in an American Presidential Election. Nobody knows what happened, in the last few hours before the vote, to upset the predictions. Perhaps there was some last minute shift of public opinion between the time the samples were taken and the opening of the polling booths, it matters not. The facts serve to show what a really precarious business it is to predict what will happen tomorrow, let alone what will happen in two thousand years time. It is the ever present problem of those who would predict, that few things either in private lives or in international affairs proceed as the human mind would anticipate.

## WHO WOULD HAVE THOUGHT IT?

"Who would have thought it?" is a well-used phrase among we mortals and a testimony to the fact that few things go as we would anticipate. It's repetition enshrines the inability of men to see what lies ahead of them.

In 1933 Germany was on her knees, bowed down with the heavy burden of reparations following the infamous treaty of Versailles, torn apart by the cavortings of the Communist and Nazi thugs, weakened by inflation and with seemingly no will to recover. Who could have foreseen that within a decade Germany would have conquered virtually the whole of Europe, smashing through the more powerful French army and dismissing the British expeditionary force from the continent of Europe?

Hitler was the implacable enemy of the Soviet Union, yet they joined hands in a treaty over the prostrate nations of Poland and Finland — **WHO WOULD HAVE THOUGHT IT?** A year on and things had changed again, Nazi Germany sent it's hordes plunging deep into the heart of the Soviet Union and the Russian army recoiled from the onslaught, leaving in it's wake a burning trail — the scorched earth policy. "All is finished for the Russians", said the world as the German armies prepared for their final blow against Moscow, the capitulation of Russia was thought to be close at hand. Just three years later the conquering Russian hordes marched triumphantly into Germany with the battered and beaten German army in full flight before them – **WHO WOULD HAVE THOUGHT IT?**

In 1945 British, American and Allied soldiers clasped the hands of Russian soldiers and hugged each other as they met in conquered Germany. Just five years before the Russians and the British had been bitter enemies – **WHO WOULD HAVE THOUGHT IT?**

Sir Harold Wilson, a truly great Labour Prime Minister of Great Britain, once said "A week in politics is a long time". History tells us how right he was, but these days a week is a long time in almost any sphere of human activity.

Do you remember the eminent British astronomer who predicted that man would never land on the moon — just three years before man landed on the moon?

Remember those who said the four-minute mile would never be run? That man would never survive at speeds which involved breaking the sound-barrier?

History is littered with pronouncements and predictions that have proved to be incorrect. Prediction is a dangerous business indeed!

We are not concerned in this volume with men who predict 'Tomorrow's World', we are concerned with prophets who looked down through

thousands of years of time to OUR DAY, and, as we shall see, got it right!
I hope that by the end of the book you will consider prophecy nothing less than — HISTORY PRE-WRITTEN.

# 2.
# Is 'Something'
# 'Somewhere' Trying
# to Contact the
# Human Race?

"Therefore I should infer from analogy that probably all the organic beings which have ever lived upon this earth have descended from one primordial into which life was first BREATHED BY THE CREATOR."

Charles Darwin. The Origins of the Species.

Our first question: Whether the ancient seers did, in fact, have powers of prediction and whether there is an 'invisible hand' controlling the destiny of mankind, begs the question whether there is a universal intelligence able both to determine and communicate. Is there an 'it' out there?

I use the words 'it' and 'something, somewhere' because there are few descriptions of the great universal spirit which have not through the ages become euphemisms for God and I do not, for the present purpose, wish to commence with the assumption that a god, that is to say a god cast in the traditional theological mold, exists. If I say : Let us approach this unbiassedly, I am asking the impossible! It is given to very few of us, less of us than one would imagine, even among scientists, to approach a subject with a completely unbiased mind. Perhaps, however, I can ask you, for the purpose of the more enjoyable pursuance of our subject, to become temporarily as unbiased as you are able. It is better to start with as primitive and ill-formed an idea of what, if anything, started the multiplicity of phenomena we see around us, as possible.

We are all, unfortunately, the prisoners of prejudice and preformed notions. I only have to write the word 'God' especially with the capital 'G' and each of us will mentally picture that being which, either by early training, environment or later study, has become his or her idea of what God should be. To a very large number of Westerners that image will be of a rather genial old gentleman, sitting on a golden throne and surrounded by plump little angels. Maybe they will see as the image of God those paintings which abound in religious art, in our churches, in our art galleries and Bible illustrations. Few intellectually will really believe in the 'god of the golden throne' but we have always been taught that religious inexplicables are best not questioned, have we not?

A Buddhist who had been converted to Christianity, for example, told me that even many years later he thought of the deity in terms of the bodily likeness of Buddha. Similarly, a coloured man, a man with professional qualifications, found that, though now a Christian, he thought of God in the image of the local gods of his childhood.

I wish to reason from as loose a concept of the great universal spirit as possible, as primitive a concept as possible, an 'it' somewhere, although even 'somewhere' suggests a physical existence which is possibly not so. Perhaps the great universal spirit does not even relate to time and space.

My purpose is to get away from any concept which may, because of preconceived notions, be rejected in the mind of my reader. The agnostic puts his question mark where theology ends. I wish to place mine prior to the point at which theology commences.

Unfortunately, there has been much fallacious reasoning regarding the existence or non-existence of a universal force: If there is a God why does he allow it? That's the same as saying: 'That dog just bit me, I don't believe that dog exists'. Then, of course, there is the assumption among some that a belief in an unseen universal power is an indication of eccentricity. That is certainly not so: A belief in the existence of a supreme being, a first cause, a great universal spirit or a 'god' is to be found among leaders in all the sciences, political leaders and the expert and famous in all walks of life. Scientists, however, are quick to point out that their opinions on the existence of non-existence of a great universal spirit have no more weight than those of any other person.

Sir James Jeans, in his book "The Mysterious Universe", has written:

> *Today there is a wide measure of agreement which, on the physical side of science, approaches to almost unanimity, that the stream of knowledge is heading towards a non-mechanical reality; the universe begins to look more like a great thought than a great machine. Mind no longer looks like an accidental intruder into the realm of matter; we are beginning to suspect that we ought rather to hail it as the Great Creator and Governor of the realm of matter, not, of course, our individual minds have grown, exists as thought. We discover that the universe shows evidence of a designing or controlling power that has something in common with our own minds.*

Very explicit words for an eminent scientist!

Possibly, though Mr. Average may profess either a belief or disbelief in a supreme being, many people are really agnostic, that is, they really don't know.

Atheism is, of course, a very difficult position to maintain intellectually since one is committed to proving a negative. It is difficult enough to prove a negative given a limited canvas, but, when the scenario is the whole of existence in time and space, it becomes impossible.

Most people have either a sneaking suspicion or perhaps rather more than a sneaking suspicion that there is 'something out there', a 'one above' or a 'first cause'. Even refusal to walk under a ladder is an admission of belief in the possibility of there being a cause capable of bringing retribution upon one, a cause that is other than rational cause-and-effect.

All superstition, not breaking mirrors because we fear we may be afflicted by seven years bad luck, not crossing knives, throwing salt over our shoulders if it has been spilt, and touching wood, are testimonies to our belief in the existence of inexplicable forces which have intelligence and a power to interfere in our lives. Superstition is indicative of human uncertainty as to whether all things which happen around us happen because of causes which are normal and explicable. Every man or woman who believes in a good luck charm, or a bad luck omen, testifies to a belief in a power beyond our ken.

Of course, superstition is one thing and reasoned assumption another. I do not equate the two. However, may it not be that we all believe rather more than we admit in public? As the Cosmologist we have previously quoted put it: "We discover that the universe shows evidence of a Designing and Controlling Power that has something in common with our own minds".

If, in fact, we are of those who will categorically deny there is any mind other than the human mind in the universe, and all else happens by chance, then we are not in accord with scientific opinion because as Sir James Jeans said: "Today there is a wide measure of agreement which ... approaches almost to UNANIMITY, the stream of knowledge is heading toward a non-mechanical reality. We discover that the universe shows evidence of a Designing or Controlling Power that has something in common with our own minds".

Then there are those words of Charles Darwin quoted at the head of this chapter in which he affirms his belief in a first cause "... into which life was first breathed by the Creator".

Note well the words, the words of two scientists one of whom, Charles Darwin, has often been put forward as the father of unbelief. Certainly one cannot accuse Charles Darwin of being hidebound by conventional belief, for was it not he who tore aside accepted beliefs when he published his theory of evolution?

There must, in view of such statements and the declared beliefs of many other eminent scientists, be reasonable grounds for asking our question: Is 'Something' 'Somewhere' trying to contact the human race?

Just as most people have doubts, so, I imagine, do most people have, on times, doubts about their doubts. Few people would find it reasonable to believe that even the simplest china cup had come by chance, and it is only natural, therefore, that our intellect revolts against a concept which holds that something as diverse, complex and wonderfully designed as our planet and the living things upon it came about by chance. Just to gaze into the sky at night, contemplate the most distant star and wonder what is beyond that, and beyond that and beyond that. Where does it all end? Nowhere? That's something beyond our comprehension — the mind boggles. We suddenly realise that as our bodies are confined within a small part of the universe so our minds are confined within incredibly restricted limits.

## HAVE YOU EVER TRIED TALKING TO YOUR GOLDFISH?

Suppose, just suppose, that there is something 'up' there, 'out' there or around us everywhere, which started this process we call life, that thing Charles Darwin called 'the Creator'. That thing which scientists call 'Mind' with a designing and controlling power which has something in common with our own minds. I ask you, is it not reasonable to assume that such a power, being intelligent and creative, able to design and control, that power with a mind vastly superior to, but also akin to, our own minds would seek to contact that which it had created?

Then why cannot we point to some clear-cut communication? Why, for example, does no voice boom from the heavens and make clear the will of this 'super-power' to men? Why does 'it' not stand among us so that we can behold it's presence?

Perhaps you will have the answer if you will spend the next ten minutes trying to explain the refrigerator to your pet goldfish. Yes, the gulf between us and 'it' may be that great! I find it incredibly difficult to understand someone who does not speak my language, but, at least, we all live on the same planet, are surrounded by much the same bric-a-brac of living, wear the same kind of clothes and share the same environment. How would an 'it' relative neither to time nor space, without a body and therefore without the ability, normally, to appeal to our five senses, communicate? We cannot see non-matter, so how would 'it' make itself visible to us? The concepts of it's existence, too, may be beyond us, for as with your goldfish, very little of 'its' existence would impinge upon the senses we have.

## MANKINDS MOST IMPORTANT QUEST:

"It is futile, then", someone will say, "to even attempt to know of this being." I would submit that, if we feel it to be a reasonable assumption that there is an 'it' somewhere with absolute power, intelligence and the ability to communicate, there can be no more important quest for mankind than to seek and interpret any communication that may have come from that 'it'. Whatever problems present themselves as obstacles in that task would seem to fade into insignificance compared to the importance of the quest. In this book we shall sift through the many ancient records which purport to be communications from the great universal spirit and see if there is anything which would appear to be supernormal communication.

That is not to say we should be overcome by credulity, for there is no person more exasperating than he who, every time the door squeaks, hears in it some voice of the divine and does not oil the hinges. Let us never forget that the pendulum has two extremities — credulity is one and incredulity the other — there is a centre point.

Could the 'seers' have had a special sense which allowed them to pick up communications from the universal 'mind' which ordinary mortals cannot receive? Regrettably I have no exciting tales to tell of the apparitions I have seen nor of the supernatural voices I have heard. I have never seen an apparition nor heard a voice, the source of which was not human, and neither, I suspect, have most people. I would go so far as to say that I discount the larger amount of so-called 'psychic experience', the seeing of apparitions and mystical experiences, believing them to be explicable naturally or of psychological origin. I think, however, that we cannot discount ALL such experiences and we should recognise that if only one such experience, in the whole of the human history, is shown to be a real contact with a supernatural of supernormal force, the existence of the supernatural is proven.

## AN EXTRA SENSORY GIFT WE NO LONGER HAVE?

Did the ancient seers exercise a gift we no longer have? If the 'IT' did speak to mankind did it warn of things it had foreseen or tell of things it had predestined? Perhaps it gave mankind due notice that, despite the elevated opinion the leaders of men have of themselves, they and we really swim helplessly in the tide of predestination, the waters of which will eventually engulf us.

The great days of the ancient seers were between 1000 B.C. and 500 B.C. though there were a number of predictions uttered outside that period. Was that period a time when the great 'IT' for some reason came very close to mankind? As we have said, the problems attendant to such supernormal contact are immense and varied. Where can a human being begin his comprehension of a being which may exist in 'spirit form' only?

Traditionally humanity has given it's gods hands, feet and forms which have varied from a perfect likeness of Western civilized man to the totem pole. We like to think of our gods as being people, and consequently we run into intellectual difficulties when we try to visualise them being without eyes yet able to see, without ears yet able to hear and without vocal chords yet able to speak. The human mind strains at the 'spirit' concept of the supreme being, and something which exists beyond the bounds of time and space is beyond our comprehension.

## THE SILENT VOICE

Yet ears and eyes are only means of receiving messages, and vocal chords simply a method of transmitting messages. We know there are animals and plants able to receive communications without them being audible in our sense of the word, and without bringing the normal organs of comprehension into play. There is evidence, too, that under certain circumstances human beings are able, in a very limited way, to receive telepathic communication. It is of interest to note that telepathy is successful only with certain people and then only in very special situations.

Perhaps we are being restrictive when we think of the human mind being forever limited within it's present bounds. Could it be when the ancient records say 'And the Lord spake unto ...' that is what actually happened? Perhaps we dwell too much on whether what the prophet heard was a REAL voice.

No migratory bird actually HEARS the vast voice of nature call 'Fly away' and yet unerringly the voice of nature does speak to their inner selves, and millions of birds fly away punctually and accurately to climes they have never before visited, and cannot have known existed, but which are more suitable environments for them at certain times of the year. The inexplicable voice is more certain, more sure than their reasoning capabilities.

Consider the crocus bulb. It is dormant until it is instructed by nature to spring forth. Why do trees bud in the Spring, blossom in the Summer and lose their leaves in the Autumn? There IS a voice, not spoken with the mouth, not heard with the ears it's true, but a voice none-the-less which communicates.

One shrinks, sometimes, from discussing the possibilities because one feels either arrogant in the presence of the inexplicable or, on the other hand, too humble at the grandness of it all. On the one hand we say "I insult my intelligence by seeking after that which may not exist.", and on the other "Who am I that I should perceive that which others have failed to perceive." We should be neither too arrogant nor too humble to seek. There is nothing foolish about trying to push the boundries of one's knowledge beyond what they are at a given time — that's the stuff human progress is made of. There is nothing foolish about asking questions, for the alternative to questioning is to make the assumption that there is either nothing we do not know or to resign ourselves to not caring. The former is intellectual arrogance of the worst kind and the latter the sleep of reason — a sleep akin to intellectual death.

I hope to show in the following pages many things which defy explanation, things which have happened throughout the millenia of recorded history; things which, in our present state of knowledge, would appear supernormal. There are many things happening today which we do not understand. Why, for instance, are nations in this twentieth century to be found gathering in the political alliances and geographical locations foretold by the ancient seers three or more thousands of years ago? Do nations, as do animals, migrate under the influence of an 'invisible hand'? We are not conscious of these things being so but neither, one imagines, is the migratory bird in flight or the eel from a British river, swimming under an unseen influence.

King Solomon said "He that answereth a case before he heareth it is a fool." I can imagine there are thousands of people who have set themselves to believe there is no mind other than the human mind in the universe. They are entitled to their opinion. Their view does not, however, absolve them from their duty, a duty they owe to themselves and the rest of mankind, to sift as dispassionately as it is possible for a human mind, through the evidence.

This is a book of speculation. I do not believe it will PROVE anything, it is not meant to. Every advance of human knowledge has proceeded from a speculation, a hypothesis. It is the nature of things that questions must be asked before answers are found.

In passing, I should say I have a specific readership in mind, certainly not the theologian, enough books have been written for the theologian. Rather the men and women who sit in the evening either in their homes or the lounge bar of the pub, talking 'pub' politics and 'pub' philosophy. I see as my readership that vast majority of people who, amid their busy and yet somewhat humdrum lives, seek some novelty, enlightenment and sometimes truth. And let those who would sneer at such people recall that had we listened to 'pub politicians' we would have wrung old Hitler's neck in 1933 and Stalin's sooner.

I want to 'get through' too, to those who have previously had no inkling of this subject. The only way to be meaningful to an uninitiated readership is to be simple. Whatever may be said of this book I hope no-one will say they could not understand it; I would regard that as the ultimate condemnation.

From here on I shall 'float' the proposition that much of earth's history has been pre-written, because, if it is anything, then that is exactly what prophecy is — history pre-written and pre-spoken by the seers. I suggest that there is evidence that the history of planet earth is rather like a railway timetable, planned both in destination and in time of arrival. I will spare you the almost obligatory joke about British Rail.

# 3.
# The Amazing Scientific Accuracy of the Ancient Seer who Pre-empted Darwin by 3500 Years

In 1859 Charles Darwin published his derivative work "The Origins of the Species" and set religion back on it's heels. Darwin, as we have seen, did not in that work deny the existence of a creator though he did deny the very basis of the churches teaching about the way in which the world had come into being.

About 1500 B.C. — some three thousand five hundred years before Darwin was born — an ancient seer, Moses, gave an account of the beginnings of the earth and the life which is upon it, which is more up-to-date today than the theory of evolution as propounded by Darwin.

How did the ancients know those many years ago how the earth and the life upon it came into being? Of course some didn't because there were, and still are, many fantastic theories of how things began. This one seer, however, told the complete story, and it is only a matter of MONTHS SINCE SCIENCE CAUGHT UP WITH HIM!

Doubts are now being cast on the theory of evolution as it used to be taught. It is now generally acknowledged that the gradual evolution of man from lower forms of life cannot be accepted as the whole explanation Science is coming to believe the 'great leap forward' theory though still at a loss to explain what caused the genetic impulse which caused the 'great leap'.

It is beyond the scope of this volume to discuss, in any detail, the theory of evolution. However, if we are to maintain the credibility of the ancient seers and support the proposition that there is an intelligence trying to contact humanity through them, then we should expect that that intelligence would have something to say through the ancient seers, which is scientifically accurate, about how planet earth, the things upon it and the beings which inhabit it came to be.

Almost every ethnological group has it's own creation story and very fanciful many of them are. The pre-Darwin teaching of the church was, though not quite as ridiculous as some theories, ridiculous enough to be demolished over a relatively short time as science began to produce evidence that the earth had not been in existence for a mere six thousand years and had certainly not been created in 'six' days.

## SOME ANCIENT BELIEFS AS TO HOW THE WORLD CAME INTO BEING

Among the Crow Indians it is believed that long ago there existed only water on which swam ducks. The sun, the creator, became merged with the transformer known as the 'Coyote' and told the ducks to dive into the waters. From the mud attached to the webbed feet of one of the ducks he created the earth and caused it to be inhabited by living creatures.

The Egyptian creation story tells of everything being created from the dry land which appeared out of the abyssmal ocean. Amon, god of the sun and father of all the other gods, also came from the abyss. One legend has it that he appeared as a child sitting in the centre of a lotus bud.

Babylonian creation myth has it that Marduk the god of Babylon made the earth from the two parts of the body of Tiamat, a chaos dragon. Marduk is said to have destroyed Tiamat after a protracted battle.

Hinduism postulates a universe of immense proportions — in which postulation it is, of course, quite correct. The 'Day of Brahma' is the fundamental cosmic cycle, a cycle which lasts for some 4,320,000,000 years. At the beginning of this day Vishnu is said to have lain asleep upon the cobra Shesha who floats upon the cosmic ocean, the primaeval chaos. From Vishnu's navel grew a lotus from the bud of which is born the god

Brahma, who in turn created the universe on behalf of Vishnu. Vishnu then awoke and controls the cosmos during the 4,320,000,000 years.

Shaktas believe that a mother goddess gave birth to the universe after an act of sexual intercourse with her husband Shiva.

Norse legends have as the prime mover a giant 'Ymir' who created a six-headed giant by rubbing his feet together and produced a son and daughter who, it is believed, appeared from under his armpit. The god Odin and his two brothers killed Ymir and created the world from his body "earth from his flesh, mountains from his bones, sky from his skull and sea from his blood".

Such were the ancient views of creation and it is against the background of such fanciful theories that we should look at the record of the prophet Moses as to how the earth was formed and populated.

Unfortunately, the church took an ancient yet scientific account of how the earth was formed and how man came to be, and, by sheer misrepresentation and dogma, turned it into a myth just a little better than the Babylonian myths of creation.


## THE CONFLICT BETWEEN THE THEORY OF EVOLUTION AND THE DOCTRINE OF CREATION

I have always found it difficult to understand why there should be a conflict between the concept of 'evolution' and the concept of 'creation' for the terms themselves are not opposites.

There are two ladies with whom I was once acquainted who, though otherwise quite unexceptional, had the extra-ordinary ability of each being able to talk on a different subject, each to the other, simultaneously. One would be happily talking about the price of groceries while the other would be talking about her holidays. They were quite oblivious of the fact that they were not talking about the same thing and I am sure it was, to them, a satisfactory, if unintentional, arrangement.

Those ladies are little more odd than some of the protagonists in the debate evolution -v- creation, who do not seem to comprehend that they are not talking about the same thing. Darwinians continue to argue the case for evolution as though a belief in creation is an affront to that theory, whilst many Christians still argue the case for creation as though evolution was it's opposite — it is not.

Charles Darwin, as we have seen, believed in a 'creator' and, it will come as a surprise to many theologians to learn, the prophet Moses propagated the Theory of Evolution 3500 years before Darwin was born.

To everyone with preconceived ideas I would say: Read what Darwin really taught, read what Moses really wrote, bring yourself up-to-date with present day scientific thinking and you will discover that Moses had the most mysterious piece of foreknowledge in history.

Do not, I appeal to you, defend what you THINK Moses wrote, read

WHAT he wrote and believe what he DID write not what you have always been taught to believe he wrote. It is futile for the Christian to try and gainsay the many facts which science has brought before us. It is equally futile for the sc ientist to deny that there is something very mysterious about a man, who lived 3500 years ago, knowing exactly how planet earth came into being.

Men of science found it very easy to dispose of the theories of those who taught that the world came into being 4004 B.C. — a theory never expostulated by Moses but by an Irish cleric Usher, and then printed for many years in the MARGINS — not the text, mark you — of our Bibles. Nowhere in their writings do either Moses or any of the ancient seers purport to tell us how long the earth, in it's present form, has existed.

## THE MIRACLE THE MEN OF RELIGION MISSED.

The history of misinterpretation of the prognostications of the ancient seers is the history of preconceived ideas being allowed to take pre-eminence over fact. Because they were so caught up in their own preconceived ideas, students of the writings of the prophet Moses missed one of the great wonders of the Book of Genesis, a wonder which stamps the book surely with an authority beyond human authority: IT REVEALED THE EXACT SEQUENCE OF THE COMING INTO BEING OF THE EARTH AND THE LIFE UPON IT 3500 YEARS BEFORE THE WORLD HEARD THE NAME DARWIN:

Only in one vital respect does the Moses account differ from the conclusions of Darwin — it explained, which Darwin could not explain, a phenomenon which science 3500 years later was to call 'the missing link'. Now 125 years after Darwin, science is beginning to get it right.

Let us compare what Moses DID say with the facts of the coming into being of the world as it exists today:

*In the beginning God created the heaven and the earth and earth was WITHOUT FORM AND VOID.*

I want you to notice the word "was" for from the Hebrew the literal translation is "became". There is therefore in the original text a distinct statement that the earth was in existence before it "became" without form and void. Note too, that there is no statement as to how long, before it BECAME without form and void, the earth had been in existence. There is enough time latitude in those unexplored eras of earth's history to take into account the many facts of science which show our earth to be millions of years old.

## THE EARTH WAS WITHOUT FORM AND VOID.

*The earth was without form and void.*

24

A most unusual phrase to use, for what element is "without form and void"?

Moses, living in a time when, as we have seen, many fanciful theories of how the earth came to exist were accepted, tells us that in the beginning the earth was "without form and void".

The only element that can truly be said to be without any form and void is — GAS! Is it not surprising that it is only in recent years that science has come to the conclusion that our earth was originally a cloud of gas which later solidified?

How did Moses know that in the beginning our earth was a cloud of gas — WE HAVE ONLY RECENTLY FOUND OUT!

## THE 'SIX DAYS' OF CREATION.

Much has been made of Moses' assertion that the world was made in 'six days'. Atheists have scoffed at it and Christians have become hot-under-the-collar defending the concept. Some evangelical Christians, especially, have felt it necessary, in all sincerity, to insist that the world was created in six literal 'days'.

The word translated 'day' is the Hebrew word 'Yom' and is variously translated 'day', 'time', 'age' and 'season' — it is certainly not necessary to insist upon it indicating a twentyfour hour day.

More than sixty-five times the prophets Zepheniah, Isaiah, Zechariah and Joel refer to a period of time they call "The day of the Lord" — a period of time at the end of earth's history when they foresee the 'Lord' taking control. The word they translate 'day' is the same word we find in Genesis translated 'day' — 'Yom'. No-one surely feels it necessary to insist that "the day of the Lord" is to be confined to one twentyfour hour day?

Ferrar Fenton, in his translation of Genesis, expresses the first verse like this:

"By periods God created that which produced the solar system; then that which produced the earth".

In his explanatory note he writes:

"Literally 'by headships' it is curious that all translators from the septuagint have rendered this word b'reshith into the singular, although it is plural in the Hebrew so I render it accurately."

Moses said, and science agrees, that at it's inception the earth existed as a dense cloud of gas. How did Moses know, from whom or what did he receive his information? It's not the kind of thing you would cull from observation of the phenomena around us. What made him make the rather unusual pronouncement that "In the beginning ... the earth was without form and void"?

## THE FIRST STAGE OF CREATION.

Science has it that gradually the gas solidified and that during the solidification process the atmosphere was so dense that no light penetrated to the earth's surface.

The 'first day' is one of the more controversial of the periods of the creation story as written by Moses. His words: *"And God said, let there be light: and there was light"* have been the centre of many a controversy. Yet that, agrees science, is precisely what happened! The gas solidified, the atmosphere thinned and the earth became light — rather as a sea fog lifts mid-morning before a warm day.

It is often pointed out by those who are more intent upon criticism than understanding, that the sun, moon and stars are not said to have been created until the fourth 'day' and yet light is said to have appeared on the first 'day'.

Moses was not so naive a person that he was unaware he had written of the existence of light before he had mentioned the existence of the sun, moon and stars. Moses was a very intelligent man — he knew well what he was writing. He could quite easily have written that the sun, moon and stars appeared in the heavens on the first 'day' but had he done so he would have been scientifically wrong. He was aware, too, that all the earth's light comes from the sun and moon, and a very little from the stars. Then why did he write that light appeared BEFORE the sun, moon and stars?

We know today that that is exactly how it happened. There is light on a cloudy day but one cannot see the sun, moon or stars. With the complete honesty of one receiving a revelation from an outside source Moses left in the narrative something he undoubtedly did not understand — how there could be light before the sun or moon were in the heavens. How could he know that 3500 years after his death science would show that what he had written was absolutely correct? We know today that light appeared on the surface of the earth before the sun and moon could be seen from the earth's surface. From whence did Moses' knowledge come?

## THE SECOND STAGE OF CREATION.

It is accepted today that during the early millions of years of earth's existence and after it had solidified, the earth was covered in vapour. The whole of the earth's surface was dank, wet swampland. We are told there was no rainfall at that time. That is the modern scientific view. But let us see what Moses said of that period in earth's history:

*For the Lord God has caused it not to rain upon the earth and there was not a man to till the ground but there went up a mist from the earth, and watered the whole face of the ground.*

Would not the evidence of Moses' eyes tell him that the earth had always been as he saw it during his long lifetime? How did he reach conclusions which science would not reach for another 3500 years? From whence came his information?

What happened next in the development of the earth? Gradually, the mists cleared from the earth's surface and the clouds formed in the heavens. The earth now began to experience it's first rainfall. At this time the system of evaporation to dry the earth, and condensation to form the raindrops, began. Here's how Moses described it:

*And God said, Let there be firmament in the midst of the waters, and let it divide the waters from the waters. And God made the firmament, and divided the waters which were UNDER the firmament, from the waters which were ABOVE the firmament.*

## THE THIRD STAGE OF CREATION.

Both science and Moses agree that the next stage in the creation or evolution of the earth was the separation of the land masses from the water and the coming forth of the first vegetation:

*"And God said, Let the waters under the heaven be gathered together in one place, and let the dry land appear: and it was so. And God called the dry land Earth; and the gathering together of the waters called he Seas ... And God said, Let the earth bring forth vegetation, the herb yielding seed, and the fruit tree yielding fruit after it's kind, whose seed is in itself, upon the earth: and it was so.*

## THE FOURTH STAGE OF CREATION.

Scientists tell us that it was at this time that the clouds which had girdled the earth in a seamless garment of vapour began to break up and there were periods when the skies were clear. For the first time, had there been life on earth with eyes to behold them, the sun, moon and stars would have been visible.

That is the next step in Moses' account of creation or evolution, too:

*And God said, Let there be lights in the firmament of the heaven to divide the day from the night; and let them be for signs, and for seasons, and for days, and years;*

## THE CONTROVERSIAL FIFTH DAY OF CREATION.

This is the point at which the religious thought of his day and Charles Darwin came into bitter and direct conflict. I think it fair to say that the church was so put out by what Darwin had to say about the emergence of life on earth that they organised a verbal 'lynching party' to discredit him.

Now what did Darwin teach to cause such a furore? He taught that ALL animal life originated from lower forms of life which had first formed in the waters on the earth's surface. Both Moses and science agree that plants and vegetation were the first forms of life on earth but Darwin went further, he taught that the first really living things, single cell life forms, the first animal life on earth, developed in the waters.

Later simple life forms developed into higher forms of life: Jellyfish, sea anemones, corals, comb jellies, flat worms and nemertine worms. Then came the cartilaginous fish and the bony fish such as lung fish and sturgeon, followed by the amphibians, reptiles, birds and mammals.

Darwin was laughed to scorn, and not only by religious activists, I would hasten to add, for many of his fellow scientists were in the forefront of the bitter attacks upon him. Had Darwin gone no further than proposing that fish had a common ancestry in the waters of the world, perhaps Darwin would not have met quite so much opposition, but how could anyone with commonsense imagine that birds and mammals actually originated in the water?

No scientist, nor any good sane Christian man or woman, could possibly comprehend, or even tolerate the proposal, that the monkey, lion, ostrich, goat, sheep or, for that matter, the dinosaur, had originated in some murky pool.

You have to admit that, had you not been taught it at school, it would be difficult to envisage that the ancestors of the pet cat or dog originated in a swamp, but that is what Darwin taught: You wouldn't know it by merely looking at Tibs or Bonzo, would you? Darwin and others did a lot of exacting investigation before they convinced themselves that the theory they were about to launch upon the world was supportable. Darwin was not unaware that his professional reputation was at stake.

If we rely on commonsense we must realise that birds do not come out of the water, they are born in nests. Observation certainly does not lead us to the conclusion that ALL animals and EVERY living thing originated in the waters of the world.

Yet you know, had Moses been alive, he would have been the first to shake Darwin by the hand and tell him how right he was. Perhaps he would have chided him on the fact that the human race had taken so long to find out and perhaps said "I told you so". Indeed, Moses had told us so, 3500 years ago:

> And God said, Let the waters bring forth abundantly the moving
> creature that hath life, and fowl that may fly above the earth in

revolutionary as Darwin's. Of course, Copernicus was reviled not only by his scientific contemporaries but also by some of the religious authorities of his day.

Today Nicolas Copernicus is regarded as the founding father of modern astronomy. Copernicus was both a religious man and a scientist, being at one time canon of the cathedral at Frauenburg.

There were numerous theories of how the earth was 'held up' before and during the time of Copernicus. One, and that not the most imaginative, which tells of the world being held aloft by a man, who stood on the back of an elephant which in turn stood on the coils of a great snake.

Perhaps Copernicus, in his spare moments in the cathedral, read the prophet Isaiah who 2200 years before had said:

*It is he [God] who sitteth on the Circle of the earth.*

40:22

How did Isaiah know the earth was round 2200 years before the fact came to be accepted by science? Was it because he was writing under the guidance of a superior intelligence?

The prophet Job, writing in the year 1000 B:C., pre-empted Copernicus by 3475 years when he wrote:

*[The Lord] hangeth the earth upon NOTHING.*

26:7

Can you imagine the many smiles people living before Copernicus must have had reading those two statements "the circle of the earth" (everyone could see it was flat) and "He hangeth the earth upon nothing" — why, it was quite easily demonstrated that it is not possible to hang anything on 'nothing'. Two statements which we know to be true but which are not apparent to the naked eye, that the world is round and that the earth quite literally is held up by nothing.

How did Isaiah and Job know what it took science thousands of years after their day to find out? They were both prophets, ancient seers and they both claimed to have this special rapport with the great universal spirit.

In A.D.1630 Galileo discovered that the wind was regular in it's paths, that rain was caused by heat evaporating the waters of the seas and rivers, and, that the wind carried the vapour in clouds until it condensed and fell as rain. Mark the date. A.D.1630.

How did the writer of the Book of Ecclesiastes, writing about 1000 B.C., all those years before Galileo was born, know what it took science 2600 years to find out? Listen to what the writer of Ecclesiastes has to say:

*The wind goeth towards the South and turneth about unto the North; it whirleth about continually, and the wind returneth again*

*according to it's circuits. All the rivers run into the sea; yet the sea
is not full; unto the place from whence the rivers come, thither
they return again.*                                              1:6,7.

Reason and observation could not tell the writer of Ecclesiastes that —
he would never have seen a river run uphill anymore than you or I have.
One thousand years before Christ and two thousand five hundred years
before Galileo — the ancient seer knew!

In the great space in the heavens of the North there are no stars. We
know because we have very powerful telescopes which tell us so, they let us
probe into the depths of space. Job had no such equipment when he wrote
over 2500 years before science became well enough equipped to establish
the truth of his statement:

*He [God] stretcheth out the North over an empty place.*

26:7

He was speaking of the heavens, as you will see if you read the context.

From whence did such knowledge come? The prophets I have mentioned
in this chapter claimed to speak in the name of the 'Lord': Certainly they
all had a knowledge of the world about them which we have only acquired
in fairly recent times. Had they a supernatural source of knowledge?

# 4.
# A Trip
# In a Time-
# Machine

I am going to charter, just for a short while, a time-machine, for I want to take you on a journey back into history long past, to a city which no longer exists.

We shall travel, in distance, some thousands of miles and, in time, some 2582 years. When we land in this city the birth of Christ will be yet some 550 years in the future.

Our 'date-clock' is set for 600 B.C. and our destination is a certain city on the banks of the great River Euphrates which flows through the country we, in the twentieth century, call Iraq.

Soon, below us we see the waters of the mighty river shimmering in the heat, for the sun is high in the heavens. Before us there stretches a vast fertile area and in the distance the city. At first we may think the city to be a mirage, for it has a certain fairytale quality, but as we draw nearer we realise it is very real indeed.

The city is walled about with great high walls and the River Euphrates flows into the city through a leaved gate in one of the walls, through the centre of the city, and out again through a leaved gate in the far wall. The river virtually divides the city into two parts.

It takes us some little time to comprehend that such a vast city, a city with a peculiar etherial quality, could exist in such unusual surroundings. We, from the twentieth century, would not expect to see a city of this size, or this sophistication, either here on the banks of the Euphrates or in this period of time.

As we continue to survey the city from the air we are struck by a certain familiarity of layout. We ponder for a while: Where have we seen a city laid out like this before? Suddenly we realise, yes, that's it — New York. This city is laid out rather like New York. It is traversed by absolutely straight, wide roads running the length of the city and these are crossed by equally wide roads running absolutely straight and parallel with each other across the width of the city. This city is quite unlike any of the other cities we have flown over in our journey here. Unlike Jerusalem, for example, with it's narrow winding streets. The streets of this city compare well with the main roads of our major modern cities, and are wider than most.

Let us find a spot where we can land unnoticed. We shouldn't find it too difficult because there is plenty of parkland down there within the city walls. We can already see vast areas of trees and shrubs. Absolutely perfect for hiding this strange machine of ours from the prying eyes of the inhabitants.

So, and it is with some trepidation, lest the inhabitants be unfriendly, that we guide our machine down toward a clearing.

We land and make our way through gardens such as we have not seen in our civilisation, their beauty is breath-taking and the planning and terracing beyond anything we know today. Several notices proclaim and extol the virtues of 'The Hanging Gardens' and we appreciate why they are so named, for flower laden foliage hangs down from the trees and terracing in a plentitude which is spectacular. But we will not tarry, for our curiosity and excitement mounts as we see the first wide street of the city before us.

The street is thronged with people as, we will find, are all the streets in this town. Each street has a name, though few of the names are familiar to us: A notice tells us we are in Shamash Street. The natives seem friendly enough, they all seem too busy with their own interests to care very much about us, so let us ask one of them where Shamash is or who Shamash is.

"Excuse me, sir", we say to a passer-by, "we are strangers here, and we were just wondering, since this street is named 'Shamash street' where

Shamash is and what it's importance is that it should have a street named after it?"

"You've never heard of Shamash? Where have you been all your life? Everyone has heard of Shamash, but if you want to know where he is, he's up there." Our eyes follow the pointed finger and we redden with embarrassment as the small crowd which has gathered laugh good naturedly at our ignorance. We shield our eyes, for we find ourselves looking directly into the sun.

"Up there, up where? We can't see anything!"

"Up there, the sun, Shamash the sun god, there he is, up there, that bright light in the sky — you do have the sun where you come from don't you?"

Just our luck to pick the 'life-and-soul-of-the-party' of whom to ask our question, wasn't it?

We laugh with the little group of people, hoping they won't turn nasty. No need to worry, they are already hurrying on their way as though they are trying to live two days in one. We ask our informant one last question:

"Thank you for that information but who is that street," we point to a street which intersects Shamash Street, "named after?"

"That's Morshick Street."

"Who's Morshick?"

"Another god. All the streets are named after gods. Have a nice day."

"Thank you, and goodbye."

We walk on and notice the names of other streets, there's Adad street, Mergal street, Zabab street and hundreds more that we shall not see.

As we walk the streets there is a certain similarity between what is going on here and life in the towns back home. Of course, the clothing of the people is different, as is their method of transport, but their activities are identifiable. People are going to, and coming from, work. The shoppers are hurrying and bustling, laden down with shopping. There are shops and offices, cafes, and there are barrow boys trading in the streets from their barrows. Dealers peddle their wares and offer services both dubious and honest; caravans, laden to exhaustion, cram the thoroughfare and there are traffic-jams here and there.

Among the shoppers and workers, as they hurry to and fro, there are tourists, some of whom obviously do not speak the language. There are pilgrims, who, it would seem, regard this as a holy place, and there are priests making their way to the temples. Among it all there is the ever present sprinkling of army personnel.

Here is a notice for tourists and pilgrims giving information about the things to see and do in the city. Let us read it: "In this city there are 53 temples to the chief gods, 55 chapels of Morduk, 300 chapels to the earthly deities, 600 for the heavenly deities, 180 altars to the goddess Ishtar, 180 for the gods Nergal and Adad and 12 other altars for different gods". Little wonder there are so many pilgrims and priests about!

Another surprise awaits us as we walk around the corner, for before us is a tower which we adjudge to be about 300 feet high, built on seven levels. It is an impressive sight, each side of the base measures over 290 feet and on top of the tower is a large temple. Let us ask another passer-by what this tower is called, for it is certainly one of the wonders of the city.

"Excuse me, can you tell me what this structure is and what it is called?" We ask a man who looks as though he may be a man of the cloth.

"This? Oh, this is the Tower of Babel. It's the tower from which this city and our empire takes it's name — Babel — Babylon, see? It's been here for over 1400 years, when they built it they said it's top might reach to heaven. The Hittites tried to destroy it and they did make rather a mess of it, but our present King has had it restored and though it doesn't quite reach to heaven, that's still what it symbolised to us."

"What is the name of your king?"

"You mean you haven't heard of our mighty King, the King of Babylon? Where have you been all your life?" I do wish they would stop saying that!

"I'll probably know him if you mention the name." A bit weak, but what else can one say in such circumstances?

"Our king is the 'King of Kings', the mightiest King in all the earth. He's built this city and this empire. Now no-one can withstand us — even the Jews here admit he is the 'King of Kings'. If you haven't heard his name before you'll hear it often enough again. His name is Nebuchadnezzar. Now have you heard of him?"

Perhaps because he has seen the colour drain from our faces our informant does not wait for an answer. Giving us a weak smile he goes on his way. We don't really notice that he has gone, we stand in awe for we have heard about the Tower of Babel in Sunday school. We never thought of it as a real place, just one of those little stories it seems obligatory to teach children while their parents have a quiet afternoon. But here it is, not a myth at all, the 'tower that was to reach up to heaven'.

We must be on our way, for there is little time left for us to stay in this place. It is obvious to us that the two great pillars of Babylonian life are religion and commerce — there is an apparent working relationship between them. The temples and the department stores, the priests, the financiers and the shop managers, work closely together. The food departments in the stores sell the meat from the sacrificial altars and the remainder of the gifts and tithes of the faithful are sold also. How else could these things be turned into cash for the use of the king, the temples and the priesthood? You can't store perishables forever and god's don't wear clothes or jewellery, so why waste these things? It is an aspect of Babylonian life which makes us feel there is a certain timeless bond between commerce and organised religion.

At the very heart of Babylonian commerce is the 'Gold Standard' and the finance houses upon which the merchants and the people depend and to whom they are enslaved.

Babylon is undoubtedly prospering, for on our way back to the 'Hanging Gardens' to board our time-machine for the flight home, we see the banks, estate agents offices, lawyers offices and a large exchange building where exchange rates and prices are fixed just as they are in the financial centres of the world in our own time.

We are in no doubt that we are visiting the capital city of an empire in it's ascendancy. On everyone's lips are stories of the Babylonian conquests of the past few years, the army personnel are obviously national heroes for the soldiery walk with confidence and, from time to time, a military man with receive a pat on the back from a passer-by. Above conquest, however, and above the military fortunes of Babylon, there is adoration of the king Nebuchadnezzar to be heard everywhere. Quotations from his speeches are to be seen displayed in every street. One quotation especially seems to be the favourite —

"Is not this the mighty Babylon that I have built?"

The most impressive feature of this city is the buildings and the amount of building still going on, for everywhere there is new building work in progress. Let us stoop and pick up a brick. It is stamped just as brick manufacturers today stamp their products. We see that all the bricks are stamped in a similar way, millions of them, with a one word inscription — NEBUCHADNEZZAR.

"Is not this the mighty Babylon that I have built?" is no vain boast, for the city is set foursquare and each of it's walls is 14 miles in length and the city is no less than 56 miles in circumference. Within the 56 miles of walls there is the richest city on earth, a city growing richer by the hour. It has it's prosperous commercial centre, it's unquenchable water supply in the mighty river, and an abundant supply of home-grown food in it's orchards, fields and plantations. This is a city indeed to which no-one could lay siege, even if there was a nation on earth reckless enough, or powerful enough, to challenge the might of Babylon.

The walls are 300ft. high and at least 80ft. thick.It is said that intrepid drivers often turn chariots drawn by four horses full circle at speed on it's walls. Atop the wall 250 towers militarily dominate the surrounding countryside.

These mighty and seemingly impregnable walls have one hundred gates, 25 in each wall, and the whole city is surrounded by a deep, wide moat. No wonder Nebuchadnezzar boasts of his city, no wonder the Babylonian soldier preens himself as he walks the streets, no wonder the people of Babylon fear no man for there can be no doubt that Babylon is here to stay.

"Is not this the mighty Babylon that I have built?" As we wander through the hanging gardens, those peaceful serene gardens, we can identify with the pride King Nebuchadnezzar has in this city. Prosperous, fertile, mighty Babylon: It's walls are impregnable to any army on earth and any weapon on earth. It is safe from siege because of it's ample water and food supply — there are provisions for a twenty year siege — but who is there to besiege this city anyway?

Even as we board our time-machine for home the Babylonian army is rolling back the armies of the nations as though they were chaff on a threshing floor, they have crushingly defeated the Egyptians in battle, defeated and occupied Assyria, occupied Palestine, taken the majority of the Jewish nation captive and a major part of the treasures of King Solomon's Temple are now in King Nebuchadnezzar's storehouse.

## THEY DON'T TELL IRISH JOKES IN BABYLON.

Oh, just before we take off, let me tell you another thing we have found out about the Babylonians — they don't tell Irish jokes. Well, we don't think so, anyway, perhaps because the Irish at that time were not known as Irish but as 'Beth-Cumri', and they, or rather their forefathers, were wandering about further down the Euphrates in Assyria. But the Babylonians do tell Jewish jokes, and a lot of them are about this Jewish fellow who would not come to Babylon when Babylon conquered Palestine, but stayed in Jerusalem. Mind you, it is funny, this story, when you listen to it. You do get some funny stories about the Jews in Babylon.

It seems that when Jerusalem fell in 586, that is, of course, B.C., this fellow was given the choice by Nebuchadnezzar of either coming to Babylon or staying with the poor remnant of his people in Jerusalem. The chap was a bit silly, the Babylonians thought, because if they had one grouse about Nebuchadnezzer it was that he had exalted so many young Jews to positions of high office in the state. Obviously Nebuchadnezzer had big plans for this particular Jew but, no, he preferred Jerusalem — certainly not a nice place to be at the time.

This fellow, by the name of Jeremiah, is now saying that the voice of 'God' has spoken to him and told him what is going to happen not only to Babylon but also King Nebuchadnezzar.

He's even written a book, a book which would have him in deep trouble with the authorities if it were to be taken seriously. "The Book of Jeremiah the Prophet" it is called — just read some of the things he says in just one of it's chapters (Chapter 50). He is writing, don't forget, of this mighty Babylonian empire:

Destroy her utterly: let nothing of her be left.
The broad walls of Babylon shall be utterly broken, her high gates shall be burnt with fire.
Babylon shall become heaps.
A drought is upon her waters; and they shall be dried up.

As God overthrew Sodom and Gomorrah and the neighbouring cities thereof, saith the Lord; so shall no man abide there, neither shall any son of man dwell therein.
All nations shall serve (Nebuchadnezzar), and his son, and his son's son, until the very time of his land come; and then many nations and kings shall serve themselves of him.

You can't blame the Babylonians laughing when people write things like that, can you? Those broad walls "Nothing left"; this great city " A heap"; this broad rushing river "dried up"; this great commercial civilisation "no man dwell therein" and all this to happen during the reign of Nebuchadnezzar's son's son — a sick joke indeed.
Of course, Jeremiah foretells that all this will happen long after he and Nebuchadnezzar are dead — that, of course, is the big joke in Babylon. It's easy to foretell something is going to happen after you're dead, isn't it — you're not going to be here to 'face the music' if your prophecy goes wrong. An easy way to fame whilst alive, and what does it matter if the prophet is wrong after he's dead? No, they are not taking Jeremiah seriously in Babylon.
We are about to take off, but a thought crosses my mind — I remember learning about Jerusalem at school and Damascus at school, but my twentieth century teacher never once mentioned Babylon. I don't recollect seeing any advertisements for package tours to Babylon either! I wonder what happened to Babylon? Funny! I know, let's not go straight home, let's stay right here in Babylon but get our machine to take us back to the twentieth century. We'll stay in Babylon but return to 1984.
As we set the date-clock to 1984, the mists of time enshroud us, the howling rush of history speeded to a crescendo engulfs us, we are blind and deaf for a short time as we journey through the ages to our day.
A few moments to adjust and we are ready to step out of our machine and walk the streets of twentieth century Babylon. Let us see how it has changed.

## THE CITY THAT DISAPPEARED:

Something must be wrong with our time-machine for we programmed it to stay in the same place but at a different time in history. Here we are in a desert, not only is there no Babylon but there is no River Euphrates either.
Ah, over there! There's a notice in the desert sand, perhaps that will give us some clue as to where we are. We brush the sand away from the board and we see that it identifies a stopping place on the Bahgdad railway "Babylon Halt". All around is utter desolation. The only sign of a city are the trenches the German archaelogists have left behind and even these are becoming covered by the desert sands.
So where is Babylon? There's a little Arab settlement called "Babil"

named after the famous Babylon — but that's several miles away. The fact of the matter is that the mighty Babylon Nebuchadnezzar built no longer exists in any meaningful form. Let's go home to our history books and find out what happened to Babylon the Great.

You will remember that Jeremiah wrote his 'peculiar' prophecies in 620 B.C. and he predicted not only the utter destruction of Babylon, but in whose reign the dismemberment of the mighty empire would take place.

He said it would take place in the reign of Nebuchadnezzar's son's son — mark this well — Jeremiah did not say in the reign of Nebuchadnezzar's grandson, he specified the reign of Nebuchadnezzar's son's son.

Nebuchadnezzar was succeeded as King of Babylon by his son Evil-Merodach, who was assassinated after he had reigned for two years.

Nebuchadnezzar's sister's husband then took the throne and he was killed in the fourth year of his reign.

Neriflissar's son, Laborosoarchod, a grandson of Nebuchadnezzar, came to the throne but he was Nebuchadnezzar's DAUGHTER'S son, not his son's son — that's near enough for any prophet, don't you think?

Not a bit of it! By the time you have finished reading this book you will realise that the ancient seers are never NEARLY right, they are always EXACTLY right.

But how could the prediction of Jeremiah now be fulfilled because the royal lineage of Babylon had gone off into a different branch of the family? The Babylonian empire did not come to an end under Nebuchadnezzar's daughter's son.

Laborosoarchod was succeeded by another son of Evil-Merodach, Belshazzar by name, Nebuchadnezzar's son's son, and it was under him that the empire came to it's end precisely as Jeremiah had predicted more than 75 years before.

This is a pattern we shall see time and time again in the predictions of the ancient seers. The unlikely is predicted, events seem to move in a manner which preclude their fulfilment, then, at the 'appointed time' the prediction is fulfilled exactly and precisely. Had we lived in the days when Laborosoarchod took the throne of Babylon there would have been no way in which a reasonable person could have done other than doubt whether the prophecy of Jeremiah could be fulfilled. Yet, events turned full circle and the prophecy was fulfilled with a precision which would be beyond belief were it not a FACT OF HISTORY.

## THE RIVER THAT CHANGED COURSE.

As we have seen, Babylon was divided into two parts with the river Euphrates flowing through the centre of the city. Jeremiah said: "A drought is upon her waters; and they shall be dried up." It would be unthinkable to the Babylonians that the mighty river would dry up. That, of course, is not what Jeremiah said, he was precise "Her waters ... they shall dry up.'' Not the waters of the Euphrates but the waters of Babylon. The river Euphrates did not dry up but the waters of Babylon did and the drought was upon HER waters.

Now since the waters of the river Euphrates were not to dry up and the waters of Babylon were to dry up, and the waters of the Euphrates were the waters of Babylon, how could that prediction be fulfilled? Seems impossible, doesn't it?

The answer would be unbelievable if it were not a proven fact of history. Hundreds of years after Jeremiah had spoken those words, for some reason unknown to us, the river changed it's course. Now, in the twentieth century, standing at 'Babylon Halt' only the palm trees in the distance testify to the course of the river Euphrates — BYPASSING COMPLETELY THE AREA WHERE BABYLON ONCE STOOD.

"Neither", said Jeremiah, "shall any son of man dwell therein.'' That, at the time, was rather like someone today saying that London, New York or Moscow would not be inhabited a few hundred years from now. The ancient seer Isaiah also predicted that Babylon would not be inhabited — writing in 700 B.C., about 170 years before the event, he predicted:

> And Babylon, the glory of kingdoms, the beauty of the Chaldeans excellency, shall be as when God overthrew Sodom and Gomorrah. It shall never be inhabited, neither shall it be dwelt in from generation to generation; neither shall the Arabian pitch tent there; neither shall the shepherds make their fold there.
> Book of the prophet Isaiah. Chapter 13.

No Arab today will remain in the Babylon area, or in the unearthed ruins of the ancient city, after dark let alone dwell there or keep sheep there. Babylon is now an uninhabited area of ruins, covered largely by the sands of the desert, which cannot be cultivated because of the nitre content of the ruins of the ancient city.

How did Jeremiah and Isaiah know what would happen to ancient Babylon? When they were alive there was no sign that Babylon would meet such a complete and disastrous end. How did Jeremiah know that:

1. Babylon would "become a heap"?
2. The fall of Babylon would take place in the reign of Nebuchadnezzar's son's son?
3. The waters of the river Euphrates would bypass Babylon, flowing in another channel miles from the city?
4. How did Isaiah know that the Arabs would refuse to pitch their tents there?

How did they know? Both Jeremiah and Isaiah claim 'the Lord' told them. Certainly it was not just a series of guesses. Then let us ask again: Is there an 'it' out there who has contacted certain people at certain times?

Be careful before you answer in the affirmative that there is an 'it' trying to contact, and seemingly succeeding in many cases, mankind for the prophecies of the ancient seers did not cease with the disappearance of Babylon. The ancient seers predicted things which have happened in our generation and things which have yet to happen in the very near future.

Is there an 'invisible hand' guiding the destiny of mankind? Is there a silent 'voice' whose bidding we unwittingly obey? If you answer those questions in the affirmative then this book may well change your politics, your religion and indeed the whole of your life!

You have been warned!

# 5.
# The Man
# who Pre-wrote
# History

It has been said that prophecy is history pre-written. How true that is you will be able to judge for yourself in this chapter.

Daniel is probably best known by most people for his lion's den experience — a favourite story among Sunday school teachers. Few, however, realise that Daniel was a great predictor of future events. Most of the Book of Daniel, when it was written, was written to foretell the future.

The time scope of the Book of Daniel is extraordinary, for his predictions span dates as widely apart as 604 B.C. and 1992 A.D. Thus there are events yet future to OUR time which Daniel foretold over 2600 years ago.

Daniel was a Jew who was taken to Babylon in the first deportation under Nebuchadnezzar. Despite his predictions of the downfall of Babylon, Daniel became one of the three high officials of the land. Daniel predicted the course of history from his time to our day and his prognostications came to be the pivot of the Messianic prophecies.

In this chapter I want to show how Daniel wrote the following predictions in 539 B.C. All the quotations in this chapter are taken from the eleventh chapter of the prophetic Book of Daniel.

The date of the prophecy is given in the first verse which reads "In the first year of Darius, the Mede, even I, stood to confirm and to strengthen him. And now I will show thee the truth ...."

539 B.C. was the FIRST YEAR of DARIUS the Mede.

---

## PROPHECY

*"And now I will shew thee the truth. Behold there shall stand up yet three Kings in Persia; and the fourth shall be far richer than they all; And by his strength through his riches he shall stir up all against the realm of Greece."*                                                                v.2

## FULFILMENT

Cyrus was the King of Persia when Daniel uttered his predictions as to what would happen to Persia in the years which lay ahead. After Cyrus, Daniel predicted, there would be three kings but he saw nothing eventful happening until a fourth king took the throne. The fourth king after Cyrus would, Daniel predicted, attack GREECE.

### XERXES I

Xerxes I was the fourth king after Cyrus. The ancient historian Heridotus tells us of the immense wealth of Xerxes I. He was, exactly as Daniel had predicted, the wealthiest of the four kings. The great ambition of Xerxes was to conquer Greece. His immense wealth enabled him to raise an army of five million two hundred and eighty three thousand men. He defeated the Spartans and destroyed Athens.

Xerxes had not been born when Daniel foretold his invasion of Greece, predicted the great army Xerxes would muster and his immense wealth.

## DATE OF FULFILMENT

486 B.C. 53 years after the prediction.

## PROPHECY

*"And a mighty king shall stand up, that shall rule with great dominion, and do according to his will. And when he shall stand up, his kingdom shall be broken, and shall be divided towards the four winds of the heaven; and not to his posterity, nor according to his dominion which he ruled:"*                                                                 v.3

## FULFILMENT

### ALEXANDER THE GREAT

150 years after Xerxes' attack on Greece came Alexander the Great. History records that he did 'according to his will' for Alexander was renowned for his autocratic behaviour. It was Alexander who was responsible for the destruction of the Persian Empire in 333 B.C.

In verse 3 Daniel foretells that the empire of this autocratic person would be divided into four parts! North — South — East — West. The succession of kings would not be through Alexander's family. All this was fulfilled 233 years after it had been predicted by Daniel.

## DATE OF FULFILMENT

333 B.C. 206 years after the prediction.

## FULFILMENT

### ALEXANDER'S EMPIRE DIVIDED

After Alexander died, four of his military governors divided the kingdom between them. In 306 B.C. Antigonus proclaimed himself King of the whole empire but Casander, the military governor of Macedonia, Seleucus, the military governor of Syria and Ptolemy, the military governor of Egypt, proclaimed themselves king of their own region.

## DATE OF FULFILMENT

306 B.C. 233 years after the prediction.

Thus, precisely as had been predicted by Daniel over 200 years before, was the empire of Alexander the Great divided into four and 'not to his posterity'. Nor was the empire 'after his dominion' because, being divided into four the empire was quite different territorially from that of Alexander.

Here the question must be asked, which we ask ourselves time and time again during the reading of this book: How did the prophet KNOW what would happen those many years after his death?

## PROPHECY

*"And the king of the south shall be strong, and one of his princes; and he shall be strong above him, and have dominion; his dominion shall be in great dominion. And in the end years [that is the end years of their struggle] they shall join themselves together; for the king's daughter of the south shall come to the king of the north to make an agreement:"*

v.5 - 6

## FULFILMENT

The centre of all the geographical reckoning of the ancient seers is PALESTINE. Therefore the 'King of the South' is the power existing in Egypt or to the South of Palestine and the 'King of the North' is Syria or a power existing to the North of Palestine. The word 'King' is often used to denote the nation and not always the king himself.

After the death of Alexander and the division of his kingdom, a long struggle for possession of Palestine ensued. This struggle lasted from 301-207 B.C.

## DATE OF FULFILMENT

301-207 B.C. 231-325 years after the prediction.

## FULFILMENT

The kings of Egypt for the period were:
(B.C.)
306-285 Ptolemy I, 285-247 Ptolemy II, 247-222 Ptolemy III, 222-205 Ptolemy IV, 205-181 Ptolemy V.

The kings of Syria for the period were:
306-301 Antigonus the One Eyed, 301-280 Seleucus Nicanor, 280-261 Antiochus I, 261-246 Antiochus II, 246-226 Seleucus II, 226-223 Seleucus III, 223-187 Antiochus III.

## ANTIOCHUS II AND BERENICE

The strife between the two kingdoms came to a head in the reigns of Ptolemy Philadelphus, King of Egypt and Antiochus II, King of Syria. The disruption was ended by a political marriage between Berenice, daughter of the King of Egypt (king of the south) and Antiochus II, King of Syria (king of the north). Antiochus disowned his wife to marry Berenice and also the two sons of his previous marriage.

So it was that the two kings 'joined themselves together' and the 'King's daughter of the South' came to 'the king of the north' to make an agreement. It all happened exactly as predicted almost three hundred years before.

## PROPHECY

*"But she [the daughter] shall not retain the power of the arm; neither shall he [the king of the North] stand nor his arm [power]: but she shall be given up, and they that begat her, and he that strengthened her in these times. But out of a branch of her roots shall one stand up in his estate."*

v.6 - 7

## FULFILMENT

Two years after the marriage of convenience, the father of Berenice, King Ptolemy, died. King Antiochus, the reason for his marriage to Berenice now being at an end, reinstated his wife and sons.

The restored wife, Laodice, still filled with hatred and burning for revenge, had Antiochus put to death (249 B.C.) after which she persuaded her son Seleucus to kill the deposed Berenice.

So it was that all who were party to this political arrangement suffered from it exactly as the prophet foretold. Within three years of the arrangement: 'He that brought her' — King Antiochus 'He that begat and strengthened her' — King Ptolemy, and Berenice herself were dead. Berenice did not 'retain the power'. King Antiochus did not retain his power. AND IT ALL HAPPENED THREE HUNDRED YEARS AFTER THE PROPHET DANIEL HAD PREDICTED IT! What was to happen next?

## PROPHECY

*"Which shall come with an army, and shall enter into the fortress of the king of the north [Syria], and shall deal against them, and shall prevail: And shall also carry captive into Egypt their gods, with their princes, and with their precious vessels of silver and gold:"*

v.7 - 8

## FULFILMENT

When Berenice and her only child were murdered that seemed to be the end of the matter. But the prophet had foretold that a 'branch of her roots shall stand up in his estate'.

Following the death of Berenice, Selucus, the murderer of Berenice and the son of Antiochus, came to the throne. How now could a branch out of Berenice's roots stand up in the King of Syria's estate? As is so often the case, it seemed the prophecy was incapable of being fulfilled.

## EUERGETES

Then King Ptolemy III of Egypt invaded Syria. King Ptolemy III was none other than Euergetes, BROTHER of Berenice. Euergetes attacked Syria in revenge for his sister's death. Exactly as the prophet had said 'out of her roots' stood one in Antiochus' estate.

Euergetes came, as foretold, with an army and prevailed. Syria was about to fall when news came to Euergetes that revolution had broken out in Egypt. He quickly returned to Egypt, taking many prisoners with him together with 2,500 idols and many vessels of silver and gold which the Syrians had taken from Egyptian temples. Thus was the prophecy, uttered over 300 years before, fulfilled, to the letter 'And he shall carry captive into Egypt their gods, with their princes, and with their precious vessels of silver and gold.'

## PROPHECY

*"And he shall continue more years than the king of the north. So the king of the south shall come into his kingdom, and shall return into his own land.*
*But his sons shall be stirred up and shall assemble a multitude of great forces: And one shall certainly come and pass through: Then shall he return, and be stirred up, even to his fortress. And the king of the south SHALL BE MOVED WITH CHOLER, and shall come forth and fight with him, even with the king of the north: And he shall set forth a great multitude; but the multitude shall be given into his hand. And when he hath taken away the multitude, his heart shall be lifted up; and he shall cast down many ten thousands but shall not be strengthened by it."*

v.8 - 12

## FULFILMENT

Ptolemy III (Euergetes) did 'continue more years than the king of the north' for he reigned for 25 years whereas Seleucus II reigned only 20 years.

The sons of Seleucus were indeed 'stirred up' by the treatment of their father at the hands of the Egyptians and they swore to avenge themselves on Egypt. The two sons, first Seleucus Ceraunus and then Antiochus the Great tried to rebuild the Syrian war machine to it's former strength. They did indeed 'assemble a multitude of great forces'.

## PTOLEMY IV

Ptolemy IV (Philopater), son of Euergetes, became King of Egypt in 222 B.C. His record was one of inactivity — certainly not the kind of man one would expect to take his country to war. Yet, history tells us, he was stirred with anger (choler) when he heard of the plans of Antiochus the Great to attack Egypt. Exactly as the prophet predicted he came forth to fight 'the king of the north'. The Syrian army was defeated at Raphia in 217 B.C.

DATE OF FULFILMENT

222 B.C. 317 years after the prediction.

PROPHECY

*"And in those times there shall many stand up against the king of the south; also the robbers of thy people shall exalt themselves to establish the vision, but they shall fall. So the king of the north shall come, and cast up a siege mound, and take the fortified cities; and the arms of the south shall not withstand, neither his chosen people, neither SHALL THERE BE ANY strength to withstand."*

v.14, 15

FULFILMENT

ANTIOCHUS IV

The exact translation of the phrase 'also the robbers of thy people shall exalt themselves to establish the vision' from the original is 'also the sons of the robbers of thy people shall lift themselves up to establish the vision; but they shall fall'.

Antiochus IV (Epiphenes) looted and defiled the temple. He took spoils of the City of Jerusalem, took women and children captive and possessed their cattle according to 1 Macc. 1: 29-32 and 2 Macc. 5:24. Robbery was one of his major vices as history attests. In the course of time the Jews rebelled against the oppression of Epiphenes. The last straw came when officers of Epiphenes' forces entered El-Mediah, as it is known today, and tried to force the priest Mattathias to foresake the law, offer sacrifices and burn incense. Mattathias refused and even killed one of his compatriots who did sacrifice on the altar, together with the king's commissioner. Mattathias pulled the altar down. He was supported by his fellow Jews, the revolt spread and the Wars of the Maccabees had started.

The son of Mattathias, Judas Maccabaeus, became the leader of the revolutionaries. Such was the power of the uprising and the contempt and fury that inspired it that these untrained men, men with little equipment with which to fight, set the army of Antiochus to flight. Judas Maccabaeus captured Jerusalem in 164 B.C., more than three and a half centuries after the prophet had predicted the event.

Excavations have shown that the struggle centred around Beth-Zur is a mound today known as Khirbet et-Tubeka. Two American architects, O.P.Sellers and W. Albright, excavated the site in 1931 and found over three hundred coins stamped with the names of Antiochus Epiphenes and Antiochus Eupator.

DATE OF FULFILMENT

164 B.C. 375 years after the prediction.

## PROPHECY

*"But he that cometh against him shall do according to his own will, and none shall stand before him; and he shall stand in the glorious land, which by his hand shall be consumed. He shall also set his face to enter with the strength of his whole kingdom, and upright ones with him; thus shall he do; and he shall give him the daughter of women, corrupting her, but she shall not stand ON HIS SIDE, neither be for him.*
*After this shall he turn his face unto the isles and shall take many, but a prince on his own behalf shall cause the reproach offered by him to cease; without his own reproach, he shall cause IT to turn upon him. Then shall he turn his face toward the fortresses of his own land, but he shall stumble and fall, and not be found."*

v.16 - 19

## FULFILMENT

### CAESAR AND CLEOPATRA

This is probably one of the most startling of all the predictions Daniel made. He had said of the armies of Antiochus Eupator 'but they shall fall'. For many years it seemed the prophecy was doomed not to be fulfilled, then from Carthage came the news that the armies of Rome had overthrown the armies of Hannibal and were pushing into Asia Minor.

Here are the things the prophet predicted would happen 476-481 years after his prophecy:

★ The Syrians would fail
★ Another would come and take their place who would do 'according to his own will'.
★ None would be able to stand against him.
★ He would stand in the 'glorious land' — PALESTINE.
★ He would give another person the 'daughter of a woman' and corrupt her.
★ She would not 'stand at his side', that is, she would not support him.
★ He would turn his face to the 'Islands'.
★ He would take many away from the 'Islands'.
★ A prince was to cause the reproach offered by him to cease.

Obviously Daniel regarded this person as one of the key people in history. In 63 B.C. Pompey, the Roman General, heading an all-conquering army, entered Jerusalem and it is certainly true to say that he did 'according to his own will'. It is an equally true statement of the policy of Rome in general.

It is also true that none were able to stand against the Roman Empire, they had defeated Hannibal, they sat astride the old Greek empire, they had subjugated Syria, conquered Palestine and stood at the gates of Egypt.

In 51 B.C. King Ptolemy Auletes of Egypt died. He ordered that his son

Ptolemy and his daughter Cleopatra (the Cleopatra of "Anthony and Cleopatra" fame) should marry and rule the kingdom. This with the blessing of the Romans they did.

Families do not, however, always live as 'happily ever after' as their parents hope they will, and, far from keeping the throne intact, and in the family, the arrangement had the opposite effect. Young Ptolemy drove his sister from Egypt and she sought shelter in Syria.

In 47 B.C. Cleopatra met Julius Caesar in Alexandria and became his mistress. They subsequently had a child, Caesarion. Ptolemy was killed in battle and, whilst Cleopatra was still the mistress of Caesar he prevailed upon her to marry her younger brother Ptolemy XV. Thus Caesar, in the words of the prophet 'corrupted her' by causing her to undertake a second incestuous marriage and by, after that marriage, retaining her as his mistress.

Caesar later caused Cleopatra to leave her husband and live in Rome. So utterly had she been corrupted by Caesar that when he died she returned to Egypt, arranged for her brother to be killed, and her son to be made joint ruler of Egypt with herself.

'He will turn his face to the Islands'. Julius Caesar did, as we well know, invade the British Isles. We shall see in a later chapter how very significant those two words 'the Islands' are in the writings of the ancient seers, there was no doubt among them where the 'Islands' were or of the identity of the nation that dwelt there.

Caesar 'turned his face to the Islands' quite literally. His invasion of Britain was no chance passing through. Caesar turned his face to the Islands because of the constant support given by the British in the fighting in Gaul against Roman oppression.

Some have tried to interpret the word 'islands' as 'coast-lands', but this is an unworthy devise for there are twelve words in the Hebrew which can mean 'coastlands' but only this ONE which is capable of the translation 'islands'. The word 'islands' used in this way was not at all unfamiliar to the ancient seers as we shall see in our chapter "The Mystery of the Missing Millions".

It is perhaps a coincidence that the story of Caesar and Cleopatra gained world wide fame through the writings of a bard, William Shakespeare, who wrote, those many years ago, in a tiny hamlet in 'the islands' — one wonders!

'He shall stumble and fall'. Is it not amazing that these are the exact words history uses to record the death of Julius Caesar and the very words the prophet used to predict his death 500 years before it happened? Caesar, you will remember, was stabbed to death, on the Ides of March, in an attack so frenzied that his killers wounded each other. History tells us that Caesar stumbled, then, pulling his cloak over his head as if to protect himself, he fell.

Can you really believe that it is coincidence that:

★ The Romans did cause the Syrians to fail?
★ The Romans did do according to their will and no-one was able to stand against them?
★ The Romans did stand in the 'glorious land'?
★ Julius Caesar did, in world renowned circumstances, corrupt a woman?
★ Caesar did turn his face to the Islands?
★ Caesar did 'stumble and fall' as he died?

How did Daniel know?

## DATE OF FULFILMENT

63 B.C. - 54 B.C. 476-481 years after the prediction.

## PROPHECY

*"Then shall stand up in his estate a raiser of taxes in the glory of the kingdom, but within a few days he shall be destroyed, neither in anger, nor in battle".*                                                              v.20

## FULFILMENT

### AUGUSTUS CAESAR

Just seventeen years before Jesus was born in Bethlehem, Augustus Caesar became the first Emperor of Rome. Exactly as the prophet had foretold over 500 years before, Augustus Caesar was to gain a reputation as a great raiser of taxes. Augustus Caesar was Emperor of Rome when Jesus was born and the record of the birth of Jesus bears witness to Caesar's tax-gathering expertise:

*"And it came to pass in those days, that there went out from Caesar Augustus, that all the world should be taxed"*

Luke 2:1

It has been held by some that the word 'taxed' in that passage would be better rendered 'registered'. Be that as it may, there is no doubt that the registration was for the purpose of extending and perfecting the Roman system of taxation. The 'descriptio orbis', a state paper which equated with the treasury papers of a modern nation, was written in the hand of Augustus Caesar himself. These papers contain 'the budget', how much tax had to be raised and how much spent on the military, secret service, subsidies etc.

How was the end of the 'raiser of taxes' to come about? The prophet tells us! "Within a few days he shall be destroyed, neither in anger nor in battle." Unlike other leaders of Rome Augustus Caesar was not struck down by an assassin nor killed in battle, he died peacefully. The nation mourned, he was deified by his people and his name was revered.

## DATE OF FULFILMENT
17 B.C. 522 years after the prediction.

## PROPHECY
*"And in his estate shall stand up a vile person, to whom they shall not give the honor of the kingdom; but HE SHALL COME IN PEACEABLY, and OBTAIN THE KINGDOM BY FLATTERIES. And with the arms of a flood they shall be overflown from before him, and shall be broken; yea, also the prince of the covenant."* v.21

## FULFILMENT
### TIBERIUS CAESAR
In the estate of Augustus Caesar 'stood up' his son-in-law Tiberius Caesar. The prophet had foretold that the person to follow Augustus Caesar would be a 'vile person'. It is an indication of the vileness of Tiberius Caesar that even secular historians are ashamed to describe fully the depth of his depravity. Suetonius, the ancient Roman historian writes: "On retiring to Capreae he (Tiberius) made himself a private sport house, where sexual extravagances were practised for his secret pleasure. Bevies of girls and young men, whom he had collected from all over the empire as adepts in unnatural practises, and known as spintriae, would copulate before him in groups of three, to excite his waning passions ... SOME ASPECTS OF HIS CRIMINAL OBSCENITY ARE ALMOST TOO VILE TO DISCUSS, much less believe. Imagine training little boys, whom he called his 'minnows' to chase him while he went swimming and get between his legs to lick and nibble him. Or letting babies not yet weaned from their mothers' breast suck at his breast or groin — such a filthy old man had he become!"

A vile person indeed! Is it not amazing that Suetonius, who incidentally was not born until almost 600 years after the prophet Daniel had died and had certainly not read Daniel's writings, used the very word of the prophet — 'VILE' ?

Seneca said of Tiberius "He was only drunk once and that was all his life".

Mallonia, who ultimately committed suicide because of his unnatural sexual demands upon her, called Tiberius "That filthy-mouthed, hairy, stinking old man".

Even when he sacrificed to his god the lust of Tiberius ran amok, for he indecently assaulted both the male incense carrier and his brother: Because they had the temerity to complain Tiberius had their legs broken.

This 'vile person' had an incestuous relationship with his mother and his homosexuality caused him to have a young man castrated so that he could take him as a lover. Certainly the prophet was correct when he described him thus!

There was something else which the prophet foretold would happen in the reign of Tiberius which was to be an outstanding event in world history. The 'Prince of the Covenant' was to be destroyed, or 'broken'.

The word 'Prince' in the original is exactly the same word used by the prophet Isaiah to describe the coming Messiah — 'Sar' — "The Prince of Peace".

Is it therefore a further coincidence that Jesus of Nazareth was crucified during the reign of Tiberius the 'vile person'?

We have seen how accurately Daniel predicted the course of history from the time of Cyrus to the death of Jesus of Nazareth. Daniel predicted the course of history beyond the coming of Jesus, beyond the coming of Mohammed, beyond the year 1917 and beyond our day to the year 1992. But all that is for later chapters.

# 6.
# Breaking
# the
# Code..........

The thunder of anti-aircraft guns reached a crescendo as I sat at my desk preparing a document for transmission via the transatlantic cable to the United States of America. It was Winter, it was dark outside and the light inside was confined to that shining on my papers. The windows were shrouded in blackout drapes, without which the slightest glimmer of light in the office would have been greeted by the familiar roar of the air-raid warden — "Put that light out!"

They were dark days in more ways than that, for, though the tide of battle had turned in our favour, the war was not yet won. Important events were afoot, we were standing on a threshhold, the other side of which were the momentous events which are now part of the history of the Second World War.

Every nation wanted to know what the other was doing, information was at a premium. Men and women risked their lives to gather it and others risked their lives to make sure they did not.

The document before me was a communication from the United States Naval Base and, though I prepared it for transmission and read it several times, I do not know to this day what information that document contained — it was in code. The message was intended for somebody, somewhere, at a particular time, and it was important that that person understand it, but it was equally important that other people should not understand it. A message designed both to inform and to conceal information.

Two world wars have familiarised us all with the reasons for coding messages. Those who do not remember the war will undoubtedly have read in books, or seen on film or television, the clandestine activities of those whose work required messages intended for one person to be made unintelligible to others, and those whose job it was to break the codes. I think everyone knows the reason for code is to inform the people of one's choice, while rendering the message incomprehensible to those who have not got the 'key'.

'The voices' of old were not slow to realise the necessity for coding their messages. They knew that those against whom they spoke would spare no effort in their attempts to destroy not only them but their writings. They knew also that there would be those who, for personal gain, would attempt to pervert their prophecies.

The Jewish prophet writing about 539 B.C. makes it plain that there is a key to prophetic writings:

*And I heard but I understood not. Then said I, O my Lord, what shall be the end of these things?And he said, Go thy way Daniel; for the words are closed up and sealed till the time of the end.... none of the wicked shall understand but the wise SHALL understand.*

Book of Daniel 12: 9-10

Daniel, one of the most prolific of the ancient seers, says there is a time in human history when the things he wrote will be understood, that period of history he calls 'the time of the end'. He tells us, too, that there is a state of mind which is essential to the understanding of his writings. He places the state of mind he calls 'wicked' in apposition to the state of mind he calls 'wise'.

When one reads the Christmas story of how Herod, having heard the prophecy of the Messiah's birth, slaughtered the innocents in his attempt to kill the Messiah, one is brought to realise the lengths to which men will go to further, or maintain, their own position of power in the world: For good reason the seers coded their messages. Today the Soviets suppress and eradicate literature which does not conform to the party line, as did the Nazis during their short reign of terror. Little has changed throughout the ages, we can well imagine what would have happened to the documents of the ancient seers had they not carefully veiled the meaning of their writings.

We have already mentioned the difficulty an 'It' would have in communicating with a people of not only lesser intelligence but also a people without experience of an entirely different form of existence from their own. There is, too, the problem of the developing technology! Even today, when technological advance is all around us and part of our everyday lives, experts have to speak to us in similes, showing us simplified diagrams and graphs. How many of us really know how a nuclear reactor works? How many of us fully understand how our own body works? We have an inkling of how the wonders around us work only because someone simplifies them for us.

How could a prophet, having had a vision of our age and seeing an aeroplane, describe it? To get an idea of how difficult that would be, and so you will appreciate the more the reason for the imagery used by the ancient seers, just try it for yourself: Sit for a moment and imagine that you have to explain what an aeroplane looks like, and what it does, to someone who has never seen an aeroplane — someone who lived two hundred years ago.

The seers were face to face with the eternal problem; how to make the truth available to all generations. Try to describe an army tank and it's function to someone who has never seen anything more sophisticated than a horse and trap! Explain a television set and it's function to people who have not even known electricity. Some of the seers were talking of things many thousands of years forward from their time. Is it any wonder that they had to use imagery and code?

## THE TIME CODE.

It is generally accepted that numbers have a significance in the writings of the ancient seers. It may, however, come as a surprise to many to realise that the major events in the history of our earth were foretold by the ancient seers and exact dates given when the prophecies would be fulfilled.

General Allenby's victory at Jerusalem in the First World War was foretold by the seer Daniel more that 2500 years before it happened — I'll give you the details in a later chapter.

The establishment of the Jewish state of Israel in 1948 was foretold a similar number of years before it happened.

A few people recognised these dates in the writings of the ancient seers as early as the end of the last century. As we have said previously, Dr. Grattan Guiness wrote a very well-known work "Light for the Last Days" — published in 1887. In it he said:

> "There can be no question that those who live to see this year 1917 will have reached one of the most important, perhaps the most momentous, of these terminal years."

Eleven years later, in 1898, Dr. Aldersmith wrote a book under the title "The Fullness of the Nations" in which he said:

> "Students of prophecy are agreed that when the times of the Gentiles are fulfilled, and Jerusalem ceases to be trodden down, we may expect it to pass into the hands of it's rightful owners. This period may end about A.D.1917. Time only will show."

That is not being wise AFTER the event, is it? They were but two among the many who waited patiently for that momentous year, 1917, the year which commenced the terminal years of earth's history. Both predicted from dates revealed by the ancient seers — neither of them claimed to have any prophetic gifts themselves.

## ONE PROPHETIC DAY – ONE YEAR.

The prophet Moses gives us the key to the time scale referred to as ' a day' in the prophetic writings: In the year 1450 B.C. he wrote:

> *After the number of days in which ye searched the land, even forty days, each day for a year, shall ye bear your iniquities ....EVEN FORTY YEARS.....*
>
> Numbers 14:34

Ezekiel the seer also reveals the code of one day representing one year when seven hundred years later he wrote:

> *......and thou shalt bear the iniquity of Judah forty days; I have appointed thee each day for a year.*
>
> Ezekiel 4:8

A day, therefore, in prophetic terms represents one year. We'll see later the fascinating predictions that are revealed by this breaking of the 'time code'.

## A 'TIME'.

There is a period which is referred to by the prophets as a 'time'. We shall see later how important it is to the breaking of the prophetic code and we should find out what length of time a 'time' is.

Very early on in the writings of the prophets we are told that the period of punishment on Israel for national apostacy would be a period of 'seven times'. Moses, speaking on behalf of his source of inspiration, which he describes as 'The Lord your God', writes:

> *And if ye will not be reformed by me by these things, but will walk contrary unto me, Then will I also walk contrary unto you, and will punish you yet SEVEN TIMES for your sins.*
>
> Leviticus 26: 23-24

It is indicative of the single source from which all the seers drew their inspiration that it is not until over 1500 years later that John the Divine uttered a prophecy which allowed us to understand the length of a 'time'.

Remember that a day is a year in prophecy!

The prophet John is on the Isle of Patmos, receiving the vision which we now know as the Apocalypse or the Book of Revelation. I quote at length because it is vital to the identification of the period referred to as a 'time' and the identification of that period is essential to the understanding of the predictions of the seers as they affect the history of our world today.

> *And there appeared a great wonder in heaven — a woman clothed with the sun, and the moon under her feet, and upon her head a crown of twelve stars. And she, being with child, cried, travailing in birth, and pained to be delivered.*
>
> *And there appeared another wonder in heaven; and, behold, a great red dragon, having seven heads and ten horns, and seven crowns upon his heads. And his tail drew the third part of the stars of heaven and did cast them to the earth; and the dragon stood before the woman who was ready to be delivered, to devour her child as soon as it was born.*
>
> *And she brought forth a male child, who was to rule all nations with a rod of iron; and her child was caught up unto God, and to His Throne. And the woman fled into the wilderness where she had a place prepared by God, that they should feed her there a thousand two hundred and threescore days.*
>
> The Apocalypse Chapter 12: 1-6

In this second quotation John sees the same woman, beset by the same dragon, fly into the same wilderness.

> *And when the dragon saw that he was cast unto the earth, he persecuted the woman who brought forth the male child. And to the woman were given two wings of a great eagle, that she might fly into the wilderness, into her place, where she is nourished for a time, and times, and half a time, from the face of the serpent.*
>
> The Apocalypse Chapter 12: 13: 14

The same woman, the same dragon, and the same wilderness, therefore she must be in the wilderness for the SAME length of time.

So the 1260 days ("... a thousand two hundred and three score days") stands for 1260 years. What then is a time, times and half a time? Three and a half times, of course. One time, two times and half a time — three and a half times. So three and a half 'times' equals 1260 years. Now let us divide 1260 by 3½ to find how long a 'time' is. 1260 divided by 3½ equals 360, the exact number of days in the ancient Hebrew year.

A 'time' is shown to be a year of days. One 'time' equals 360 years. The punishment on Israel for apostasy was seven times or 2520 years.

The prophet Daniel gave a starting date and a period of 1260 years which ended in 1917 —. what happened in that year? The story is fascinating and awe inspiring.

Daniel also gave a time period of 1290 years which expired in 1948 — we shall see what happened in that year.

## THE SEA.

John wrote the Apocalypse around the year A.D. 95.

The declared intention of the book is to tell of the past, record the present and foretell the future. 'The present' to John was, of course, A.D. 95, 'the past', things which happened prior to that date and the things 'hereafter' events after that date. The 'voice' John heard instructed him to

*Write the things which thou has seen, and the things which are, and the things which shall be hereafter.*

The Apocalypse 1:19

We are often told we should not 'bother' with the Apocalypse, 'it is much too difficult to understand.' Surprising advice, indeed, since it is supposed to be a 'revelation' — who ever heard of a revelation which was not to be understood? Of course, you cannot sit and read the Apocalypse as you would a novel and admittedly, on first reading, it is difficult to understand. Shorthand is difficult, people study it for years to become proficient in writing and reading it, so why should we expect not to have to gain some proficiency if we are to understand a book such as the Apocalypse? That something is in code does not mean it is not to be understood, but, rather that it contains information of such importance that it should be the subject of much effort to understand it.

The writer of the Apocalypse makes it plain that he wrote the book to be read AND understood. In Chapter one of the Apocalypse we read "Blessed is he that readeth, and they that hear the words of this prophecy, and keep those things which are written in it; for the time is at hand." How can we be 'blessed' by things we cannot understand? How can we 'keep' the words of something we cannot understand? Both the words

'Apocalypse' and 'Revelation' mean DISCLOSURE OF THAT WHICH IS PREVIOUSLY HIDDEN OR UNKNOWN.

Having said that, I can quite understand why the Apocalypse, and indeed some of the writings of the prophets Ezekiel and Daniel, can be offputting. Beasts rising from the sea, frogs coming out of the mouth of a dragon, mountains being thrown into oceans, the moon being turned to blood — it's all very confusing stuff unless one knows how to crack the code. You must at the moment accept my word that once the code is cracked such prophecies become fascinating and leave one with the exhilaration of discovery.

## 'MOUNTAIN' IS THE CODEWORD FOR A MIGHTY NATION.

Here is one quotation which refers to the casting of the burning mountain into the sea.

*And the second angel sounded, and, as it were, a great mountain burning with fire was cast into the sea; and a third part of the sea became blood;*

Revelation 8:8

One of the outstanding features of the ancient seers is that their predictions, though separated in time by many hundreds of years, are all separate parts of the same picture. Each writer provides a piece that fits the jigsaw and it is not until the pieces are correctly put together that the picture as a whole can be appreciated. Thus one has to 'cross reference' the writings of one seer with the writings of the others if the code is to be broken. A part of the jigsaw we do not understand often becomes understandable when we compare what is missing with a part 'cut' by another seer several hundred years before.

Thus, if we want to know the meaning of that 'great mountain burning with fire' which was 'cast into the sea' written of by John in A.D.95, we have to refer to the prediction of the prophet Micah written eight hundred years previously.

*But in the last days it shall come to pass, that the mountain of the Lord's house shall be established in the top of the mountains, and it shall be exalted above the hills, and people shall flow into it.*

Micah 4:1

The prophet Isaiah uses exactly the same word 'mountain' in the second verse of his second chapter, whilst Daniel the prophet records a vision of 'a stone which is cut out without hands' which becomes a mountain, and fills the whole earth.

A mountain symbolised a kingdom. The great mountain of Revelation

8:8 is therefore a great kingdom and the symbolism of 'burning with fire' is evidently that that kingdom is to be consumed by a conflagration. But what does being 'cast into the sea' mean? Let us look at the symbolic use of the word sea.

## SEA IS THE CODEWORD FOR THE RESTLESS MASSES OF PEOPLE.

David King of Israel, writing 1000 years before Christ, says of his God:

*Which by his strength setteth fast the mountains; being girded with power: Which stilleth the noise of the seas, the noise of their waves, and the tumult of the people.* Psalm 65

David the prophet equates the restless sea with the restless masses of the people.

Over one thousand years later the 'angel of God' is recorded by John in the Apocalypse as saying:

*The waters which thou sawest, where the whore sitteth, are PEOPLES, and MULTITUDES, and NATIONS, and TONGUES.* Apocalypse 17:15

The sea is an apt codeword for the troubled and unstable masses of people, at one time placid and at another tempestuous. That mighty ocean we can sail in the most fragile craft in the sunshine, into which the old lady may dip her toe on Bank Holiday, and in which children may splash with joy, can, in hours, turn into one of the most powerful agents of destruction known to man. Villages have disappeared in minutes in vast tidal waves on occasion, and, more usually, massive concrete bastions which have been built against it are torn away in a roar of fury, and mighty ships splintered, to disappear forever in the depths.

Well does the sea represent the troubled masses of people who now populate this earth!

Does the prophecy of the great mountain burning and being thrown into the sea now begin to make sense? A great kingdom, being consumed by a conflagration or revolution, is submerged beneath the troubled mass of people to disappear without trace forever.

We will come back to that prophecy, and how it fits into the events which are happening around us, later.

## 'THE EARTH' IS THE CODEWORD FOR THE SUBJECTED, DOWNTRODDEN PEOPLE.

The earth is the foundation upon which the mountains stand and the towering grandeur of the mountain hides it from view, it receives little credit for it's massive feat of upholding the mighty mountain. The earth is compressed beneath the mountain, and one can literally say OPPRESSED by it. The earth represents the ordered mass of society, of the human beings who have always upheld kingdoms but who have rarely benefited from the grandeur of those kingdoms.

## THE BEASTS.

There can be few who do not know a little, all be it a garbled little, of the prophecies of the Apocalypse, since the film 'The Omen' was released. I doubt if very many took the trouble to obtain a copy of the Apocalypse to read the real story of the beast — 666. Yet the real story is even more terrifying, more interesting and more awe-inspiring than the book or the film version, and what's more it has existed and is existing in the real world, not the world of fiction.

Here's a short extract from the thirteentn chapter of Apocalypse in which John introduces his readers to the beasts:

*And I stood upon the sand of the sea, and saw a beast rise up out of the sea, having seven heads and ten horns, and upon his horns ten crowns, and upon his head the name of blasphemy.*

Then again:

*And I beheld another beast coming up out of the earth; and he had two horns like a lamb, and he spoke like a dragon.*

In the seventeenth chapter of the Apocalypse John gives us the key to the symbolism of the beast:

*And the angel said unto me, Why didst thou marvel? I will tell thee the mystery of the woman, and of the beast that carrieth her, which hath the seven heads and ten horns.*
*The beast that thou sawest was, and is not, and shall ascend out of the bottomless pit, and go into perdition; and they that dwell on the earth shall wonder, whose names were not written in the book of life from the foundation of the world, when they behold the beast that was, and is not, and yet is.*
*And here is the mind which hath wisdom. The seven heads are seven mountains on which the woman sitteth. And there are seven kings: five are fallen, and one is, and the other is not yet come; and when he cometh, he must continue a short space.*
*And the beast that was, and is not, even he is the eighth, and is of the seven, and goeth into perdition.*
*And the ten horns thou sawest are ten kings, who have received no*

*kingdom as yet, but receive power as kings one hour with the beast.*
*These have one mind, and shall give their power and strength unto the beast.*                                    Apocalypse Chapter 17:7—13

Thus we know that the seer is quite aware that there is not, at any time in human history, going to be a literal animal rising out of the sea to afflict the nations.

The beast is a montage of world powers contributed to at various times by many nations and kings. Many empires and alliances in the history of mankind illustrate the political power with a single destiny though not single purpose or nationality.

*Those four Great Beasts that you have seen are four Empires, which will be established on the earth.*                    Daniel 7:17

*Then he said, 'The Fourth Beast is a Fourth Empire on earth. It will be different from all the Empires, and devour all the earth, and thrash it, and break it.*
*And the Ten Horns of the Empire, are Ten Kingdoms that will arise; but another will arise after them, and it will differ from these kingdoms, and will depose three kings. It will also speak in opposition to the HIGHEST and persecute the Saints of the MOST HIGH and determine to change the Times, and the Laws; and they will be given into his hand for a period, and periods, and half a period.*                                          Daniel 7:23-25

## THE DRAGON.

The ancient seers believed that just as there was a living God so there was a living Devil. Who are we, who see after many thousands of years of civilisation such unbelievable cruelty among men, to deny that?

We are familiar with our science fiction films which depict the goodling with supernormal powers fighting the badling with supernormal powers. Is there a rational explanation as to why educated people, living in a scientific and allegedly enlightened age, should still settle their differences on the battlefield?

The dragon is the symbol in prophecy of all Satanic effort directed against the Kingdom of Israel. John leaves us in no doubt as to the entity depicted as the 'Dragon' in the prophecies:

*And I saw an angel come down from heaven, having the key of the bottomless pit and a great chain in his hand. And he laid hold of the dragon, that old serpent, who is the Devil and Satan, and bound him a thousand years.*                            Apocalypse 20:1,2

It is of vital importance in trying to understand the message of the prophets to realise that they saw the destiny of the world as being in the hands of supernatural agents rather than the destiny of the world being steered by the will of man. They regarded nations as being the earthly agents of the supernatural powers that motivated them. The seer Paul said:

*We wrestle not against flesh and blood, but against principalities, against powers, against the rulers of the darkness of this world, against spiritual wickedness in high places.*

Ephesians 6:12

How a nation such as Germany could, in a few years, have become the habitation of monsters, especially in their dealings with the Jews, is astounding. What happened to this brave, friendly and cultured people? The Germans were not by nature a cruel race and they are not a cruel race today. The whole of Europe is indebted to them for their great contribution through the years to civilisation, culture, and the arts. Admitting the traumatic effect upon the German nation of the ill-conceived Treaty of Versailles, their subsequent plunge into hyper-inflation, mass unemployment and their desire to regain lost territories, none of that explains the depths of cruelty to which some in that nation sank and to which others acquiesed. Was that unbelievable phenomena really just the admittedly thin veneer of civilisation — for civilisation is an unbelievably thin covering on all of us — being torn away or was it something altogether more sinister, a nation being controlled by some supernatural power? Certainly the events of the decade prior to 1945 were uncharacteristic of the German race.

We read of exorcism being practised more frequently these days. Indeed, exorcism, once reported as a matter of curiosity, is now reported by the press as a matter of fact. We read of houses, places of distress and turbulence and in the grip of evil, becoming places of peace after exorcism. Is it possible that these evil forces, which many believe afflict individuals and infest buildings, may also afflict nations? The prophets taught it is so and who are we, having witnessed the events of our lifetime, to gainsay it?

## SUN, MOON AND STARS.

In Moses' Book of Genesis we read:

*And God said, Let there be lights in the firmament of heaven to divide the day from the night; and let them be for signs, and for seasons, and for days and years; and let them be for lights in the midst of the firmament of the heaven to give light upon the earth: and it was so.*
*And God made two great lights; the greater light to rule the day,*

*and the lesser light to rule the night: he made the stars also.*
Genesis 1: 14, 15, 16

There is little need for me to spend much time proving that the sun, moon and stars in prophecy refer as follows:

*The sun*
Primary rulers in earths history
*The moon*
Those of lesser stature who rule by the power or reflected glory of the primary rulers
*The stars*
Those petty authoritarians of whom there are millions, who, like the stars, do not shed much light but still form the background of the power structure

I do not know of one student of the ancient prophets who would not agree with that interpretation and the conclusion would seem too obvious to gainsay.

I would like you to note, however, the functions Genesis attributes to the sun, moon and stars:

## TO DIVIDE THE DAY FROM NIGHT.
*For signs*
The star of Bethlehem almost 1500 years after Genesis was written was but one example of such a sign and the wise men of the day recognised 'his star'.
## FOR SEASONS.
*For days and years*
They are the method by which days and years are fixed.
As rulers of the day and night.

Here is a prophecy from the Apocalypse which is meaningless until we have the key to unlock the mystery of the symbolism in the words 'sun, moon and stars'.

*And the fourth angel sounded [the fourth trumpet] and the third part of the sun was smitten, and the third part of the moon, and the third part of the stars.* Apocalypse 8:12

The prophecy only becomes meaningful when we realise that it speaks of the day when anarchy replaces authoritarian government. Even today there is probably no leader in the world who can sleep peacefully. Everywhere authority is being questioned, everywhere old loyalties are breaking down. Ferment from the lower stratas of society, not only in

Britain and America but in the Soviet block, are an indication of the trend towards 'grass roots' government.

## THE FIG TREE AND THE VINEYARD.

It is understandable that the ancient seers of Israel should prophesy mainly about Israel.

In a later chapter we shall deal with the mystery of the missing millions: Suffice it here to say that in 970 B.C. the Kingdom of Israel split into two separate entities — the House of Judah and the House of Israel. The House of Judah (later known as the Jews) consisted of the Tribe of Judah, the Tribe of Benjamin and a few of the priestly Tribe of Levi. The ten tribes formed the House of Israel.

The land the world knows as the nation of Israel today is NOT the Kingdom of Israel, though it is a part of the Kingdom of Israel. It is not either the House of Israel and it is not any part of the House of Israel. The nation of Israel as it exists in the world today is the old House of Judah, the tribes of Judah, Benjamin and a few of the tribe of Levi. This, by the way, is a fact recognised by leaders in the Jewish faith.

It has been well put as follows: All Jews are Israelites but not all Israelites are Jews, just as all Welshmen are British but not all Britons are Welshmen!

Unlike many commentators, the seers never speak of the House of Judah when they mean the House of Israel or the House of Israel when they mean the House of Judah.

We shall never interpret the seer's prognostications correctly unless we are careful to differentiate between things that really differ.

The Kingdom of Israel means the twelve tribes.
The House of Judah (the Jews or modern Israel) the two tribes.
The House of Israel the ten tribes which were scattered abroad.

In prophetic code 'vine' or 'vineyard' represent the House of Israel, the ten tribes which are not part of present day Israel nor have they been united with the House of Judah since that fateful day in 970 B.C. when unacceptable taxation demands caused them to go their separate ways — and we think our Chancellors of the Exchequer present us with NEW problems!

The prophet Isaiah identifies the symbolism of the vine in prophetic utterance when he says:

*The vineyard of the Lord of hosts is the house of Israel, and the men of Judah his pleasant plant.* Isaiah 5:7

Jeremiah the prophet, writing 700 B.C., reveals the symbolism of the fig tree:

*The Lord showed me, and, behold, two baskets of figs were set before the temple of the Lord ... One basket had very good figs, even like the figs that are first ripe; and the other had very bad figs, which could not be eaten they were so bad.*
*Then said the Lord unto me, What seest thou Jeremiah? And I said Figs; the good figs, very good; and the bad, very bad, that cannot be eaten, they are so bad.*
*Thus saith the Lord, the God of Israel, Like those good figs so will I acknowledge those who are carried away captive of Judah.*
The prophet Jeremiah. Chapter 24: 1-5

The symbol of the fig tree is of vital interest to us. Throughout the centuries men have speculated about the 'end of the world'. At one time people who talked about the world coming to an end were considered at the very best eccentric and at the worst positively insane. As modern weapons became more destructive, more people began to see, especially in the late 1800's and the early 1900's that the possibility of world wide destruction was ever more plausible.

Nuclear weapons have turned the tide of thinking. Not so many years ago the man who believed in the possibility of this old world of ours coming to an end was considered a crank, few people today would doubt that there is a distinct possibility that the world will one day come to an end in a nuclear holocaust.

Do you know that men were speculating about the end of the world when Jesus was on earth? In fact Jesus' disciples asked Him when the end of the world would be — AND HE GAVE THEM THE ANSWER.

*And they [the disciples] asked Him [Jesus], saying, Master, when shall these things be? And what shall be the sign of Thy coming and of the end of the world?*                    Matthew 24:3

In His reply Jesus said:

*Now learn a parable of the fig tree: When it's branch is yet tender and it putteth forth leaves, ye know that summer is near.*
Matthew 24:32

In other words when the fig tree (the Jews) begin to bear fruit and show new life, that is the sign that the bitter winter is coming to it's close and the first warming rays of the sun are near.

Someone will say : "Summer? What's so good about the end of the world? I wouldn't liken the end of the world to summer!"

Well, here's news for you! The seers make it plain that this world is NOT going to come to an end. There are a lot of hard times ahead yet, there is the most frightful battle of earth's history, but the world will not be destroyed — ACCORDING TO THE PROPHETS, SUMMER IS NIGH!

The word in the question to Jesus translated 'world' means 'age' or 'dispensation'. "What will be the sign of thy coming and the end of the age!"

According to the prophets we are rapidly approaching the end of the age, but take heart for they make it plain that as this age dies in the most terrible of death-throes, a new and glorious age for all mankind is being born. Though the prophets take us by the hand and lead us through the valley of the shadow of death they give us a message of ultimate hope.

Great Britain will never be called upon to suffer nuclear war on her territory nor will the United States of America be the victim of nuclear war, as we shall see in a later chapter.

Since that glorious day when a British General walked bare-headed through the Jaffa Gate and into the old city of Jerusalem to pronounce that he had "not come as conqueror but as deliverer," the Jewish 'fig-tree' has sent forth it's shoots, it has born so much fruit that we may rightly say it is laden down with fruit. The summer is nigh!

I want you to mark well the difference between the 'fig tree', the House of Judah (the Jews) and the 'vine' the House of Israel (the ten lost tribes) because without keeping that constantly before us we can never understand what the prophets have to say. The 'fig tree' and the 'vine' are both very important code words.

Israel, that is the House of Israel, is never spoken of as the fig tree but as the 'vine': The prophet Hosea makes it plain in his tenth chapter.

*Israel is an empty vine, he bringeth forth fruit unto himself:*
Book of Hosea 10:1

## THE SHEEP.

Jesus Christ was a prophet even by the most specific definition of the word 'prophet', that is, one who foretells future events.

He described Himself as the good shepherd, but who are the sheep? Many of the great hymns liken the 'sinner' to the sheep and of course that is a legitimate spiritualisation, but in fact the real usage of the word 'sheep' is in respect of the people of Israel.

David, King of Israel, gives us the key to the codeword 'sheep' when he writes:

*But [the Lord] made his own people to go forth like sheep, and guided them in the wilderness like a flock.* Psalm 78:52

And again:

*For he is our God; and we are the people of his pasture, and the
sheep of his hand.*                                                    Psalm 95:7

I think most people to be familiar enough with King David's 23rd Psalm
"The Lord is my Shepherd" for it not to be necessary to quote it here.
The prophet Isaiah wrote:

*Israel is a scattered sheep; the lions have driven him away: first the
king of Assyria hath devoured him; and last this Nebuchadnezzar
king of Babylon hath broken his bones.*                  Jeremiah 50:17

The prophet Ezekial leaves us in no doubt as to the identity of the
'sheep' of the prophecies when he writes:

*For thus saith the Lord God; Behold I, even I, will both search my
sheep, and seek them out. As a shepherd seeketh out his flock in
the day that he is among his sheep that are scattered; so will I seek
out my sheep, and will deliver them out of all places where they
have been scattered in the cloudy and dark day. And I will bring
them out from the people, and gather them from the countries,
and will bring them to their own land, and feed them upon the
mountains of Israel by the rivers, and in all the inhabited places of
the country ... I will feed my flock.*                      Ezekiel 34.

When Jesus was preaching outside Palestine, in the country around
Tyre and Sidon, Gentile country, a Syro-Phoenician woman asked Him to
come and heal her daughter. Jesus Christ replied "*I am not sent but to the
lost sheep of the House of Israel.*"
Such sayings we are pleased to ignore because they do not fit in with the
picture we humanitarians like to paint of the supreme being, a supreme
being it has taken us thousands of years to make in our own image.
Ask most religious people who the 'sheep' of the scriptures are
symbolic of and you will most surely receive the reply 'those who have
wandered from the fold, and those who have sinned, those who have
transgressed.' Not so! The word 'sheep' is used to denote the children of
Israel, both the House of Judah (the Jews) and the House of Israel (the ten
tribes). Until we realise that we will not be able to appreciate the prophecy
hidden and enshrined in that otherwise unintelligible saying of Jesus:

*And other sheep [The House of Israel] I have which are not of this
fold [the Jews]; them also must I bring, and they shall hear my
voice: and there shall be one fold and one shepherd.* John 10:14-16

Unless one understands the 'code' it is easy to miss the fact that in that seemingly simple statement is enshrined, as we shall see in a future chapter, a prediction by Jesus the prophet of Nazareth of an event to take place which is yet future, an event which will be one of the most momentous events of earth's history. That event will take place within the next few years.

Who were the 'other sheep'? Obviously not the Jews because He was speaking to the Jews, the Jews were 'this fold'. The 'other sheep' were none other than the missing millions of the House of Israel who had been expelled from their homeland over nine hundred years before. In the chapter "The Mystery of the Missing Millions" we shall see that we are living at the time in which the prophetic words spoken by Jesus those many years ago are about to be fulfilled. We live in the age of the 'one fold' and 'one shepherd'. It is to be, as we shall see, an event that will turn world politics upside-down.

So the seers spoke and wrote in code. We have not dealt comprehensively with their code by any means, some of it we have not yet managed to decipher, but we have examined enough of their code to serve the purpose of this book and acquaint us with the 'things which are yet to be.'

THE INVISIBLE HAND

72

# 7.
# The Most
# Mysterious Man
# who Ever Lived!

The idea that one day an extra-terrestrial being will come to earth and somehow either persuade or force mankind to turn it's back on violence and war has persisted throughout the ages. Some people today like to think that such a being will come from an advanced civilisation which has developed on another planet, and others see in the 'flying saucer' phenomena the beginnings of an outer-space intrusion into the affairs of man.

Many of the ancient seers predicted the coming to earth of such a being — a supreme being. They believed that the great universal spirit would one day visit the earth and, having clothed himself in human nature, would walk among men. They called this person the 'Messiah' and foretold the date of his coming and a considerable amount of detail about his birth, life and death.

Jesus of Nazareth was one of the many hundreds of people who throughout history have claimed to be the 'Messiah', the 'God' of Israel come to earth. Because the carpenter of Nazareth was just one of the many who have claimed the awesome distinction of being a 'godman', some have argued this as being a reason for rejecting his claim out-of-hand but that cannot be done. After all, if a hundred people claim to be the Queen of Britain that does not preclude the possibility that one of them is.

Whatever one may think about the claim of Jesus of Nazareth to be an embodiment of the great universal spirit, there is one thing of which I can assure you — there is something very mysterious about this Jewish prophet who was crucified nigh on two thousand years ago. In fact I would say that Jesus of Nazareth is THE MOST MYSTERIOUS MAN WHO EVER LIVED.

Why I say that, is the subject of this chapter, and I would like to draw your attention to a prediction written by the ancient Jewish seer Daniel in the year 510 B.C.

*Seventy weeks are determined upon thy people and upon thy holy city, to finish the transgression, and to make an end of sins, and to make reconciliation for iniquity, and to bring in everlasting righteousness, and to seal up the vision and prophecy and to annoint the most Holy.*

*Know, therefore, and understand, that from the going forth of the commandment to restore and to build Jerusalem unto the Messiah the Prince shall be seven weeks, and threescore and two weeks; the street shall be built again, and the wall, even in troublous times.*

The Book of Daniel. 9:24,25

The prediction is that 69 'weeks' after 'the going forth of the commandment to restore and rebuild Jerusalem' the Messiah-God would come. As we shall see, this prediction foretells precisely the year in which the Messiah would come.

To the seers of ancient Israel the coming of the Messiah-God was the most important of events. No-one in those days would have subscribed to the modern view that the Messiah was to be just an earthly deliverer, a supreme leader or an ordinary king. They were in no doubt whatsoever that the Messiah was to be Jehovah (one of their names for God) himself.

The prophet Isaiah made his expectations as to the identity of the Messiah quite plain when he wrote some 700 B.C.:

*For unto us a child is born, unto us a son is given, and the government shall be upon his shoulder; and his name shall be called Wonderful, Counselor, THE Mighty God, THE Everlasting Father, THE Prince of Peace.*

*Of the increase of his government and peace there shall be no end, upon the throne of David, and upon his kingdom, to order it, and to establish it with justice and with righteousness from henceforth even forever.* The Book of the Prophet Isaiah 9:7

It was, in Israel, blasphemy to apply any of the names of God or any of his attributes to a human being. We can be sure, therefore, that when Isaiah applied the names 'The Mighty God' and 'The Everlasting Father' to the coming Messiah, there was no doubt in his mind that it was none other than the great universal spirit, 'Jehovah-God' who was to be that Messiah.

The predictions that the Messiah would be 'God manifest in the flesh' are too numerous to deal with fully, but I quote a few predictions taken from the ancient seers' prognostications at random, to reinforce the view that they expected the coming to earth of a Messiah-God. We have the concept amplified by the prophet Isaiah in his 43rd chapter:

*Ye are witnesses, saith the Lord, and my servant whom I have chosen, that ye may know and believe me, and understand that I am He: before me there was no God formed, neither shall there be after me. I, even I, AM THE LORD, AND BESIDE ME THERE IS NO SAVIOUR.*

The prophet Zechariah, too, makes it plain that the King of Israel was to be the 'God' of Israel:

*And the Lord shall be King over all the earth; in that day there shall be one Lord, and his name one.*
The Book of the Prophet Zechariah 14:9

King David said:

*For the Lord is our defence, and the Holy One of Israel is our King.* Psalm 89

Remembering what we discovered in our chapter on breaking the prophetic code, let us look further at what Daniel predicted.

1. The Messiah/God/King was to come to earth.
2. He was to come at the end of a period of time given as "Seven weeks and threescore and two weeks" — Sixty nine weeks.

3.  The period of counting was not to commence when he, Daniel, gave the prophecy, but from "the going forth of the command to restore and to build Jerusalem ..."

Referring again to our chapter "Breaking the Code" we see that 'a week' in prophecy is a week of years or seven years. The coming of the Messiah-God was therefore to take place 483 years after the "going forth of the command to restore and rebuild Jerusalem."

The first thing we must do, then, to find out the year in which, according to the prophet, this supernatural being would come, is to determine when the commandment to restore and rebuild Jerusalem was issued. We must then look at the records of the year which was 483 years after that date to see if anything took place in that year which we may equate with the coming of a supernatural being to earth.

A prerequisite of our deliberations must be to very carefully read what Daniel DID predict and not colour his prediction with our own prejudices or any preconceived theory. The ancient seers spoke with precision, we must interpret them with precision.

The 483 years was to commence with the 'going forth of the command to restore and rebuild Jerusalem' not from the actual restoration and rebuilding of Jerusalem.

A command went forth to rebuild the temple in Jerusalem but we must be careful not to let that mislead us because the prophecy is very specific that it is the command to restore and rebuild the city not the temple that is the starting point of the 483 years.

There was also a command to allow the Jews to return to Jerusalem but that is not the command either, for at that time there was no command to rebuild the city.

Various edicts were issued over the years ordering all the things I have mentioned above to be done, but the prophet is very specific indeed, even to adding, just to make sure no-one mistakes the edict referred to *"The street shall be built again, and the wall, even in troublous times."*

We must note also that from the command to "restore and rebuild" it was to be 483 years to 'the Messiah Prince', not, I would point out, to the birth of the person who would become the Messiah.

There were four decrees issued which may vaguely fit the prophecy but there is only one which PRECISELY fits:

The decree of Cyrus 538-537 B.C. was to 'build this house of the Lord God of Israel.' Fifteen years later no action had been taken in response to that decree, and the house remained unbuilt.

Darius issued a decree reaffirming the decree of Cyrus. The decree of Darius was around 519 B.C. This decree was also specifically to 'build this house of the Lord God of Israel.'

The third decree was issued by King Artaxerxes (Ezra 7:7) in B.C. 458-457 and it gave authority for the restoration of the Jews in Jerusalem and the setting up of Jewish national life.

King Artaxerxes issued another separate and entirely different decree in 445-444 B.C. (Nehemiah 11:1)

The decrees of Cyrus and Darius were not concerned with the restoration and the building of Jerusalem, they were specifically concerned with the rebuilding of the 'House of God', the temple, so they do not fit precisely the words of the prediction.

The two decrees of King Artaxerxes fulfil EXACTLY the words spoken by the prophet 'to restore and build'. The first decree authorised Exra to organise a Jewish state in Jerusalem and the second specifically concerns itself with the building of the walls of the city. As a result of the first decree Exra appointed magistrates and judges to judge the people, and, as a result of the second decree, the walls of Jerusalem were rebuilt: It is worth mentioning that by the time the decree was issued the prophet who had foretold the happening had been dead for over three quarters of a century — is that not in itself an AMAZING prediction?

*The street shall be built again, and the wall, even in troublous times.*

The prophet had predicted, and he was absolutely correct, for Nehemiah records of the event:

> *But it came to pass that, when Sanbalat, and Tobiah, and the Arabians, and the Ammonites, and the Ashodites heard that the repairing of the walls of Jerusalem went forth, and that the breaches began to be closed, they were very angry, and conspired all of them to come and to fight against Jerusalem, and to hinder it .... And it came to pass from that time forth, that half of my servants wrought in the work, and the other half of them held the spears, the shields, the bows, and the coats of mail ... They who built on the wall, and they who bore burdens, burdened themselves; everyone with one of his hands wrought in the work, and with the other hand held a weapon.*
>
> Book of Nehemiah Chapter 4

"Troublous times" indeed, exactly as the prophet had foretold.

So we have the two decrees of Artaxerxes to 'restore' and 'build'. The dates are 458-457 and 445-444 B.C.

Now let me quote the prophecy of Daniel more fully:

> *While I was speaking in prayer, even the man, Gabriel, whom I had seen in the vision at the beginning, being caused to fly swiftly, touched me about the time of the evening oblation [about four o'clock in the afternoon].*
>
> *And he informed me, and talked with me, and saith, Oh Daniel, I am now come forth to give thee skill and understanding.*
>
> *At the beginning of thy supplications, the commandment came*

*forth, and I am come to show thee; for thou art greatly beloved. Therefore understand the matter, and consider the vision.*

*Seventy weeks [490 years] are determined upon thy people and upon thy holy city, to finish the transgression, and make an end of sins, and to make reconciliation for iniquity, and to bring in everlasting righteousness, and to seal up the vision and prophecy, and to annoint the most Holy.*

*Know, therefore, and understand, that from the going forth of the commandment to restore and to build Jerusalem unto the Messiah, the Prince, shall be seven weeks [49 years], and threescore and two weeks [434 years]; the street shall be built again, and the wall, even in troublous times.*

*After threescore and two weeks shall Messiah be cut off, but not for himself; and the people of the prince that shall come shall destroy the city [Jerusalem] and the sanctuary [the Temple], and the end of it shall be with flood, and to the end of the war desolations are determined.*

*And he [Messiah] shall confirm the covenant with many for one week [7 years]; and in the midst of the week he shall cause the sacrifice and the oblation to cease, and for the overspreading of abominations he shall make it desolate, even until the consummation, and that determined shall be poured upon the desolate.* The Book of the Prophet Daniel. Chapter 9.

I have said that the Jews were waiting for Messiah-God and that it was the coming of Messiah-God which Daniel foretold. The general concept was that, when the Messiah-God came, all the problems of the Jewish nation would be over, a new age would dawn, the enemies of Israel would be confounded, he, the Messiah, would reign for ever and ever.

But that is not what Daniel foretold: He foretold something quite different from the general accepted concept of what would happen when the Messiah-God came:

★ He would die!
★ He would cause the sacrifice and oblation to cease!
★ Jerusalem would yet again be destroyed!

Messiah-God to die? Had not the great prophet Isaiah foretold that the Messiah would be "The Mighty God, The Everlasting Father, The Prince of Peace"? Who could conceive of Messiah-God dying?

Daniel went further and even more unacceptably, if that were possible, he foretold that the Messiah-God would cause the daily sacrifice and oblation to 'cease'. The most sacred thing the Jews knew, that which had been commanded of 'God' from the time of their father Moses, the pivotal point of their beginning of years, the passover, to cease. The sacrifice and the oblation to cease? It would be rather like a Christian prophet of today saying that God was going to come down and banish Jesus Christ from the Christian faith. No Jew could conceive of it!

Jerusalem to be destroyed yet again! But surely was the Messiah not supposed to bring everlasting peace? Was that not what Messianic teaching was all about. The prediction was most unwelcome and improbable.

## 483 YEARS LATER.

We have seen that prophetic weeks are weeks of years and that Daniel foretold that from the going forth of the commandment to restore and build Jerusalem to the coming of Messiah the Prince would be sixty nine weeks. Messiah-God would come at the close of the sixty-ninth week. 69 weeks of 7 days equals 483 days or years.

It is now 483 years exactly since Artaxerxes gave his first decree and we stand on the banks of a muddy river. In the river, with the waters swirling around him, is a man, wild looking, yet fascinating. Along the banks throng a multitude of people listening to the desert preacher as he exhorts them, with much urgency in his voice, to 'Repent' for the 'Kingdom of heaven is at hand'. One after the other the repentant step down into the waters of the river Jordan, and are baptised; the preacher is none other than John the Baptist. In the burning heat of the day the ceremony goes on and on, until suddenly .... John the Baptist falters in his rhetoric ... his eyes are fixed on a young man standing amidst the crowd on the bank of the river ... he exclaims, pointing to the young man ... "BEHOLD THE LAMB OF GOD WHO TAKETH AWAY THE SINS OF THE WORLD."

The young man to whom John the Baptist pointed was none other than Jesus of Nazareth, proclaimed Messiah exactly 483 years after King Artaxerxes had issued his first proclamation. "From the going forth of the command to restore and build Jerusalem to the coming of Messiah the Prince shall be sixty-nine weeks."

What did John proclaim this young man as being?

*John bore witness of him [Christ], and cried, saying, This was He of whom I spoke, He that cometh after me is preferred before me ... And this is the witness of John, when the Jews sent priests and Levites from Jerusalem to ask him, Who art thou?*

*And he confessed, and denied not; but confessed, I am not the Christ. And they asked him, What then? Art thou Elijah? And he saith, I am not. Art thou that prophet? And he answered, No. Then said they unto him, Who art thou? that we may give an answer to them that sent us. What sayest thou of thyself? He said, I am the voice of one crying in the wilderness, Make straight the way of the Lord, as said the prophet Isaiah ... The next day John seeth Jesús coming unto him, and saith, Behold the Lamb of God who taketh away the sins of the world... And I saw, and bore witness that this is the Son of God.*

Parts of John. Chapter 1.

John proclaimed Jesus as 'the Christ' and 'Christ' is the Greek word for 'the anointed' just as Messiah' is the Hebrew word for 'the anointed'. There was never any dispute that the Christ and the Messiah were one and the same person, nor that 'God' and the Messiah were one and the same. That's why when Jesus claimed to be the 'Christ' he was automatically accused of blasphemy because he had pronounced himself 'God'.

The leaders of the Jewish faith of his day refused to accept Jesus' claim to be the Christ, the Messiah-God. They leave us in no doubt that he did claim to be both Messiah and God because they killed him for that very reason. I wonder if they stopped to ask themselves, those 483 years after the command of Artaxerxes to 'restore' and 'build' the walls of Jerusalem, why the prediction of the prophet, for Daniel was read often enough in their places of worship, had not come to pass? Did they, I wonder, ask themselves, since the Messiah—God was to appear in that year, and if that Messiah-God was not Jesus, who came in that year who WAS the Messiah-God? Or did they, as so many of us, not really care as long as they could be left to pursue their religion of formality?

## FURTHER PREDICTIONS OF THE ANCIENT SEERS REGARDING THE COMING OF THE MESSIAH-GOD.

Is it coincidence that Jesus of Nazareth was presented to the Jewish nation as the Messiah in exactly the year the prophet had foretold the Messiah would come?

Were that the only prophecy fulfilled in the lifetime of Jesus we may just think it to be a coincidence. All the seers of ancient Israel, however, had something to say about this mystic person the Messiah-God. Do any of these other predictions find fulfilment in the birth, life or death of Jesus of Nazareth? We shall look at other predictions than those of Daniel, predictions concerning the coming Messiah-God uttered over a thousand years before Daniel was born and fifteen hundred years before the birth of Jesus.

The ancient seers foretold, in addition to the year he would come:

★ The name of the family into which the Messiah-God would be born.
★ The town in which his family would live.
★ The town in which he would be born (different from his home town).
★ The place from which the Messiah-God would emerge.
★ The form of transport the Messiah-God would use.

★ The betrayal of the Messiah.
★ Who would betray him.
★ How much money would be paid to the person who betrayed him.
★ What the betrayer would do with the money.
★ What would be purchased with the money.
★ How the Messiah-God would die.
★ What his executioners would say while he was dying.
★ What his executioners would do while he was dying.
★ What drink they would offer him while he was dying.
★ The kind of people he would die with.
★ The kind of tomb in which he would be buried.

Yes, all foretold between one thousand and five hundred years BEFORE he was born.

## THE FAMILY INTO WHICH THE MESSIAH-GOD WOULD BE BORN.

Foretelling the birth of the Messiah *eight hundred years* before Christ was born, the ancient seer Isaiah wrote:

*And there shall come forth a rod out of the stem of Jesse, and a Branch shall grow out of his roots; And the spirit of the Lord shall rest upon him, the spirit of wisdom and understanding, the spirit of counsel and might, the spirit of knowledge and fear of the Lord.*

The Book of the Prophet Isaiah 11:1,2.

Here is the lineage of Jesus:

Jesus
|
Joseph
|
Jacob
|
Matthan
|
Eleazer
|
Eliud
|
Achim
|
Sadoc
|

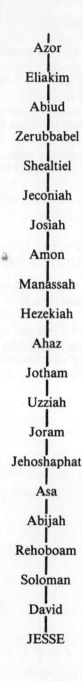

Azor

Eliakim

Abiud

Zerubbabel

Shealtiel

Jeconiah

Josiah

Amon

Manassah

Hezekiah

Ahaz

Jotham

Uzziah

Joram

Jehoshaphat

Asa

Abijah

Rehoboam

Soloman

David

JESSE

So the man who appeared on the scene in exactly THE YEAR the prophet Daniel foretold the Messiah would come, and was proclaimed the Messiah, was also born into THE FAMILY into which the prophet foretold the Messiah would be born.

## THE PLACE MESSIAH-GOD WOULD BE BORN.

Here it must be admitted the ancient seers would appear to be in disagreement. The prophet Hosea had predicted eight hundred years before Jesus was born that the Messiah would come out of Egypt when, under inspiration as he claimed, he spoke the words uttered by God

*Out of Egypt have I called my son.*

A prophet of whom we have no record, but whose utterences were well known in Palestine at the time of Christ, foretold that the Messiah would be a Nazarene.

*And He [Jesus] came and dwelt in a city called Nazareth, that it might be fulfilled which was spoken by the prophets, He shall be called a Nazarene.* Matthew 2:23.

Yet another prophet, Micah, writing in the 8th century B.C. foretold that the Messiah would come out of Bethlehem:

*But thou Bethlehem Ephrathah, though thou be little among the thousands of Judah, yet out of thee shall come forth unto me that is to be ruler in Israel, whose goings forth have been from of old, from everlasting.* The Book of the Prophet Micah 5:2

We have three different prophets, writing at different times and predicting three different origins for the coming Messiah-God.

Hosea, a well respected seer of Israel, predicted that the Messiah would come out of **Egypt.** A prophet, unknown to us but obviously known to the Jews before and during the life of Jesus, foretold that the Messiah would be a Nazarene – be of the town of **Nazareth.** Yet another well respected prophet foretold that the Messiah would be born in **Bethlehem.**

It must have seemed obvious to the custodians of the ancient writings that these statements were, on the face of them, contradictory. Yet, as we shall see often in this book, no attempt was made to alter what the ancient seers had said or 'make sense' of their predictions. Such was the faith of these custodians in the words of the prophets that they believed, however unlikely a prophecy seemed at the time, ultimately it would come true.

The story of Jesus is too well known for me to elaborate upon here. In hindsight we know, as no-one who lived before the event could have known, that all three of the ancient seers were correct.

Mary and Joseph, the parents of Jesus, had their home in Nazareth, thus Jesus was entitled to be called a 'Nazareen'.

Just prior to the birth of Jesus, Caesar Augustus sent out an edict that 'all the world' should be taxed and as Mary and Joseph were passing through Bethlehem, travelling for the purpose of obeying the edict, Jesus was born in a manger in Bethlehem.

When Herod heard of the birth of the Messiah-King, and he seems to have been more conversant with the predictions of Daniel regarding the coming of the Messiah than the priests, he was 'troubled'. He ordered a massacre of children to ensure he destroyed the boy born to be king. Thus it came about that Jesus' family fled into Egypt and the prediction of the prophet that the Messiah would come out of Egypt came to be fulfilled.

Is there not something very mysterious about a person who is born:

1. In the year foretold for the birth of the Messiah 500 years before his birth.
2. Into the family into which it is foretold the Messiah would be born.
3. And who fulfills predictions concerning the three different places of origin?

## THE STAR OF BETHLEHEM.

When I was a child, a favourite pastime around Christmas was to look heavenward on a frosty night and see if we could see the 'Star of Bethlehem'. Of course we often did, because part of the magic of childhood is that it is often possible to see exactly what one expects to see.

Someone once said that we all become children at Christmas, and perhaps it is inevitably so, for no story has so moved the world as the story of the babe in the manger at Bethlehem. At Christmas, reason takes a holiday and we question not whether herald angels did actually appear in the shepherds fields at Bethlehem: The antiseptic manger and the obligatory haloes seem somehow to be right, and the star of Bethlehem fits snuggly into the pattern, along with Father Christmas and the plum pudding. Few I think give much thought as to whether a star did actually go before the wise men as they made their way toward the place where Jesus was born.

Though I do not wish to debunk Christmas, it is far too nice a festival for that, I would like to ask you, my reader, if you really DO believe the Christmas story as historic fact as distinct from believing the Christmas message, which I would hope, we all believe.

The Star of Bethlehem is a very important part of the Christmas story. The star the wise men are said to have followed to Bethlehem is, yes, and demands to be, depicted on all the Christmas paraphernalia. What would

Christmas be without the star on the tree, the star on the cards and the star dangling from the ceiling? What would the nativity play be without the wise men, colourful all, who follow the star? It's wonderful, magical and scintillating. But did it happen or is it just a very pleasant myth? You see, the veracity of the prophets depends upon that star, for, if they have inserted one such bit of nonsense into their writings 'bang' goes their claim to divine inspiration! We all like fairy stories, but who wants a prophet who creates fairy stories?

Astronomy and astrology were taken very seriously in the days of the prophets. Few kings or leaders of nations were without their court astrologer and there were schools of astrology where budding young star-gazers studied.

Little wonder that archaeological excavations have, in recent years, brought to light very extensive information about astronomical patterns stretching back many thousands of years. There is now a considerable amount of information from Chinese, Babylonian, Egyptian, Greek, Roman and Jewish sources available to the expert.

Comets were regarded as being portentious, and ancient believers in 'what the stars foretell' were able to point to the assassination of Caesar (44 B.C.) and the suicide of Nero, as being among the many events which had been preceded by awesome comets rushing through the night sky.

The Jewish rabbinic writer Abarbanel maintained that the Messiah would appear when there was a conjunction of the stars Jupiter and Saturn. According to Jewish tradition Jupiter was thought of as the kingly star and Saturn was the protector of Israel. Saturn was regarded by some non-Jewish astrologers as being the 'god of the Jews'. Pisces was the sign of the Messiah.

In the early 1600's there lived an Imperial mathematician and Astronomer Royal, who resided in Prague. His name was Johannes Kepler. Unfortunately, apart from being a brilliant man, he was also regarded as something of a visionary and for that reason his work lost credence among his contemporaries. Kepler became a mystic when mysticism was definitely unfashionable.

On the night of December 17th, Kepler had his telescope trained on the heavens, for he knew that an exceptional event was to take place: Saturn and Jupiter were to enter a conjunction in the constellation of Pisces. A "conjunction", as far as the layman is concerned, merely means the positioning of two stars on the same degree of longtitude. As he watched, the two stars seemed to come closer together until all he could see in the sky was one bright star of wonderful brilliance. Probably the awe-inspiring sight was the reason his mind leapt back to something he had read years before but had forgotten until that moment — the prophecy of the writer Abarbanel that the Messiah would appear when there was a conjunction of Saturn and Jupiter in the constellation of Pisces. Few astronomers would have delved so deeply, but we owe it to

Kepler's mystical turn of-mind that he did delve, and publish his findings, but it is also due to his mystical turn of mind that his findings were discredited and ignored.

The excited Kepler wondered about the meaning given to the two stars Jupiter and Saturn and to the constellation Pisces by the astrologers of the ancient world. Pisces 'the sign of the Messiah', Jupiter 'the Kingly star' and Saturn 'the protector of Israel'. You don't have to be a mystic for that to excite you, do you? But where was the Messiah? What had happened to Israel that day in 1603? Nothing!

Fortunately it is possible for astronomers to know relatively simply exactly what the sky looked like and how the stars were positioned at any given time thousands of years before their time. There is little difficulty, the result of such an investigation will not be a product of mysticism but of science, and will be scientifically accurate.

In his planetarium Kepler turned the heavens back over sixteen hundred years and checked and checked again his calculations, and yes, he was right, exactly the same conjunction of the two stars Jupiter and Saturn had occurred in the constellation of Pisces in the year 6-7 B.C.

As I have said, Kepler was a rather odd mixture of a man, brilliant in some ways and unbelievably naive in his mysticism in other ways. His astral discovery was published but never given great credence. It can be said that it was dismissed as a novelty, unworthy of scientific consideration but interesting for those of a superstitious turn of mind.

It was not until the year 1925 that a German by the name of Schnabel deciphered the records of a famous school of astrology that had existed in Babylon in ancient times, the school was the School of Astrology at Sippar in Babylon. Among the veritable mine of information he found in the ancient writings the proof for which astrologists had been waiting. Jupiter and Saturn had been in conjunction in the constellation of Pisces in the year 7 B.C.

Kepler had been right, Jupiter and Saturn did meet in Pisces three times in the year 7 B.C.

Every few years one reads of astronomers packing their telescopes, and departing for various parts of the earth to get a view of an eclipse or some such heavenly happening. The reason they travel so far, so often, is that astral happenings cannot be seen from all parts of the earth's surface. So the next step was to find out from which part of the earth's surface the conjunction of Jupiter and Saturn in the constellation of Pisces would have been visible in 7 B.C. Mathematical calculations showed that the happening would have been especially brilliant in the land of Israel and the Medditerranean area.

## THE EVENTS OF THE YEAR 7 B.C.

The great astrological event of the year 7 B.C. was, as we have seen, the conjunction of the stars Jupiter (the star astrologers of those days knew as 'the Kingly star') and Saturn (the star known as 'the protector of Israel') in the constellation of Pisces (known among the ancient astrologers as 'the sign of the Messiah').

They had, as we have today, in ancient writ, the predictions of the many ancient seers concerning the coming of the Messiah-God. The prediction of the prophet Micah "But thou Bethlehem Ephrathah, though thou be little among the thousands of Judah, out of thee shall come forth unto me that is to be ruler in Israel, whose goings forth have been from of old, from everlasting" would be known to them.

Thus the 'wise men', 'Magi' or 'Astrologers' would know exactly where the birth of the Messiah-King was to take place. The message of the stars was so powerful that no astrologer could ignore it — the 'Kingly star' and the 'Protector of Israel star' in the constellation of the 'Sign of the Messiah'.

At the end of February in the year B.C. 7, the ancient astronomers watched the heavens as Jupiter moved into the constellation of Pisces and towards Saturn — what was about to happen was long awaited and significant. In the event the sighting was disappointing because the brilliance of the conjunction was subdued by the light of the sun, the sun being on that day also in Pisces.

At daybreak on April 12th, however, the astronomers were able to get a better view of the conjunction and were undoubtedly keeping in the forefront of their minds the three words 'Israel'. 'Messiah' and 'King'.

On the morning of May 29th it is believed the stars were visible for two hours and, on December 4th of 7 B.C. Jupiter and Saturn met in the constellation of Pisces for the last time.

Was anyone of importance born in 7 B.C. who could be said to fulfill the prophecies regarding the coming Messiah? Yes, Jesus of Nazareth. 'But', someone will say, 'Jesus was born on December 25th A.D.1'. The answer is, he was not born in A.D.1 and he was not born on 25th December. The A.D. system of dating is inaccurate: It is a system of dating which owes little to the birth of Christ and rather more to the imagination of a Scythian monk Dionysius Exiguus who was instructed in A.D.533 to commence a new calender working backwards from his day to the birth of Christ. As is to be expected, he was years adrift in his reckoning. We know roughly when Jesus was born from the New Testament narrative:

*Jesus was born in Bethlehem of Judea, in the days of Herod the King*                                                                    Matthew 2:1

It is a fact of history that Herod died in the year 4 B.C.

Between the birth of Jesus and the death of Herod there were several events which necessitate there being a period of years separating the two events. There was the 'slaughter of the innocents' which drove the Jesus family into Egypt. Herod dare not have mounted that until the census ordered by Caesar had been completed and such a census could not be completed in a few months. People had to travel from far and wide to census points and the whole operation, including the necessary checks which would be undertaken, would take a long time. Thus the Bible narrative indicates that the birth of Jesus could not have been very much later than B.C.7.

We can see, therefore, that what sounds, when read at Christmas-time, like a myth is fact:

> *Now when Jesus was born in Bethlehem of Judah in the days of Herod the King, behold there came wise men from the east to Jerusalem, saying, Where is he that is born King of the Jews? For we have seen his star in the east and we have come to worship him.*
> Matthew 2: 1,2.

The words "in the east" can be more correctly translated "We have seen his star appear in the early dawn". That is exactly when Jupiter in conjunction with Saturn did appear — as a startingly bright, seemingly single source of light, in the early dawn.

"His star" — why his star? Because Pisces was the Messianic constellation!

"Where is he that is born King of the Jews?" Why did they seek the King of the Jews? Because Jupiter was the 'Kingly' star and Saturn the star considered to be the protector of Israel. Why did they come to Bethlehem? Because that is where the ancient seers had foretold the Messiah would be born.

## HEROD WAS TROUBLED.

> *When Herod, the king, had heard these things, he was troubled and all Jerusalem with him. And when he had gathered all the chief priests and scribes of the people together, he demanded of them where the Christ should be born. And they said unto him, In Bethlehem of Judaea; for thus is it written by the prophet.*
> Matthew 2: 2,3.

The events of the year 7 B.C. were indeed dramatic. Why should the mighty Herod, backed by the power of Rome, be troubled by the birth of a baby in a cattle shed? We are told that "all Jerusalem" was troubled with him — why?

Flavious Josephus, the ancient Jewish historian, tells us that at the time of the birth of Jesus it was said in Jerusalem there had been a sign in the heavens proclaiming the birth of a Jewish king.

Jerusalem at that time had a very well developed centre for astrological study and there is little doubt that the significance of the conjunction had been widely rumoured, both by astrologers and by the many devout people who studied the ancient seers.

Perhaps next Christmas, when you gaze at the star atop your Christmas tree, you will think again of the year 7 B.C. and the conjunction of Jupiter and Saturn in the constellation of Pisces, and agree with me that Jesus of Nazareth is the most mysterious man who ever lived.

## THE MOST MYSTERIOUS STATEMENT EVER MADE.

Herod was troubled! Jesus of Nazareth has been 'troubling' people ever since and especially those who involve themselves in religious studies — they find him terribly difficult to explain away. Sometimes one is under the impression that that body of people who like to call themselves 'The Christian Church' spend a considerable amount of time explaining that Jesus did not mean what he said or say what he meant.

The Jewish Messiah has been transformed from a Messiah-God into a 'good-man', a 'prophet' and sometimes a philosopher, almost imperceptibly he has been changed from being 'wholly God' to being just 'wholly good'.

Jesus cannot be said to be simply a good man. Either he was what he claimed to be, or a raving fanatic, an arch-deceiver or a blasphemer. The magnitude of his claims leaves no neutral ground.

The town of Emmaus was but a little way from Jerusalem and the discussion to which we now refer took place between Jesus and two Emmaus disciples. What he said to them is probably the most mysterious statement ever made and destroyed forever his right to be called a 'good man'.

*Then he said unto them O foolish ones, and slow of heart to believe all that the prophets have spoken!*
*Ought not Christ [the Messiah] to have suffered these things, and to enter into his glory? AND BEGINNING AT MOSES AND ALL THE PROPHETS, HE EXPOUNDED TO THEM, IN ALL THE SCRIPTURES, THE THINGS CONCERNING HIMSELF.* St Luke. Chapter 24: 25-27.

What scriptures? The Jewish Scriptures, which we today call the Old Testament — the New Testament was, of course, not at that time written. So Jesus claimed that ALL the prophets and ALL the scriptures referred to HIM. That doesn't leave much room for the present day 'good man' assessment. I say again, if Jesus was not what he claimed to be then he was a raving madman.

One has only to read the early Christian writings to realise that among the apostles there was no doubt as to who, and what, Jesus claimed to be and there is no doubt that they accepted without qualification his claims. The doctrine that Jesus Christ was simply a good man was quite foreign to the early church teachers.

John opens his Gospel with the words:

*In the beginning was the Word, and the Word was with God, and THE WORD WAS GOD.*
*The same was in the beginning with God.*
*All things were made by him; and without him was not anything made which was made .... and the WORD was made FLESH, and dwelt among us.*

Parts of John 1: 1-12.

There can be absolutely no doubt at all what the apostle meant by those words.

In his first Epistle, John refers to Christ in this way:

*This is the true God, and eternal life.*                    Chapter 5 v.20

The apostle Paul in his Epistle to the Hebrews makes his views of the nature of Jesus quite plain, writing of Jesus he says:

*Thy throne, O God, is forever and ever.*                    Hebrews 1-8.

In verse 2 of the same chapter Paul refers to Jesus as being "Heir of all things, by whom also he made the worlds."

In the first book of Corinthians, Christ is called "The Lord of Glory" and in the Acts of the Apostles, Chapter 10 verse 36 as "Lord of All".

No student of the Jewish scriptures could doubt that the word 'Saviour' referred to God. "I am the Lord, and beside me there is NO Saviour." Isaiah had written, claiming to be writing under the inspiration of God (Chapter 43: 10,11). Then again he addresses God in this way "O God of Israel, THE SAVIOUR."

We today are so used to using the word "Saviour" that we are unaware it had a very specific meaning in those far off days of the ancient seers. There was only one worthy of the name "saviour" they believed, and that was God himself.

When, therefore, Jesus and his disciples used the word "saviour" all who heard him would clearly understand he was claiming to be none other than God, since Israel expected no other saviour than God.

Throughout the New Testament Jesus is given the name of Saviour. For example, we read in Luke Chapter 2 "For unto us is born this day in the city of David a saviour who is Christ the Lord."

In the fifth chapter of the book to the Ephesians it is written "Christ is the Saviour of the world."

Chapter 2 of the first book of Timothy speaks of Jesus as "God our Saviour."

In the first chapter of the book of Titus, Jesus is called "God our Saviour" (v.3) "Christ our Saviour" (v.4). In Titus Chapter 2 the two doctrines proclaimed by Jesus Christ are referred to as "...the doctrine of God our Saviour."

Jude, the brother of Jesus, calls Jesus "The only wise God our Saviour." (v.25).

John the Divine in the Apocalypse refers to Jesus as being "The Alpha and Omega, the Beginning and the Ending, who is and who was, and who is to come, THE ALMIGHTY." Revelation 1:8

Surely any ordinary man who led people to believe such things about himself must be either a religious fanatic, a blasphemer of the worst kind or a rogue? No prophet of Israel had ever claimed such things before, and no apostle of the Christian faith ever claimed such a status for himself. Abraham, the patriarch and father of Israel, never made such a claim, neither did Isaac, Jacob or Moses. Little wonder the religious authorities of the day were hopping mad at the claims of this, the carpenter's son from Nazareth.

"But", someone will say, "all those things are what the disciples of Jesus said about him. What did he say about himself?"

Let us see what the most mysterious man who ever lived had to say about himself. That we cannot regard Jesus as an ordinary, though very good man, becomes obvious when we contemplate what we would think of the local vicar if he said the following about himself.

Jesus said *"I and my Father [God] are ONE."*     John 10:30

He also said

*I am THE way, THE Truth, and THE light; no man cometh unto the Father, but by me.*     John 14:6

Those are tremendous claims, aren't they? He claimed he was the only way, the only truth, and the only light. Contrary to what many people think today, and indeed quite contrary to the teaching of a large section of the Christian Church, Jesus taught that ONLY through Him could man contact the great universal spirit he called "The Father". Not for him any of the philosophies of toleration so beloved of our modern teachers, not for him the belief that men could come to God through any number of various religions, any number of prophets, and a multiplicity of spiritual leaders. Jesus was dogmatic in the extreme.

*No man cometh unto the Father but by ME.*

## IS THAT THE LANGUAGE OF A 'GOOD MAN'?

This man claimed to be able to dispense everlasting life to those who believed in him. Again I ask you to imagine what you would think of your local vicar if he said the following:

*Verily, verily, I say unto you, he that heareth MY word and believeth on Him that sent me, HATH [has got] everlasting life and shall not come into judgement but IS passed from death unto life.* (Jesus speaking as recorded in John Chapter 5:24)

He claimed to be able to satisfy the pangs of spiritual hunger when he said

*I am the bread of life; He that cometh to me shall never hunger, and he that believeth on me shall never thirst.* John 6:35

That is surely one of the most stupendous claims ever to have been made by a religious leader. He went further, he even claimed to be able to open heaven's gates to the dying. You remember Jesus was crucified between two thieves, one who railed upon him but the other who said!

*Lord, remember me when thou comest into Thy Kingdom.*

Jesus replied

*Verily I say unto thee, today shalt thou be with me in Paradise.* Luke 23: 42,43.

If the leaders of religious opinion today are in any doubt as to who Jesus of Nazareth claimed to be, the religious leaders of HIS day were certainly in no doubt. When speaking to the Pharisees he said to them

*I am from above: ye are of this world; I am not of this world.* John 8:23

The words 'I am' lose a lot in the translation, they are "ego eimi" a title of Jehovah God, which accounts for the sudden attempt of the Pharisees to kill Jesus because they were aware he was claiming to be God.

At the feast of the dedication in the temple Jesus was asked plainly who he was and he replied:

*I and my father are ONE.*
*Then the Jews took up stones again to stone him. Jesus answered*
*them, many good works have I shown you from my Father; for*
*which of these works do you stone me?*
*The Jews answered him, saying, for good work we stone thee not,*
*but for blasphemy; and because that thou, being a man, makest*
*thyself God.*                                                  John 10: 30-33

Undoubtedly the running battle which developed in later years between
the Pharisees and Jesus was not brought about because of the lovely
thoughts expressed in his 'Love thy enemies' speeches. Jerusalem was not
unused to prophets who preached repentance, any more than we are
unaccustomed to people who carry banners exhorting us to 'Prepare to
meet thy God'. The Pharisees didn't worry over-much about roving
preachers, because the synagogue was a forum where various views were
aired and tolerated. The one thing no Jew could tolerate, though, was
blasphemy, and to claim to be God was blasphemy. Jesus did not just
propagate unusual views, he went much further than that as in the
following example:

*Then said the Jews unto him [Jesus], Now we know that thou hast*
*a demon. Abraham is dead, and the prophets; and thou sayest, if*
*a man keep my saying, he shall never taste of death.*
*Art thou greater than our father, Abraham, who is dead? And the*
*prophets are dead. Whom makest thou thyself? ...*
*[Jesus replied] Your father Abraham, rejoiced to see my day; and*
*he saw it; and was glad.*
*Then said the Jews unto him, Thou art not yet fifty years old, and*
*hast thou seen Abraham?*
*Jesus said unto them, Verily, verily, I say unto you, Before*
*Abraham was I AM.*                            John 8: 52,53,56,57,58.

Again the words "ego eimi" 'I am' the name of the Jehovah-God.

## WAS JESUS OF NAZARETH THE MESSIAH GOD?

We have seen he came at the time the prophet had said the Messiah-God
would come, and we have seen that what has been called the Star of
Bethlehem was in fact the conjunction of Jupiter and Saturn in the
constellation of Pisces. We have further seen that this was a long awaited
astrological event portending the coming of the Messiah-King to Israel.
Let us recapitulate on the following:

★    Jesus was presented as Messiah in the year foretold by
the prophet over five hundred years before his birth.

★ He did indeed come out of Egypt, was born in Bethlehem and was a Nazareen exactly as the prophets had foretold.

★ He was born in the year the astrologers expected the Messiah to be born because of the significant conjunction.

★ He was born of the family of Jesse as the prophet had foretold.

## THE COMING OF THE KING.

Kings were not, in the days of the prophets, the democratic animals we know today. 'Walk-abouts' had not been thought of, nor had constitutional monarchy. The King was the centre of pomp and ceremony with the power of life and death over his people. Kingdom was essentially ballyhoo, the more high and mighty the King, the more his fame spread. The King was on his throne and the nation was his footstool.

We can imagine how Zechariah felt when, 500 years before Christ, he was called upon by 'The Lord' to predict regarding the coming God-King of Israel the Messiah-God, the following:

*In the eighth month, in the second year of Darius, came the word of the Lord unto Zechariah, the son of Berechiah, the son of Iddo, the prophet, saying...*

Human desire must have fought a tremendous battle that day with what Zechariah received by 'inspiration' for, as so often in the prognostications of the ancient seers, the message was unexpected in it's content. Remember that Zechariah prophesied about the everlasting, almighty, all powerful coming King of Israel. What royal splendour he must see, what a regal procession, what a mighty calvalcade of men under arms, what magnificent garments and how majestic the King. Not so!

*Rejoice greatly, O daughter of Zion; shout, O daughter of Jerusalem: behold, thy King cometh unto thee; he is just, and having salvation; lowly, and riding upon an ass, and upon a colt, the foal of an ass.*

Book of the prophet Zechariah 9:9

No mighty leader at the head of a conquering army? No pomp and no ceremony? The God King of Israel 'lowly'? How can this be? Riding on an ass? Surely nonsense!

Five hundred long years roll by and Zechariah is long dead, as is Darius

94

the King in whose reign he began to prophecy. His prophecy has not been forgotten for it is read in the Jewish places of worship, but it is by now only nominally believed, in very much the same way as we, in our day, nominally believe in the resurrection of the dead. Five hundred years is a long time, people give up hope: But come with me and stand at the foot of the Mount of Olives. In the distance there is the sound of cheering and rejoicing. Multitudes of people are throwing branches in the path of a man riding rather incongruously on an ass. The man is none other than Jesus of Nazareth. Read the contemporary report of the event and compare it with the prophecy of Zechariah.

*And [the disciples] brought the ass, and the colt, and put on them their clothes, and they set him [Jesus] theron. And a very great multitude spread their garments in the way; others cut down branches from the trees, and spread them in the way. And the multitudes that went before, and that followed, cried, saying, Hosanna to the Son of David! Blessed is he that cometh in the Name of the Lord! Hosanna in the highest!*
Matthew 21: 7,8,9.

Is it chance that Jesus of Nazareth rode into Jerusalem in exactly the way in which the prophet had foretold the Messiah-God would come? Or is it another indication that Jesus really is the most mysterious man who ever lived?

## THE BETRAYAL OF THE MESSIAH-GOD.

There are several forms which prophecy took and before we read the next prophecy regarding the betrayal of the Messiah-God let me mention just two. The first form is the seeing of a vision or the hearing of a voice by the prophet. The second form is that in which the voice of the originator of the message speaks in the first person.

King David of Israel received many of the second type of prophecies in which the originator of the prophecy 'The Lord' speaks directly in the first person. Such is the prophecy we are about to examine.

Zechariah foretold over five hundred years before the event, the following betrayal of the Messiah-God:

*And I said unto them, If ye think good give me my price; and if not forebear. So they weighed for my price THIRTY PIECES OF SILVER. And the Lord said unto me, Cast it unto the potter: a goodly price which I was prized at of them. And I took the thirty pieces of silver and cast them to the potter in the house of the Lord.*
Zechariah 12:12,13.

Three things foretold about the betrayal of Messiah-God over five hundred years before Christ.

1. The exact price of betrayal — thirty pieces of silver.
2. The money to be 'cast away' to the 'potter'.
3. The place it was to be cast away 'in the House of the Lord.'

It seems nonsensical doesn't it? You'd think sensible Rabbis would have tried to alter it and make some sense of it. But, as usual, nobody did try to alter the words of the prophet.

If Jesus was the Messiah-God as he claimed then we must expect these things to have happened to him at he betrayal.

Let us read the record of the events following the betrayal of Jesus by Judas:

> *Then Judas which had betrayed him, when he saw that he [Jesus] was condemned, repented himself, and brought again the THIRTY PIECES OF SILVER to the chief priests and elders saying, I have sinned in that I have betrayed innocent blood and they said, What is that to us? And he cast down the pieces of silver IN THE TEMPLE [the House of the Lord], and departed, and went and hanged himself. And the priests took the pieces of silver, and said, It is not lawful to put them in the treasury because it is the price of blood. And they took council, and bought with them THE POTTERS FIELD.*

Once again we see the most unlikely prediction come to pass, over five hundred years after it was uttered, absolutely accurate in every detail.

★ Exactly thirty pieces of silver as the prophet said.
★ Cast down in the House of the Lord as the prophet had said.
★ Finally used to purchase the 'potters field'.

It is of interest to note that the 'potters field' which was purchased was not known by that name in the day when the ancient seer wrote. Not only did he predict what would be done with the money, but also the name to be given to a field 450 years hence.

Unfortunately, religious art has led us badly astray in our view of Judas. In paintings of the Last Supper we see him sitting with the others, ugly of face and without the halo the others have. Judas was, in fact, a beloved disciple with no outward characteristic which distinguished him from the other disciples. Had Judas been the ugly, evil-looking character the paintings depict there would have been little point in the disciples asking

96

Jesus "Who will betray you — is it I?" for they would have immediately been able to 'pin it' on the ugly little character without the halo.

Judas had followed Jesus during his ministry and was very close to him, not at all the kind of person one would expect to perform the treacherous act. That is, of course, unless one had read the prophecy of King David about the betrayal of the Messiah, written one thousand years before the event: The prophecy is the originator speaking in the first person.

*Yea, mine own familiar friend, in whom I trusted, who did eat of my bread, hath lifted up his heel against me.*        Psalm 41:9

Friendship meant far more in those days than it does in our careless society: Great store was laid by faithfulness in friendship. Yet it was Jesus' own familiar friend who did betray him and while they were eating bread together. Coincidence?

King David's prophecy was that:

★   The Messiah-God would be betrayed by someone he had treated as his own familiar friend.
★   It would happen when the man was eating of his bread.

Both those things happened to the most mysterious man who ever lived!

## DEATH OF THE MESSIAH-GOD.

As we have previously remarked, the coming of the Messiah was considered among the Jews to be the time of deliverence for their nation, a time when peace would be ushered in and their God take the throne of their father David and rule forever. It is astonishing, therefore, that any prophet dared foretell THE DEATH of the Messiah-God. It is also astonishing that such a prophecy should be retained in the annals of Jewish prophecy. The death of Messiah-God would seem to be a contradiction in terms, yet through King David came the prophecy in 1000 B.C.

*I am poured out like water, and all my bones are out of joint: my heart is like wax; it is melted within me.*
*My strength is dried up like a potsherd, and my tongue cleaveth to my jaws; and thou hast brought me into the dust of death. For dogs have compassed me; the assembly of the wicked have enclosed me; they pierced my hands and my feet.*
*I may count all my bones; they look and stare upon me.*
*They part my garment among them, and cast lots upon my vesture*
        Psalm 22: 14-18

To appreciate fully the wonder of that prophecy, it must be realised that the death penalty as carried out in Israel in those days was stoning to death, not crucifixion. Look as you will through the Old Testament, you will not find any reference to the death penalty of crucifixion. Yet, looking forward to the coming of the Messiah, the writer of the Psalms was able to draw a complete picture of the method of capital punishment which would gain favour among the Romans hundreds of years after his own death.

Even the minutest detail of the grim crucifixion scene was foretold, one thousand years before the scene was enacted on Golgotha. In the light of all this, did Jesus die the death of a martyr, was the crucifixion a huge mistake or was it as the disciples claimed, the fulfilment of a plan laid by the great universal spirit?

What of the time between the betrayal and the crucifixion? Had the prophets anything to say about that? Yes, 700 years before the event Isaiah had prophesied:

*He was oppressed, and he was afflicted, yet he opened not his mouth; he was brought as a lamb to the slaughter, and as a sheep before the shearers is dumb, so he opened not his mouth.*
The Book of the prophet Isaiah 53:7

Now read the eye-witness account of how Jesus behaved when he was before Pontius Pilate on the judgement day:

*When he was accused of the chief priests and the elders he answered them nothing. Then said Pilate unto him, Hearest thou not how many things they witness against thee? And he answered him never a word.*
Matthew 27: 12-14

Isaiah again, another's voice speaking through him, seven hundred years before Christ, says:

*I gave my back to the smiters, I hid not my face from shame and spitting.*
Isaiah 50:6

Read what the prophet Micah foretold eight hundred years before Christ:

*They shall strike the judge of Israel with a rod upon the cheek.*
Micah 5:1

Now read the contemporary record of what actually happened to the Messiah.

*And they spit upon him, and took the reed and smote him on the head.* Matthew 27:30

*Pilate took Jesus and scourged him.* Luke 19:1

The ancient seers said the Messiah God would:

★ Be smitten on the back.
★ Hit on the cheek with a rod.
★ Have his face spat on.

Those three things happened to Jesus of Nazareth!
Speaking through King David, the Messiah-God foretells:

*False witnesses did rise up; they laid things to my charge that I knew not.* Psalm 35:11

Here's the contemporary account of what happened to Jesus:

*The chief priests and elders, and all the council sought false witness against Jesus to put him to death.* Matthew 26:59

Who was it the prophets foresaw being spat upon, smitten and humiliated? The Messiah, The Mighty God, The Everlasting Father, The Prince of Peace. Could anything more unlikely be foretold of such a personage? Could human mind devise such a story? Prophecies of the conquering hero, yes; prophecies of a successful revolutionary leader, yes, or prophecies of a king mighty in war, yes, but, as I have said, it would take either a lunatic or an inspired man to foretell this complete humiliation even unto death of the Messiah-God.

## THE CRUCIFIXION OF THE MESSIAH-GOD. PROPHESIED 1,000 B.C.

*They pierced my hands and my feet.* Psalm 22:16

There is little need to comment, everyone knows that Jesus was crucified, his hands and his feet pierced.

As I have mentioned, the ancient seers often spoke of the future in the past tense.

It is yet another indication of their speaking under inspiration. Does it not at first sight appear ridiculous for a person purporting to foretell the future to speak in the past tense and to use the personal pronoun "I" or "Me"?

If you think for a moment, however, it is the correct thing to happen for, if the messages were from the great universal spirit or whatever other euphemism for God you may wish to use, and the crucified Messiah WAS the great universal spirit, then it is quite correct for personal pronouns to be used.

But why the past tense? It is not until we read the prophecy of John in the Apocalypse that we read the reference to the Messiah as being

*The Lamb slaim from the foundation of the World.*

The past tense is used because all the events prophecied were deemed to be in the eternal purpose. That is why Jesus claimed

*Before Abraham was I am.*

Another example of the oneness of the ancient seers.

A little doctoring of the manuscripts by the Israelite priests would have saved all the speculation there has been about the personal pronouns and the tense of the wording: Why did they not decide to make the words more understandable? Because they believed them to be inspired!

The foretelling of the act of crucifying the Messiah one thousand years before the event, and many hundreds of years before crucifixion was known in Israel, is mysterious enough but it becomes the more mysterious when we realise that not only the major event, but EVERY DETAIL of that crucifixion scene was foretold many hundreds of years before it happened.

What the Messiah would say on the cross was foretold. Exactly what the Roman soldiers would say as they sat at the foot of the cross was foretold. What they would give Him to drink was foretold. What the Roman soldiers would do was foretold.

## INTENSE THIRST.

Crucifixion was accompanied by intense thirst. Walking the streets of Jerusalem in good health I found myself drinking cold drink after cold drink. Imagine the thirst of one nailed to a cross in the heat of the day. The Psalmist had prophesied

*My tongue cleaveth to my jaws.*     Psalm 22:15

Could a more dramatic description of extreme thirst have been written? That was not precise enough for the Psalmist, however, for he says

*In my thirst they gave me vinegar to drink.*     Psalm 69:21

Let us read the contemporary account of what happened to Jesus of Nazareth one thousand years after those prophecies:

*After this, knowing all things were accomplished, Jesus said, I thirst. Now there was set a vessel full of vinegar: and they filled a sponge with vinegar and put it to his mouth.*    John 19: 28-29

## THE MOCKING OF THE MESSIAH.

*All they that see me laugh me to scorn: they shoot out the lip, they shake the head.*    Psalm 22:7

The contemporary account records:

*And they that passed by reviled him, wagging their heads.*
   Matthew 27:39

I don't know how much you, my reader, know about human nature but I once had an experience which taught me a lot. Perhaps it was, though, rather a confirmation of what I had already known than something new to me. I had been called in to manage a business which several accountants had said should be put into liquidation — losses were running into massive sums each year. My job was to keep the business running if I could, but if not to give the business as quiet and decent a burial as possible. I was left to get on with the job! All the 'experts' disappeared.

Gradually the business began to change course, money flowed in, soon the business was making huge profits and they didn't leave me alone anymore! THEY ALL WANTED A BIT OF THE GLORY. The accountants suddenly took an interest, the other directors began to ask questions and take an interest, the business efficiency men began to take an interest and even the architects began to take an interest. Everybody seemed to come to life and try to 'get their oar in' as soon as the business was a success. And do you know what? They had all known exactly what to do to save the business all along, according to them. They hadn't done it but they knew. They hadn't even whispered it to me, but they knew. Now they were no different from most of us, we all like our bit of glory, we all like to associate with the successful things in life, we all like to think we know a little more than the next man. None of us like to put ourselves in the shadow of failure and have people think of us as failures.

When the disciples asked Jesus which of them would be the greatest in the Kingdom of God that was real human nature, but it is NOT human nature to write derogatory things of ourselves, not unless you do it for money, that is.

Zechariah, five hundred and twenty years before Christ, foretold that the shepherd would be smitten and the sheep would be scattered (Zechariah 13:7). Now doesn't experience tell us that human nature would never admit to running away when the Messiah was smitten? It's quite usual for followers of great people to say 'I was faithful to him' or 'I stood by him when everyone else let him down'. But how many people, aspiring to greatness, would put it on record that they had run away from their leader or the great man in the hour of his greatest need?

Matthew records:

*ALL the disciples forsook him and fled.*　　　　Matthew 26:56

Matthew, who wrote that, was one of the disciples. Why didn't he write "All bar one — me"? He was a man who wanted to influence the world and yet he set himself as a self-confessed coward. Why did Matthew write such a derogatory thing about himself? Because it was the truth, that is exactly how it happened. "All the disciples forsook him and fled."

## WHAT THE ROMAN SOLDIERS DID ON CRUCIFIXION DAY.

When the Roman army marched into Jerusalem in 63 B.C. King David, writer of the Psalms, had been dead for 900 years.

Little did the Roman soldiers at the foot of the cross realise that they were about to fulfil a prophecy that had been written over nine hundred and fifty years before they were born.

The voice of the Great Universal Spirit, speaking through the prophet King David, had predicted:

*They part my garments among them, and cast lots upon my vesture.*　　　　Psalm 22:18

Here is an eye witness record of what happened at the foot of the cross on that crucifixion day:

*And they crucified him, and parted his garments, casting lots.*
　　　　Matthew 27:35

The Romans crucified thousands of people — what caused them to perform all the acts which had been foretold as being applicable to the death of the Messiah if Jesus was not the Messiah?

## THE DEATH OF THE MESSIAH – THE GRAVE OF THE MESSIAH.

I have commented upon how incongruous to the human mind is the thought of the death of the Messiah-God. Assuming, however, that the prophets had, for some reason, accepted that the Messiah-God would die — how would the human mind envisage the King of Kings dying? One would imagine the deathbed to be regal and set in a palace of some splendour. There would, of course, be the finest medical attendants and all the comforts befitting a king of those days.

The prophets foresaw no such thing. We have seen that they foresaw the crucifixion and the events which surrounded it, even to the details of what the people at the foot of the cross would say and do.

Writing seven hundred years before Christ was born the prophet Isaiah predicted the following of the Messiah:

> *He was taken from prison and from judgement; and who shall declare his generation? For he was cut off out of the land of the living; for the transgression of my people was he stricken. And he made his grave with the WICKED, and with the RICH in his death.* The Book of the prophet Isaiah 53: 8,9.

It is known to almost everyone that Jesus was crucified between two thieves. Quite literally He died with the 'wicked', with criminals. Who, in their 'natural mind', would have thought of the Messiah dying with criminals?

What does the prophet mean by 'with the rich in his death'? The body of Jesus was taken by one Joseph of Arimathaea and buried in a new tomb that Joseph had had prepared for himself. Joseph was a very rich man, a tin trader who had made his fortune shipping tin from the British Isles. Jesus DID make his grave with the rich in his death.

If Jesus of Nazareth is not the most mysterious man who lived explain, if you can, how he came to fulfil all the prophecies the ancient seers had made of the Messiah-God.

## A VERY UNUSUAL THING HAPPENED.

As I have said, crucifixion was unknown to the Jews in the days of the ancient seers, yet they described the crucifixion of the Messiah in detail.

Though the Messiah was predicted to have to suffer crucifixion, there was one aspect of crucifixion he could not suffer, the breaking of the victims bones. Predicting the death of the Messiah one thousand years before the event David, King of Israel, had written: "He keepeth all his bones; not one of them is broken." Psalm 34:20

It was the custom of the Romans to break the legs of the crucified. Some have said this was done out of mercy to stop the dying man extending his death agony by raising himself up and thus allowing expansion of the lungs. Since crucifixion was not designed to be a merciful death and the Romans were not known for their mercy, the more likely explanation is that when the spectacle got boring and the crucified had lapsed into unconsciousness, the legs of the victim were broken to make sure the victim was dead. Whatever the reason, it was customary to break the legs of the crucified at the end of their suffering.

As predicted by King David the prophet, not a bone in Jesus' body was broken:

*Then came the soldiers and broke the legs of the first, and of the other who was crucified with him. But when they came to Jesus, and saw that he was dead already, they broke not his legs;*
John 19: 32,33

That is a much more significant happening than it would at first appear. It was the teaching of the ancient seers that the Messiah would be the sacrificial 'lamb' for the nation just as the passover lamb had been those many years before. Hence the exclamation of John the Baptist on seeing Jesus:

*Behold the Lamb of God which taketh away the sins of the world.*

One of the rules regarding the passover lamb was that no bone of it was to be broken and this rule had been kept by the Israelites in the celebration of the passover. What, or who, inspired the Romans to unwittingly obey the rules of the Israelite passover in the case of Jesus of Nazareth?

## WAS JESUS OF NAZARETH THE MESSIAH-GOD.

Is it not odd that the organisation which was set up to propagate the message of the coming of God in human form to redeem mankind has, to a very large extent, now set about explaining away that very message?

Of course, the whole concept of a God inhabiting a human body is an offence to the human intellect, but there are a lot of things we know to be true today, which at one time would have been considered an offence to the human intellect.

If an 'it', or if you like, a great universal spirit, or 'God did not contact mankind through the ancient seers, then how did it come about that in the very year predicted a person appeared in whose life the prognostications of the prophets were fulfilled? Was Jesus of Nazareth really the Great Universal Spirit come 'in the flesh' or merely the most mysterious man who ever lived?

# 8.
# What Jesus Foretold About the First World War

Do you know that Jesus foretold future events? Will it surprise you to know that he foretold a crucial battle in the 1914-1918 war, together with the events which were to precede it, and the events which were to follow it?

I did say he was the most mysterious man who ever lived, didn't I? Perhaps by now you agree with me but you may still find it difficult to believe that Jesus predicted the First World War — well, read on.

Come with me backwards in time to the Mount of Olives. Jesus and his disciples are gathered there, and undoubtedly the disciples are worried, worried because Jesus shows no inclination to rid their city and their land of the hated Romans. They had expected their Messiah-God to restore again the kingdom to Israel, and they were beginning to wonder if he would ever get round to doing it. He showed no signs of the nationalistic fervour they expected of him, much less of leading the Jewish nation in revolt against it's oppressors.

Jesus had recently delivered himself of a violent attack on the Jewish religious hierarchy, denouncing the scribes and pharisees in the most offensive terms. He had called them 'vipers' and 'serpents' and asked them how they could escape 'the damnation of hell'. Strong stuff and not calculated to win friends and influence people.

A few hours before, their hearts had sunk as he rounded on their beloved city Jerusalem and said:

*O Jerusalem, Jerusalem, thou that killest the prophets, and stonest them who are sent unto thee, how often would I have gathered thy children together, even as a hen gathereth her chickens under her wings and ye would not! Behold your house is left unto you desolate.*

There must have been a feeling of desperation among them as they sat on the mountainside looking down over the Garden of Gethsemane and past the Golden Gate at the temple building. They probably felt there was nothing they could do to arouse some nationalistic fervour in this man. When they had shown him the buildings of the temple, the most holy place in the land, he had said a most peculiar thing:

*And Jesus went out, and departed from the temple; and his disciples came to him to show him the buildings of the temple. And Jesus said unto them, see ye not all these things? Verily I say unto you, There shall not be left here one stone upon another that shall not be thrown down.*                         Matthew 24:2

You can imagine the disciples, can't you? "Come on, Jesus, look at the temple, look what a wonderful building it is, doesn't your heart fill with pride as you look at the immensity and glory of it?" No good! Back came the reply "There shall not be left here one stone upon another that shall not be thrown down."

What was there to do now but try to understand the man? Their loyalty remained firm but they were beginning to lose faith in his Messiahship, they could see no sign of him doing the things they thought the Messiah should do. Certainly they could see the end fast approaching, for they knew the establishment would not like the attacks he was making on them, and, were probably even now plotting how they could rid themselves of the prophet of Nazareth.

And so, sitting on the Mount of Olives, they asked him the question which was filling their minds at that time:

*And as they sat upon the Mount of Olives, the disciples came unto him privately, saying, Tell us, when shall these things be? And what shall be the sign of thy coming and of the end of the world?*

There are three questions in that passage:

★ When shall these things be? When will Jerusalem become desolate and when will the temple be destroyed?
★ What will be the sign of your coming?
★ What will be the sign of the end of the world (dispensation)?

The answer of Jesus must be quoted in full:

*And Jesus answered and said unto them, Take heed that no man deceive you.*
*For many shall come in my name saying, I am Christ [Messiah]; and shall deceive many.*
*And ye shall hear of wars and rumours of wars; see that ye be not troubled; for all these things must first come to pass, but the end is not yet. For nation shall rise against nation, and kingdom against kingdom; and there shall be famines, and pestilences, and earthquakes in various places. All these are the beginnings of the sorrows. Then shall they deliver you up to be afflicted, and shall kill you; and ye shall be hated of all nations for my names sake. And then shall many be offended, and shall betray one another, and shall hate one another.*
*And many false prophets shall arise, and shall deceive many. And because iniquity shall abound the love of many shall grow cold. But he that shall endure unto the end, the same shall be saved. And this gospel of the kingdom shall be preached in all the world for a witness unto all nations; AND THEN SHALL THE END COME.*
*WHEN YE, THEREFORE, SHALL SEE THE ABOMINA-TION OF DESOLATION, SPOKEN OF BY DANIEL THE PROPHET, STAND IN THE HOLY PLACE [WHOSOEVER READETH LET HIM UNDERSTAND],*
*Then let them who are in Judeah flee into the mountains;*
*Let him who is on the housetop not come down to take anything out of his house;*
*Neither let him who is in the field return back to take his clothes. And woe unto those who are with child, and to those who nurse children in those days! But pray that your flight be not in winter, neither on the sabbath day;*
*For then shall be great tribulation, such as was not since the*

*beginning of the world to this time, no, nor ever shall be.*
*And except those days be shortened, there should be no flesh*
*saved; but for the elects sake those days shall be shortened.*
Matthew 24: 4-22

*And when ye shall see Jerusalem compassed with armies, then*
*know that it's desolation is near. Then let them who are in Judea*
*flee to the mountains; and let them who are in the midst of it*
*depart; and let not them that are in the countries enter into it.*
*FOR THESE ARE THE DAYS OF VENGEANCE, THAT ALL*
*THINGS THAT ARE WRITTEN MAY BE FULFILLED.*
*But woe unto them that are with child and to them that nurse*
*children, in those days! For there shall be great distress in the*
*land, and wrath upon THIS PEOPLE.*
*And they shall fall by the edge of the sword, and shall be led away*
*captive into all nations; and JERUSALEM SHALL BE*
*TRODDEN DOWN OF THE GENTILES UNTIL THE TIMES*
*OF THE GENTILES BE FULFILLED .....*
*Verily I say unto you, This generation shall not pass away, till all*
*be fulfilled.*
Parts of Luke 21: 20-32

There are two things we must not forget, the first being that a
'generation' is forty years in prophecy. 'Forty' is a very significant number
in the Jewish scriptures. Forty days is the length of time the flood is said
to have been upon the earth. Noah waited forty days after the flood had
abated before opening the ark. Moses was forty years of age when he left
Egypt. Forty years later he was chosen to lead the children of Israel out of
Egypt. For forty years the children of Israel were in the wilderness
travelling to the promised land. Saul reigned over Israel for forty years, so
did David and so did Solomon. Israel was delivered into the hands of the
Philistines for forty years for disobeying God. Eli had judged Israel for
forty years when he died. Ishbosheth was forty years old when he began to
reign over Israel. Jehoash reigned forty years. Joash reigned forty years.

More specifically we read the following:

*And the Lords anger was kindled against Israel, and made them*
*wander in the wilderness FORTY YEARS, until all the*
*GENERATION that had done evil in the sight of the Lord, was*
*consumed.* Numbers 32:13

We must note, too, that Jesus is speaking specifically about 'this
people', the Jews, and not all the nations of the world nor about the
House of Israel.

I am afraid I have to repeat again, it is so important, the Prophets were precise and we must be precise. Because commentators have FAILED to realise that the prophecy is about the Jews and Jerusalem, some very fanciful theories have been propounded about the 'Great Tribulation' and traumatic pictures have been drawn of people all over the world 'fleeing to the mountains', dire warnings are issued to people that the greatest time of persecution ever is about to befall each and every one of us. Certainly there are very perilous times ahead but they are not foretold in this particular prophecy. It is not one of the functions of the prophets that they should provide expositors, who cannot or will not devote time to study, with the fodder of fear. The function of the prophets was to enlighten mankind as to what will take place at specific times, in specific places, to specific races.

In this case:

★   The specific time was 'This generation', that is the generation (40 years) following the time when Christ was speaking.
★   The specific place was Jerusalem.
★   The specific race was the Jews.

Here itemised, are the specific things that were to happen:

★   Within forty years Jerusalem was to be compassed with armies.
★   The temple was to suffer such destruction that it could reasonably be described as not having 'one stone upon another' that had not been thrown down.
★   The Jews to be led away captive into all nations.
★   Jerusalem would continue to be 'trodden down' of the Gentiles until the 'Times' (Seven times punishment period) of the Gentiles were fulfilled.

The only part the Gentiles have in this prophecy is that they would compass Jerusalem with armies, would destroy the temple, would lead the Jews away captive and would continue to tread Jerusalem down. The Tribulation warnings of the prophecy are specifically in respect of the Jews.

## THE POLITICAL SITUATION WHEN JESUS SPOKE

When Jesus spoke the words of that prophecy it seemed very unlikely that it would be fulfilled. What army was there, that could possibly attack Jerusalem? The mightiest army in the world was already there and, it seemed, had absolutely no intention of leaving. Who would dare to attack a city ruled over and guarded by the Roman Empire? It is accepted among historians that the Jews and the Romans had a fairly satisfactory working arrangement. Though, of course, the Jews would rather not have had the Romans in their country, the Romans actually interfered very little in their way of life. The Roman eagle displayed outside the temple was an irritant to the zealots but there was no interference in the day to day worship of the Jews. The safety of Jerusalem and the sanctity of Jewish religious worship was guaranteed by Rome. True, the city was 'trodden down' but it had seen far worse times, and there seemed little the Jews could do anyway. In those days, as Jesus spoke, there was little probability that the Romans would leave the city within the next forty years and even less probability that any other nation dare besiege the city with them there.

The events of the life and times of Jesus of Nazareth show how anxious the Romans were to keep the Jewish hierarchy happy. Pilate did not want Jesus crucified, but he acquiesed when the Jews insisted. None of the bargaining which surrounded the trial and death of Jesus need have taken place, the Romans could have enforced their will and set Jesus free but they were obviously prepared to do what the Jews asked of them to keep the peace. Ultimately Pilate said 'See ye to it' and washed his hands of the whole issue of Jesus who claimed to be the Messiah. Similarly, when the Jews requested a guard on the tomb of Christ, Pilate refused and told them 'You have guards', thus the tomb was guarded by guards appointed by the Jews, not, as commonly believed, by Roman soldiers.

Philo confirms the view that the Romans made little attempt to suppress the Jewish faith or culture. He tells of Pilate bringing shields made of gold, bearing the Roman Emperor's name, and displaying them in Herod's palace. The Jews considered this to be an affront to their faith and breach of their religious rights as guaranteed by the Roman Emperor. When Pilate refused the demand of the Jewish hierarchy to remove the offending shields, the Jews appealed directly to the Emperor Tiberius with the result he ordered Pilate to remove the shields immediately.

What persecution there was centred around political misdeeds and attempts to either undermine the authority of the Romans or attempts at insurrection. Such incidents were, of course, dealt with with a typical Roman ferocity and inhumanity. Religious tolerance, however, extended even to the Jews being allowed to put a Roman citizen to death if they found him within the temple fence.

Soon after the death of Jesus, Pontius Pilate became the subject of complaint by the Samaritans who made representation to Vitellius. Such was the degree to which Rome was prepared to go to placate the Jewish people that Pilate was sent to Rome for trial and, being found guilty, was banished to Gaul.

For a while the prophecy of Jesus seemed doomed to remain unfulfilled, at least in the time, forty years, 'this generation' which he had predicted as being the fulfilment time. Vitellius and his successor Petronius formed considerable bonds of understanding with the Jews and peace reigned. The possibility of the fufilment of the prophecy of the prophet of Nazareth receded.

In A.D.37 Caius Caligula became Emperor of Rome. He ordered his statue to be set up in the temple. Though he withdrew the order on the insistence of Herod Agrippa the damage had been done. The Jews knew that at any time the mad Emperor might renew his demand. Caligula was assassinated in the January of A.D.41 and was succeeded by Claudius (A.D.41-54).

From A.D.54 to the spring of A.D.66 tension mounted with assassinations of the Romans by the Jews and wholesale retaliation in the form of capital punishment, often crucifixion, meted out by the Romans. Festus (60-62 A.D.) tried to bring peace but the situation had gone beyond the point of no return.

Things finally came to a head under Gessius Florus (64-66 A.D.). There was a large scale insurrection in the city, the Emperors offerings were thrown out of the temple. Then the unthinkable happened, the Romans surrendered, there was now no Roman garrison in Jerusalem. The unarmed Romans were butchered after they had surrendered.

The years went by, and the 'generation' from the time that Jesus had spoken his prophecy was drawing to it's close, the last of the forty years were ticking away and were near to running out.

In A.D.67 the Romans were busy putting down resistance in Galilee, by A.D.68 the fighting was near Jerusalem, in A.D.69 Jerusalem was 'compassed with armies' and those in the city who had heard the prophecy of Jesus must have remembered his words

*And when ye shall see Jerusalem compassed with armies, then know that it's desolation is near.*

A.D.70 dawned and the Romans gradually broke down the savage resistance. On 9th August A.D.70 the temple was stormed. According to Josephus, the Roman general Titus ordered his army not to destroy the temple, but as though guided by an invisible hand, the soldiers did not for once observe the traditional discipline of the Roman army. Blood was shed in the holiest place of the holiest building in Jewry, human blood ran over the altar of burnt offering, indeed an abomination to any Jew. The sanctuary was set on fire despite the orders of Titus, and the temple was destroyed.

## FAMINE, PESTILENCE AND WAR.

Titus, however, did not destroy Jerusalem nor did the Roman army. Jerusalem was destroyed from within. The misery of the city is unprintable. Famine stalked the streets, weakening the defenders, and terrible pestilence swept through the city as though a forest fire. Jews who surrendered to the Romans were crucified or made slaves. Not until the arrival of Adolf Hitler, nineteen hundred years later, would there be such slaughter, for one authority has it that 1,750,000 men, women and children died by famine, pestilence or war.

Internal feuding among the members of various Jewish sects was a contributory factor in the downfall of the Holy City, for there were many 'messiahs' putting forward their own claims. Constant fighting between brothers and fellow Jews sapped the energy of the nation and brought about the actual holocaust in A.D.70.

To the students of prophecy of the day, the voice of the most mysterious man who ever lived must have thundered out from forty years past:

*There shall not be left here one stone upon another that shall not be thrown down.*

All subsequent attempts to rebuild the temple failed and to this day there is 'not one stone upon another' of the second temple, Herod's temple, on the temple site — only the Western Wall — the Wailing Wall — remains. Today Jews pray at the Wailing Wall which is built of stones from the temple

*When ye shall see Jerusalem compassed with armies, then know that it's desolation is near.*

Caesar ordered that the whole city and the temple be destroyed. The Romans ploughed over the ruins and, it is said, spread over it a layer of salt five inches thick so that nothing would grow there. The seven-branched candlestick and the table of shewbread, holy items, were taken to Rome and erected in the pagan Temple of Peace. They can still be seen in Rome on display in the arch of Titus in that city. Roman banners flew over the fire-blackened temple site, over which Jesus had looked just forty years before and said "There shall not be left here one stone upon another that shall not be thrown down." "Desolation" is the only word to describe Jerusalem in A.D.70, even the victorious Romans considered it almost a punishment to be sent to the utterly desolate wilderness which Jerusalem had become.

*And they [the Jews] shall fall by the edge of the sword, and shall be led away captive into all nations;*

Those Jews that had not died in the famine, the pestilence or the fighting were sold into slavery. Notice the precise words "All nations". This was an experience the Jews had not had before, for conquering nations usually kept their captives themselves. When the Jews had been taken captive in Egypt they were in one nation, when they had been taken captive into Babylon they had been one nation, but this prophecy foretold something which went against the expected pattern of captivity — they were not to be taken captive into one nation but taken captive into ALL nations. There is little need for me to tell my reader that that is precisely what happened. The final humiliation came when Emperor Hadrian built a Roman colony on the ruins, Aelia Capitolina. No Jew or Christian was allowed to set foot on any part of what once had been Jerusalem, the penalty for doing so was — death.

## BUT WHAT ABOUT JESUS AND THE FIRST WORLD WAR?

So far we have only dealt with the prophecies which Jesus foretold would take place within forty years, but there were other prophecies in response to the disciples' question "When shall these things be and what shall be the sign of thy coming and of the end of the world?"

*And they shall fall by the edge of the sword, and shall be led away captive into all nations; and Jerusalem SHALL BE TRODDEN DOWN OF THE GENTILES UNTIL THE TIMES OF THE GENTILES BE FULFILLED.*

The Jews were to have no homeland until 'The times of the Gentiles' were fulfilled and were to remain among the nations.

There used to be a phrase used by mothers to their restless children 'You're like a wandering Jew'. Reflecting on that phrase one recognises how rapidly times change. Few people under the age of forty remember the days when there was no Jewish state, we think that the Jews have always had a homeland. Not so, the 'wandering Jew' was not just a saying, it was an historic fact until comparatively recently. Anyone who had expostulated even fifty years ago that the Jews would have their own nation and their own army, capable of repulsing the might of the Arab nations surrounding them, would have been laughed to scorn. Jewry shared a common religion and were a people, but were not a nation. "And

*And they shall be led away captive into all nations ... until the 'Times of the Gentiles' be fulfilled.*

I have previously mentioned that 'seven Times' was the traditional punishment period of Israel for apostasy and those who listened to the prophecy of Jesus would be in no doubt as to what he meant by 'The times of the Gentiles', they would know he meant the 'seven times' which was the punishment period laid down for apostasy in Israel.

In our chapter 'Breaking the Code' we saw that a 'time' represented one year of days, that is 360 days. Therefore 'seven times' must represent a period of 2520 years. But at what point in time did the 'seven times' or 2520 years commence? What date was the beginning of Judah's punishment period?

The answer is fairly simple to find. The treading down 'times' commenced with the Gentile occupation of Jerusalem by the Babylonian Empire in the reign of Nebuchadnezzar, when Daniel and his fellow Jews were taken captive.

Nebuchadnezzar was the first of the succession of empires which culminated in the Roman Empire. The commencement date is the year 603 B.C. when Jerusalem was subjugated by the Babylonians and the Jews went into captivity. This 'treading down' was to continue until the 'Times of the Gentiles' were fulfilled.

A simple deduction shows that 2520 less 603 years gives us the A.D. date of 1917. 1917 was the year to which Jesus referred when he said "And they shall be led away captive into all nations, and Jerusalem shall be trodden down of the Gentiles until the times of the Gentiles be fulfilled."

As I have previously mentioned, the well-known mathematician Dr. Grattan Guiness, author of that great textbook on prophecy "Light for the Last Days" wrote in 1887 "There can be NO QUESTION, that those who live to see this year 1917 will have reached one of the most important, perhaps the most momentous, of these terminal years."

A Dr. Aldersmith, in his book "The Fulness of the Nations" published in 1898 wrote: "Students of prophecy are agreed that when the Times of the Gentiles are fulfilled, and Jerusalem ceases to be trodden down, we may expect it to pass into the hands of it's rightful owners. This period may end about A.D.1917. Time only will show."

Just as at the time of the birth of Jesus of Nazareth there were initiates who were students of the ancient seers, so at the turn of the century, long before the first gun-fire of the First World War snarled across Flanders fields, there were people awaiting the deliverence of Jerusalem in the year 1917.

## THE EXACT DAY OF DELIVERANCE FORETOLD.

Yes! They even looked for the exact day Jerusalem would be delivered in 1917. Some six hundred years before Jesus was born a prophet called Haggai wrote just two and a half pages of prophecy to Zerubbabel, the Governor of Judah, and Joshua the High Priest at Jerusalem. The two and a half pages remained in the Jewish scriptures and attracted little attention, but there, in those few pages, was the prediction of the deliverance of Jerusalem. Mysteriously, Haggai repeats the word 'consider' five times in that short prophecy, as though trying to attract his readers attention to something very special.

The message of Haggai to the Governor of Judah and to the High Priest of Jerusalem was plain. The people had to be reproved for their sins. They had failed to restore the 'House of the Lord' but they were busily engaged in providing houses for themselves. The message of the prophet was plain and the people of Judah set-to rebuilding the Temple in Jerusalem.

Haggai then gave a message of blessing to the Jews and to Jerusalem and drew their attention, and our attention, on no less than three occasions, to some special date, by asking us to 'consider':

*The four and twentieth day of the ninth month.*

The ninth month of the Hebrew year is KISLEV and because the Hebrew calendar is lunar, the dates move in relation to ours. Haggai drew our attention to the 24th of KISLEV. Jewish days do not, as our days, commence at one minute past midnight, they commence at sunset and continue until sunset of the following day.

As the sun set over the city of Jerusalem on December 8th 1917, all through that night and in the following early morning the Gentile army of occupation began to evacuate the city. By the time the sun was up on the 9th December 1917 the army had gone. IS IT CHANCE OR IS IT SOMETHING MORE THAT FROM SUNSET TO SUNSET THE NEXT DAY WAS — THE 24TH DAY OF KISLEV?

One wonders if, as the Mayor of Jerusalem came out with the white flag of surrender that morning, he realised he was surrendering the city in the year, to the day, that the prophets had foretold some twenty four centuries before. The 24th day of Kislev 1917. Perhaps the words of the Nazarene floated over almost nineteen hundred years to the Mayor's ears

*'Jerusalem shall be trodden down of the Gentiles until the Times of the Gentiles be fulfilled.'*

In 1917 the First World War still raged in the trenches on the Western front, whilst, in Russia, were being seen the beginnings of the Bolshevik Revolution. In the Middle East a bitter struggle was being waged between the Allies and the Turks, who for centuries had dominated the Holy City. By the beginning of December the British Army was encamped outside the city and the Turks, inside the city, prepared for a long fight.

General Allenby, as we shall see, a significant name indeed, was the commander of the British forces and we are told by W.T. Massey in his book "How Jerusalem was Won" that General Allenby issued the following orders to General Sir Philip Chetwood on November 26th 1917 "I place no restrictions upon you in respect of any operation you may consider necessary against Lifta, or the enemy's lines to the south of it, except that on no account is any risk to be run of bringing the City of Jerusalem or it's immediate environs within the area of operations."

The troops became frustrated by the slowing down of the operations in the Holy Land caused by Allenby's pre-occupation with not attacking or fighting in, the Holy City. Of course, there were political considerations — Jerusalem is the third most Holy City of the Moslems, and the first city of Christendom. No commander would wish to risk a backlash by destroying the shrines of either of the great religions. There was, however, something more to Allenby's hesitancy than political consideration, for Allenby was a devout Christian.

Allenby's tactics were vindicated, for on the night of 8th December 1917 the Turks evacuated the city under cover of darkness and Jerusalem was surrendered to the British Army without a shot being fired. Anyone acquainted with the bravery and ferocity of the Turkish fighting man must wonder at that fact of history!

Let us leave, for a moment, those British troops as they wait and watch on that 8th December 1917, and return to England. We shall attend a Church of England service.

Let us choose the kind of small church, set on the outskirts of a village deep in the countryside of a typical English county. Despite the war being fought in France, the spirit of Christmas is already among the people as they walk the frosty path to the church door. We cannot help feeling that this church is the model for every pretty, snow-covered church on every Christmas card we have ever seen. The only signs of war are a few uniforms and one or two war wounded, but everyone is in good spirits, the bells peal out over the chill countryside and as we approach the church door we hear the vibrant tones of the organ.

We are glad we have come to this typical village church, though really any Church of England church would have done, for we have come to hear the morning lesson and to pray for our men in France and our men encamped outside that city wall many thousands of miles away.

All the Churches of England will read the same lesson this morning, the lesson which has been set for the day for many centuries. Let me repeat that: We have come to hear the lesson which has been set for reading on this day for centuries. The lesson was not set a year before, nor a decade before, but hundreds of years before. Quiet! The lesson is about to be read: The reader reads from the 31st Chapter of the Book of the Prophet Isaiah.

*For thus hath the Lord spoken unto me, As the lion or the young lion roaring on his prey, when a multitude of shepherds is called forth against him, will not be afraid of their voice, nor abase himself for the noise of them, so shall the Lord of Hosts come down to fight for Mount Zion [Jerusalem] and the hill thereof. AS BIRDS FLYING, SO WILL THE LORD OF HOSTS DEFEND JERUSALEM; DEFENDING ALSO HE WILL DELIVER IT, AND PASSING OVER HE WILL PRESERVE IT.* v.4-5

So that's HOW the prophet had foretold Jerusalem would be delivered 'As birds flying'. The 'birds flying' would do three things — 'defend', 'deliver' and 'preserve'. But surely delivering and defending are two different things, to deliver a town you have to attack it. To defend a town you have to be IN the town. On the other hand neither attack nor defence are likely to result in the town's preservation.

We shall stay a day or two and perhaps visit our little church again. It is December 10th, let us listen to the morning lesson:

*Look upon Zion, the city of our solemnities: thine eyes shall see Jerusalem a quiet habitation, a tabernacle that shall not be taken down; not one of it's stakes shall ever be removed neither shall any of it's cords be broken. But the glorious Lord will be unto us a place of broad rivers and streams.* Isaiah 33:20

Perhaps we can be forgiven for feeling there is some kind of mysterious message, planned centuries before, being passed to us through these readings. Statements of prophets made thousands of years before, planned for reading in the established churches of this land centuries before and sounding like THIS MORNINGS NEWSPAPER.

On that day, December 10th, the British troops are inside the City of Jerusalem. Thousands of them are members of the Church of England and there are many who are not members of the Church of England who worship with them. They, of course, read exactly the same lessons which are being read in England. So through the miracle of the printed page let us, having attended morning service in England, now attend the evening service of the 10th December among the troops in Jerusalem. Listen to the officer as he reads the pre-set lesson:

*Comfort ye, comfort ye my people, saith your God. Speak ye comfortably unto Jerusalem, and cry unto her, that her warfare is accomplished, that her iniquity is pardoned; for she hath received at the Lord's hand double for all her sins.* Isaiah 40: 1-2

I ask you, could that reading have been more apt had the officer planned it that very morning? Could, in fact, anything have been more apt had it been written especially for the occasion? Is the whole thing coincidence?

★ Jerusalem was delivered in the year foretold.
★ On the day foretold.
★ The prayer book readings for the established church of the nation whose armies delivered Jerusalem, written thousands of years before, and planned many hundreds of years before, were about the event taking place on those particular days.

We leave that army service and mingle with the crowds. There is a distressing rumour, the Turks have pulled back but even now they are training their guns on the city to destroy it.

The hum of engines fills the air and flying out over the Turkish lines are the planes of the Royal Flying Corps. All commentators agree that the part played by the Royal Flying Corps in the Jerusalem operation was invaluable. Though war in the air was in it's infancy, it was very effective. The Turks gave up their plans to bombard the Holy City and, as the prophet Isaiah had predicted over two thousand five hundred years before

*As birds flying will the Lord of Hosts defend Jerusalem; defending also he will deliver it, and passing over he will preserve it.*

Isaiah the prophet, writing around 700 B.C., had foreseen a phenomenon which was then future to his time. As his prophetic vision pierced the mists of time, he saw what he could only describe as 'birds flying'. The age when man would take to the air was yet some 2,600 years in the future but the prophet, ever faithful to what he saw, told it just the way it was, as the Americans say. Is it coincidence that the city was 'delivered' 'defended' and 'preserved' exactly as the prophet had foretold? Is it coincidence that the 'birds' of the Royal Flying Corps hovered over the city that day?

Is it also coincidence that the motto of the squadron which carried out the operation was "I spread my wings and keep my promise"?

## AN OLD TURKISH SAYING.

In the days before the First World War the Turks had a saying: "When the waters of the Nile flow into Palestine, then will a prophet of the Lord come and drive the Turks out of the land."

Of course, before the First World War everyone knew that the waters of the Nile would never flow into Palestine. The waters of the Nile do not flow into Palestine today. During the First World War, however, British engineers laid a pipeline from the Nile into Palestine to supply water to the troops. So the waters of the Nile did, quite literally, flow into Palestine.

The Arabic form of Allenby, the name of the British commander, is Allah-en-Nebi. "Nebi" means "Prophet" and "Allah" means "God".

So when the man called in Arabic 'Prophet of God' came to Palestine and caused the waters of the Nile to flow into the land — the Turks WERE driven out! Coincidence?

## THE END OF JESUS' PROPHECY

Jesus did not end his prophecy with the deliverance of Jerusalem, he foretold that there was a lot to happen after that:

*And they shall fall by the edge of the sword, and shall be led away captive into all nations ... until the times of the Gentiles be fulfilled.*

At the end of the 'seven times' punishment, or 2520 years, and arising out of the deliverance of Jerusalem, a process was to commence which would result in Palestine becoming the home of the Jews once more. They were only to be scattered among the nations as long as the times of the Gentiles lasted.

Both the scattering and the return of the Jews is foretold in detail by other ancient seers, seers who preceded Jesus by many hundreds of years, and we shall deal with their prognostications in another chapter. In this chapter, however, we are confining ourselves to the one prophecy of Jesus in which he is answering the questions "When shall these things be and what shall be the sign of thy coming and of the end of the world (age)?" So let us read the rest of what he said:

*And Jerusalem shall be trodden down of the Gentiles until the times of the Gentiles be fulfilled. And there shall be signs in the sun, and in the moon, and in the stars; and upon the earth distress of nations with perplexity; the sea and the waves roaring. Men's hearts failing them for fear, and for looking after those things which are coming on the earth; for the powers of the heaven shall be shaken.*
*And then shall they see the Son of man coming in a cloud, with power and great glory.*
*And when these things begin to come to pass, then look up, and lift up your heads; for your redemption draweth nigh.*
*And he spoke to them a parable: Behold the fig tree, and all the trees:*
*When they now shoot forth, ye shall see and know of your own selves that summer is now nigh at hand.*
*So also ye, when ye see these things come to pass, know that the kingdom of God is nigh at hand.* **Luke 21: 24-31**

Now we have to remember our code. I will refresh your memory as we look at what Jesus said would follow the deliverance of Jerusalem.

1. There would be signs in the sun, moon and stars.
2. There would be distress of nations with perplexity. The sea and the waves roaring.
3. Men's hearts would fail them for fear for the powers of the heavens would be shaken.
4. The 'fig tree' and 'all the trees' were to 'shoot forth'.

# 1917 THE USHERING IN OF THE AGE OF REVOLUTION.

You will remember we discovered that the 'sun, moon and stars' represented the established order of things in human government, kings, leaders and lesser lights in the political world.

Let us not forget that in 1917 the Bolshevik revolution was raging in Russia and in the German armies. Corporal Hitler was suffering experiences which were to germinate the seeds of the Second World War. Little did those witnessing the Bolshevik revolution know that it was to transform not only Russia but the world. The World War was of much more importance to most people who thought that as soon as the war was over the small matter of the troubles in Russia would soon be resolved. As the tragedy of the Tzar and his family was played out in that snowbound land, little did we in the West know that our world, too, was coming to it's end. The Russian revolution was not to be just another upheaval but rather a fundamental change in human society.

I think none of my readers will need proof that since the Bolshevik revolution of 1917 events have taken place exactly as the prophet of Nazareth said they would. Governments, kings and leaders have fallen and there has, indeed, been distress of nations with perplexity.

"The sea and the waves roaring." You will recall we saw that in prophetic language the "sea and the waves" speaks of the troubled masses of people. In 1917 the troubled masses of Russia erupted in revolution. It was not to be an isolated incident for in almost every nation on earth we have seen, since that time, revolution, insurrection, civil commotion, terrorism and violence. The history of the world since 1917 has indeed been the history of

*"Distress of nations with perplexity; the sea and the waves roaring."*

## THE AGE OF FEAR.

"Men's hearts failing them for fear, and for looking after those things which are coming on the earth; for the powers of the heaven shall be shaken." What is the splitting of the atom if it is not the shaking of the powers of the heaven? Would you not consider the description "Men's hearts failing them for fear" to be an accurate description of the fear in which we all live? Has there ever been more fear and consternation about what may happen to our world because of the "powers of the heavens being shaken"?

More advances have been made, if one may use the word 'advance' of such a ghastly trade, in the design of weaponry since 1917 than in the whole of human history to that date. When the opening shots were fired in that bloody conflict, guns were still being pulled by horses, pilots fired at other aircraft with hand-held guns, and bombs were dropped over the side of the aircraft by hand. Such mechanical transport as there was seems very primitive to us. Yet within twenty-seven or so years, man was to have the ability to wipe out whole cities with one bomb, and a decade after that, the ability to destroy all life from the face of the earth. Indeed men's hearts are failing them for fear and for looking after those things which are coming on the earth.

Hindsight, it is said, is the most exact science in the world. Looking back over the years, with the benefit of hindsight, we are inclined to accept all that has happened with little awe. I think we gain a new perspective of the events of the years since the Great War if we recollect what the politicians were saying then. "The war to end wars" was held out as the great hope and the "Land fit for hero's" as the great incentive.

Jesus, almost two thousand years before, gave a much more accurate description of the world which would emerge from the Great War. Governments, he said, were to fall; revolution was to be the order of the day; the downtrodden masses of the world were to rise in rebellion against their long oppression and exploitation; fear was to stalk the earth because of something he described as "the powers of the heaven being shaken". We, who live beneath the blistering pall of the nuclear weapon, know what he meant!

## THE FIG TREE AND ALL THE OTHER TREES.

You will remember we said that the 'fig tree' is the ancient seers symbol for the Jews. After 1917, Jesus said, the Jewish nation would blossom forth. They did — but that is a long story which we will reserve for another chapter.

"And all the other trees." Probably the most astonishing international phenomenon to take place since 1917 is the emergence of so many new nations. Never in history has there been such a profusion of emerging nations as in the years since 1917. Can it be coincidence that Jesus was able, some two thousand years ago, to describe the events of our day so precisely?

# 9.
# A Minute to Midnight in Earth's History?

I am proposing in this chapter that there may be in existence a 'prophetic clock' and that anyone who will give a little unbiased thought to what the ancient seers had to say may quickly learn to tell the time by it.

Religious views can hardly be more divergent than those held by orthodox Jews, Moslems and fundamentalist Christians, and yet, when I spoke to three such groups of people recently in Jerusalem, each shared one belief — that the world is approaching the end of existence as we know it.

The Jews believed the Messiah was about to come — for the first time. The Christians believed that the Messiah was about to come — for the second time, and the Moslems believed that the return to earth of Mohammed was soon to take place.

Each group believed what they believed because they said the 'signs of the times' which their religion gave for the 'last days' were being fulfilled. Each believed there to be a 'prophetic clock' by which one could judge how close to the end of earth's 'day' humanity finds itself.

Stimulated by this unanimity, I have spoken to the adherents of many and varied religious disciplines and all agree that we are approaching something which we can loosely describe as a 'watershed' in human history. I found a unanimity almost akin to a deep human instinct, that something cataclysmic is about to happen.

With what we have already read of the predictions of the ancient seers fresh in our minds, an awesome record of fulfilment indeed, let us look more closely at the prophetic clock and see how close we are to the end of earth's day. Are we about to hear, tolling out sonerously, the chimes of the midnight hour or is there yet a little time remaining?

## THE JEW, PALESTINE AND THE PROPHETIC CLOCK.

The Jewish people and the land of Palestine may well be described as the prime hands moving around the dial of the 'prophetic clock'. I would like to show you how these hands have moved throughout history to denote how near to or how far we are from the 'time of the end'.

Much was predicted by the ancient seers of Israel regarding the Jewish nation throughout the ages. The sufferings of the Jewish people were predicted, their wanderings among the nations, their religious deprivations their backslidings, and, though not often did the prophets say anything nice about the Jews, they did predict their return to the land of Palestine.

Right at the centre of the predictions of the ancient seers of Israel are — the Jewish people.

Now who are the Jews? A silly question you may think, for does not the whole world KNOW who the Jews are? No, there is very little awareness among anyone, apart from the well-read of the Jews themselves, as to the origins of the Jewish people. Gentile historians are utterly confused as to the distinction between an Israelite and a Jew.

If historians are confused then it is a confusion they share with theologians, most of whom persist in using the words 'Jew' and 'Israelite' as interchangeable terms.

Accept for the moment, for I will discuss the matter fully in a later chapter, that there were twelve tribes of Israel and the Jews are the descendants of one of those tribes — Judah. The tribe of Judah was later joined by the tribe of Benjamin and a few of the priestly tribe of Levi but apart from that there is not, and has not been, since the division of Israel, any admixture of the tribes.

Little wonder the predictions of the ancient seers have remained uninterpreted of misinterpreted if we continue to apply what they say to the wrong nation.

Any reading of the ancient predictions should make it plain that two separate nations form the kingdom of Israel. The House of Judah (the Jews) and the House of Israel (the ten 'lost' tribes). The two separate peoples have never joined.

Neither Abraham, Isaac nor Jacob were Jews. Jacob was the first Israelite and father of the twelve children who founded the twelve tribes. Judah, ONE of Jacob's (Israel's) children, became the first Jew.

Does it matter? Of course it does, because if we read a prophecy which refers to the House of Israel and we apply it to the Jews (the House of Judah) and they are not the same people — how can we possibly understand it? This is especially so since the two nations were to have distinct captivities, distinct destinies, distinct religions and be found in different regions of the earth in the 'last days'.

The Jews are often referred to as 'The Chosen People' and indeed they are, but they are NOT the inheritors of the promises to Abraham, Isaac and Jacob (Israel). The line of promise was specifically passed, not to Judah, but to Jacob's grandchildren Ephraim and Manessah. This fact, which has been overlooked by all but a very few people, is of prime importance and ignorance of it has caused generations of theologians to build a theological edifice which is completely without foundation.

I say that as the briefest of outlines, because without that knowledge there is no hope whatever of understanding the predictions of the ancient seers. I ask you to accept what I have said for now and, as I have said, I will return to the subject in another chapter.

Remember! The ancient seers speak of two quite distinct peoples — they never confuse the two — the House of Judah (the Jews) and the House of Israel (the ten 'lost' tribes).

## THE PROPHETIC CLOCK OF THE ANCIENT SEERS.

Few adults are unable to tell the time but no-one is able to do so when they are born. There is a certain minimal learning and expertise we must acquire before we are able to read the message of the clock.

There are the hands of the clock; we have to differentiate between them — hence my insistence on you realising the difference between the House of Judah (the Jews) and the House of Israel. How will we ever be able to tell the time if we do not know the difference between the minute hand and the hour hand? It simply does not suffice to say 'One hand is on nine and the other hand is on twelve' because that will not tell us whether the clock is indicating nine o'clock or quarter to twelve o'clock. That is quite apparent, isn't it?

It should also, then, be apparent that we have to be very specific about the naming of the hands on the 'prophetic' clock otherwise we shall, as many others have in the past, receive and propagate an incorrect reading.

We must also have regard to certain laws of interpretation which are applicable to the prognostications of the ancient seers. On the prophetic clock, as on any ordinary clock, it is not enough to have the correct numbers on the dial, they must also be in the correct sequence. Nine, for example, must always be in the same position on the dial.

It should go without saying, but it is my experience that so many things which should not have to be said do have to be said, that we should never set the hands of the clock in the wrong positions because we find it convenient to do so. We will not stop ourselves being late for work by putting the clock back! The time is the time, nothing is solved, nothing is gained, and nothing is altered by messing about with the hands of the clock, we will make it neither earlier nor later — we will merely mislead ourselves.

Similarly, the great prophetic clock is a recorder of the time we live in earth's history. It INFORMS of the time — IT DOES NOT CREATE THE TIME!

So much should be obvious and yet, generations of well-intentioned but simplistic interpreters of the ancient seers have sought for one reason or another to change the time on the face of the prophetic clock thinking they could, by so doing, postpone the undesirable and expedite the desirable. Others, evil men like Herod, have sought to thwart the prophetic clock only to find that the inevitable follows — prophetic time rolls on.

## THE MARKINGS ON THE FACE OF THE PROPHETIC CLOCK.

Even as we agree that our clocks should be set to a uniform time, so ALL the ancient seers divided time on the dial of the prophetic clock in the same way.

The major division of time is expressed in the writings of the ancient seers as being "The Former Days" and the "Latter Days". The "Former Days" extended from the commencement of recorded history until B.C.7, and the "Latter Days" extended through from B.C.7 to the culmination of earth's history.

What authority have we for asserting that the prophets divided time into the "Former Days" and the "Latter Days" in the year B.C.7? All the prophets spoke of the time prior to the coming of the Messiah as "Former Days" and the days after the coming of the Messiah as "The Latter Days". The Prophet and Apostle Paul confirms this in his book to the Hebrews when he writes:

*God, who at sundry times and in diverse manners spoke IN TIME PAST unto the fathers by the prophets, hath in these LAST DAYS spoken unto us by his SON.* 1:1,2.

We have seen that another 'time period' used by the ancient seers was the punishment period of 'Seven Times' and we have noted what happened when that period ran out for Jerusalem and the Jews in 1917. Later we will return to the 'Seven Times' period of 2520 years and see what happened when it ran out for the House of Israel.

Another time period used by the ancient seers is that period they call 'Three Days' and it denotes a period of three thousand years.

## WHAT SHALL BE THE SIGN OF THY COMING AND OF THE END OF THE WORLD?

You will remember, that was the question the disciples asked Jesus of Nazareth as they sat on the Mount of Olives. We have commented on how the two pivotal points of his answer were fulfilled on the dates he said they would be fulfilled; the destruction of the temple, and the ending of the times of the Gentiles.

In 1917, we have seen, civilisation and existence, as we know it, entered upon that period of time which we may describe as being the 'last hour' on the dial of the prophetic clock.

The tripartite question asked by the disciples of Jesus of Nazareth was:

★ When shall these things be?
★ What shall be the sign of thy coming?
★ What shall be the sign of the end of the world?

Jesus, in his reply, referred his disciples back 550 years to a prediction given by Daniel the prophet about the year 543 B.C. It is essential, therefore, if we are to understand what Jesus was saying, to acquaint ourselves with exactly what Daniel said. The words are written as Daniel is coming to the end of his long prophecy, there are, in fact, in it's written form, only nine verses left — Daniel is told to close the prophetic book.

*But thou, O Daniel, shut up the words, and seal the book, even to the TIME OF THE END; many shall run to and fro, and knowledge shall be increased. Then I, Daniel, looked and, behold, there stood two others, the one on this side of the bank of the river, and the other on that side of the bank of the river.*

*And one said to the man clothed in linen, who was above the waters of the river, How long shall it be to the end of these wonders?*

*And I heard a man clothed in linen, who was above the waters of the river, when he held up his right hand and his left hand unto heaven, and swore by him who liveth forever, that it shall be for A TIME; TIMES; AND A HALF; and when he shall have accomplished to scatter the power of the Holy people, all these things shall be finished. And I heard, but I understood not. Then said I, O my Lord, what shall be the end of these things? And he said, Go thy way, Daniel; for the words are closed up and sealed* TILL THE TIME OF THE END. *Many shall be purified, and made white, and tested, but the wicked shall do wickedly; and none of the wicked shall understand, but the wise shall understand.*

*And from the time that the daily sacrifice shall be taken away, and the abomination that maketh desolate be set up,* THERE SHALL BE A THOUSAND TWO HUNDRED AND NINETY DAYS.

*Blessed is he that waiteth, and cometh to the thousand three hundred and five and thirty days.*

Book of the Prophet Daniel 12: 4-12

That, then, is the prophecy to which Jesus referred over five hundred years later when he said:

*And this gospel of the kingdom shall be preached in all the world for a witness unto all nations and then shall the end come. When ye, therefore, shall see the abomination of the desolation, spoken of by Daniel the prophet, stand in the holy place [whosoever readeth, let him understand], then...*

Daniel, Jesus indicated, had given dates which would indicate the answer to his disciples' questions. He adds an instruction which rebutts all those who tell us we should not 'delve' into such things by saying *"whosoever readeth, let him understand"*.

There are THREE 'time periods' given in the prophecy of Daniel to which Jesus referred and which we have quoted above. The first of these time periods is "A time, times and an half."

"A time" = One time.
"Times" (Plural) = Two times.
"An half" = Half a time.

You will remember we defined a "time" as being a year of days. A prophetic year contains 360 days, therefore 'one time' is 360 years. Three and a half 'times' is therefore three and a half times 360 days or 1260 years.

The second time period mentioned by Daniel is 1290 'days' or years.

A third time period is mentioned: *"Blessed is he that waiteth, and cometh to the thousand three hundred and five and thirty days"* or 1335 'days' or years.

128

These three periods of years were to run from the time that event, which he and Jesus describe as "The abomination that maketh desolate", was set up.

We should note that these prophecies refer not to the House of Israel but solely to the Jews and Palestine. The only circumstance in which other nations are brought into this prophecy is insofar as they affect the Jews and Palestine.

Something, both Daniel and Jesus said, was to happen in "The Holy Place" which they described as "The abomination that maketh desolate". The daily sacrifice would cease. From that time there would be three periods, all ending with events which would give indications of the 'end of the world' or 'dispensation'.

1. A period of 1260 years.
2. A period of 1290 years.
3. A period of 1335 years.

To tell the time by these 'hands' upon the face of the prophetic clock we need to know the answers to several questions:

a. What and where was 'The Holy Place'?
b. What is meant by 'The abomination which maketh desolate'?
c. What is the commencement date for each of these periods of time?

One thing is certain, we need not look for this person or phenomena described as the 'Abomination that maketh desolate' before the time of Christ because Jesus spoke of the event as being future to his time. In any case, the 'daily sacrifice' was still very much observed in the lifetime of Jesus — nothing that happened BEFORE the time of Christ can therefore be a fulfilment of the prophecy.

## WHAT AND WHERE WAS THE HOLY PLACE?

We must note the prophet's use of the definite article 'THE Holy Place'. There were many holy places in Israel but there was only one which was ever described as 'THE Holy Place'. It was familiar to every Jew living at the time of Christ, and it had been familiar to all the tribes of Israel from the days of the Tabernacle in the Wilderness.

One spot on earth and one spot alone was "The Holy Place", that was a rectangle measuring 20 cubits by 10 cubits situated in the Temple of Jerusalem.

If I were to tell you that flowers were to be placed on the tomb of the unknown warrior in Westminster Abbey, you would know precisely where they were to be placed. Every Jew would know exactly the place both Daniel and Jesus meant when they spoke of 'The Holy Place'.

We can quite certainly, therefore, identify the exact place in which 'The abomination that maketh desolate' was to stand. On the temple site in Jerusalem.

## THE ABOMINATION THAT MAKETH DESOLATE.

Who, or what, is meant by 'The abomination of the Desolation' has been a matter of speculation among those who purport to interpret the messages of the prophets for centuries. I think it true to say that only the identities of the "Beast" of Revelation (666) and the Virgins of Revelation (14) have evoked as much speculation.

I have, in my library, a charming book, written in 1939, which identifies the 'Abomination' as being "A-BOMB-ON-NATION" and foretells from this highly speculative premise that the air-power of Nazi Germany, until then only seen in action during the Spanish Civil War, would be unleashed against England. Further, the author reasoned, since THE Holy Place in England was Westminster Abbey, Hitler when he invaded England would accept the surrender of our Islands at the high altar. I will not name the book nor will I name the author, for it appears to be one aberration in an otherwise well-thought-out treatise.

The author had obviously become overawed by the momentous events which were taking place at the time, and had failed to apply the acid tests one must apply to all prophecies: To whom was the prophecy spoken? Where was the Holy Place of the people to whom it was spoken, at the time it was spoken? The answer, as we have seen, in the prophecy regarding the "Abomination of the Desolation" is: It was spoken to the Jews when their 'Holy Place' was situated in the Temple in Jerusalem.

Our author had also fallen into the classic traps of not putting present day events into historic perspective, and of taking a coincidental likeness between words and drawing a quite unjustifiable and erroneous conclusion from it. He is, of course, not alone for I know of eminent theologians who take the word 'Atonement' and make it 'At-one-ment' — it means nothing of the kind. There are also those who like to speak of 'disease' as being 'dis-ease'.

There is really no need to speculate as to who or what the "Abomination of the Desolation" is, for the words mean no more nor less than what they say. If we just accept them without trying to make something terribly clever of them, the identity of the 'Abomination of the Desolation' is obvious.

The Hebrew word translated 'Abomination' is Shiqquts it means simply a "detestable thing". Now we must interpret those words as if looking through the eyes of Jews living at the time they were spoken. The fact is that anybody, or anything, not Jewish and not The Temple, standing on the Temple site, would be "detestable". Had the most holy man in Christendom stood there he would have been considered "detestable" and an "abomination".

Some commentators have considered Antiochus Epiphanes, who sacrificed a sow upon the altar and entered the Holy of Holies, to be "The Abomination". Certainly he was AN abomination but not THE abomination. Antiochus Epiphanes committed his foul act before the birth of Jesus and Jesus said "When ye see the abomination..." so it was obviously future to his day — we must look to the A.D. years.

We have seen that the Roman general Titus destroyed the Temple, as Jesus had prophesied, in A.D.70. There was fighting and human blood was shed in the Holy Place. Undoubtedly that was a "detestable thing" in Jewish eyes and an "abomination".

Let us read carefully the exact words of the prophecy of Jesus:

*When ye, therefore, shall see the abomination of desolation, spoken of by DANIEL, STAND in the holy place ...*

Matthew 24:15

There is the key that unlocks the mystery! That word STAND, in the original Greek it is 'Histemi' and it means 'to stand', 'to continue' or 'to abide'. Jesus used the same word when he said "Every Kingdom divided against itself is brought to desolation; and every city or house divided against itself shall not STAND (histemi)" Matthew 12:25

Obviously the house would stand, otherwise it wouldn't be a house in the first place, but the meaning of the word is that it would not continue to stand. So the identifying mark of 'THE' abomination which distinguished it from the other abominations, was that 'THE' abomination was to 'Histemi' or continue and remain in the Holy Place.

A few months ago I stood just a few feet from that 15ft x 30ft area of the earth's surface, which was spoken of by Daniel the prophet and Jesus — the place that once was "The Holy Place". Over my head towered The Dome of the Rock, sometimes less accurately called the Mosque of Omar. The Dome of the Rock has stood and continued in the Holy Place for over 1300 years as if set there by providence. It survived the internal Moslem conflicts, the crusades, the hatred of the Jews, the liberation of the City of Jerusalem by the British in 1917, the capture of the City of Jerusalem by the Jews in 1967 and even an attempt by an Australian religious zealot to burn it down within the past few years. It stands with it's golden dome reflecting the sun as one of the great prophetic monuments of history.

## THE MYSTERY OF THE 1260 YEARS.

We have seen that Daniel gives three time periods, the first of 1260 years. We have seen, too, that the deliverance of Jerusalem took place in 1917, 2520 years (seven times 360 years) after King Nebuchadnezzar subjugated Jerusalem and inaugurated the 'Times of the Gentiles'.

You will have noticed that the first time period given by Daniel is half the time period given by Jesus as 'The Times of the Gentiles' or seven 'times'. Daniel writes of "a time, times and an half" — that is three and a half times compared with the 'seven times' of the Times of the Gentiles.

1917, the year of destiny! Something should have happened 1260 years before the deliverance of Jerusalem that would identify the "Abomination of the Desolation" if Daniel is right. Take 1260 years from 1917 and you have the years 656 - 657 A.D.

Jerusalem fell to the Moslem armies in A.D.655 and the building of the Dome of the Rock began, the building was completed in A.D.688. Another coincidence?

There is something else significant about that year the Moslems marched into Jerusalem, it was exactly 1260 years after Nebuchadnezzar had first conquered Jerusalem and ushered in 'The Times of the Gentiles'. 1260 years and 1260 years equals 2520 years! Coincidence or pattern?

The 'Abomination' was to bring desolation. It is a matter of history that Jerusalem and the Holy Land from A.D.655 became a desolate wilderness.

It is interesting to note that when Caliph Omar entered the city, Gibbon, in his "Decline and Fall of the Roman Empire", records:

*After signing the capitulation, he entered the city without fear or precaution; and courteously discoursed with the patriarch concerning it's religious antiquities. Sophronius bowed before his new master, and secretly muttered, in the words of Daniel, 'The abomination of the desolation is in the holy place'.*

Did the prophets write the "Horoscope of the Nations"? Can we see in all this the invisible hand ordering the affairs of men? Well may we ask ourselves at this point, if all these things have happened, if the prophets have been right, will the things they have foretold to happen in our lifetime come to pass also? In future chapters we shall try to pull back the curtains, which hide the future from prying eyes just a little, and see what lies beyond.

Mighty Nebuchadnezzar! We hear his voice echoing emptily through the hollow chambers of time: "Is not this the mighty Babylon I have built?" Do we detect a thunderous chuckle from the heavens? The dynasties of Egypt, of Babylon, of Assyria, of Medo-Persia, of Greece, of Rome and of the Moslem Empire have passed away, to the brink of their graves these, the many powerful men who led these great empires, thought that THEY made history. Did they, or were they unconsciously dangling on strings held by THE INVISIBLE HAND?

## THE MYSTERY OF THE 1290 YEARS.

Daniel gives two more periods of time (i) the period of 1290 years and

(ii) a period of 1335 years. The latter, the period of 1335 years, will be shown to be the most amazing of all.

On 2nd November 1917 the British Government issued the Balfour Declaration, pledging support for the establishment in Palestine of a homeland for the Jewish people. Then, on the 8th December, General Allenby liberated the city from the Turks. "2520 years from the 'treading down' by Nebuchadnezzar and 1260 years after the fall of Jerusalem to Omar".

Need I say that the difference between 1260 and 1290 is 30 years? Which brings us to 1948.

Let thirty years slip by, years in which the United Nations confirmed the British mandate in Palestine and years in which another world war afflicted mankind. Years, too, when the Jews suffered as they had never suffered before. The trickle of Jews back to the Holy Land became a torrent and then such a flood that ill famed, ill timed and ill fated measures were taken by the British Government to reduce the numbers of Jews returning to their own land.

The armies of the nations are once again fighting on the battlefields of the Middle East, the eighth army is fighting it's magnificent, historic battle to defend Egypt and the Suez Canal. The world wonders: Will the Axis armies smash their way through to Palestine? What would the inspirer of the 'Holocaust' find a more stimulating experience than capturing the very home of the Jews itself? Side by side, British soldiers and the soldiers of the Jewish brigade fight, throughout the war, to destroy the scourge of Europe.

In 1945 peace returns to Europe and twenty-seven of the thirty years have ticked away. Millions of Jews, sickened by the fate that has befallen them and their families, now want to make their home in Palestine.

1946 an Anglo-American committee agrees to the admission to Palestine of 100,000 displaced persons.

1947 the United Nations General Assembly adopts a plan for the establishment of a Jewish state.

1948, another year of destiny? What great happening took place in that year?

It is the 14th May, 1948. Come with me to the Museum Hall in Tel-Aviv. David Ben-Gurion rises to speak (I quote parts of his speech):

*In the land of Israel the Jewish people came into being. In this land was shaped their spiritual, religious and national character. Here they lived in sovereign independence. Here they created a culture of national and universal import, and gave to the world the eternal Book of Books ... Accordingly we, the members of the National Council, representing the Jewish People in the land of Israel and the Zionist movement, have assembled on the day of the termination of the British Mandate for Palestine, and, by*

*virtue of our natural and historic right and of the resolution of the
General Assembly of the United Nations, DO HEREBY
PROCLAIM THE ESTABLISHMENT OF A JEWISH STATE
IN THE LAND OF ISRAEL — THE STATE OF ISRAEL .. The
State of Israel will be open to Jewish immigration and the
ingathering of exiles. It will devote itself to developing the land
for the good of all it's inhabitants.
It will rest upon foundations of liberty, justice and peace as
ENVISAGED BY THE PROPHETS OF ISRAEL.*

So the JEWISH State of Israel was born, in the year the prophet
foretold over two thousand five hundred years before. Coincidence?

## IS TIME RUNNING OUT FOR PLANET EARTH?

Do you remember we said in the chapter 'Breaking the Code' that the
Jews (Judah) are symbolised by the fig tree in prophecy? Right at the end
of his prophecy about the 'Times of the Gentiles', Jesus said:

*Behold the fig tree, and all the trees; When they now shoot forth,
ye see and know of your own selves that summer is now near at
hand. So also ye, when ye see these things come to pass, know that
the Kingdom of God is near at hand.* Luke 21: 29-30

Let us couple that with Daniel's words:

*And from the time that the daily sacrifice shall be taken away, and
the abomination that maketh desolate is set up, there shall be a
thousand two hundred and ninety days [years]. Blessed is he that
waiteth, and cometh to the thousand three hundred and five and
thirty days. BUT GO THY WAY TILL THE END BE: FOR
THOU SHALT REST, AND STAND IN THY LOT AT THE
END OF THE DAYS.* Daniel 12: 11,12,13.

We live in mysterious days indeed! The hands of the prophetic clock, it
would appear, stand at one minute to midnight in the history of our world
as we know it.

## 1917 YEAR OF DESTINY. THE MOSLEM YEAR 1335.

I said that the time period of 1335 years given by Daniel was probably
the most mysterious of them all, it is mysterious in two ways, only one
of which I wish to deal with in this chapter. There are two reasons for me
dealing with only one here, the first being that I wish to concentrate on our
examination of the Jewish 'hand' on the prophetic clock and the second,

and perhaps a little unkind reason I admit, is that I want to keep you in suspense.

The A.D. year 1917 was the Mohammedan year 1335! Isn't that amazing? But why are all the other dates A.D. dates and this one date 'out of step', a Mohammedan date? Did Daniel cause this to happen so that we could more readily identify 'The Abomination that maketh desolate''?

Prophetic commentators seem just to accept the out-of-line date without question, but, having seen how fastidious the prophets were in their pronouncements, I cannot think that this date is there by chance. Certainly it is too much of a coincidence that 1917 is also the year 1335, for it not to have a meaning. Apart from it drawing our attention to the identity of the 'abomination', why quote the same date on two separate calendars? But we'll leave the matter there for the moment and discuss it further in our chapter '1922 — year of Destiny?'

## THE SHOOTING FORTH OF THE FIG TREE.

The prophets of Israel had always foretold that there would be a return of the Jews to the Holy Land, that the Jewish Nation (the fig tree) would blossom again, immediately prior to the last great battle of earth's history — the Battle of Armageddon. The picture painted by the prophets of this time in the history of the earth is apocalyptic. They see it as a time when all the horrors which have afflicted mankind during the 'Times of the Gentiles' will erupt as a volcano erupts after years of rumblings.

Following the end of the Times of the Gentiles there was to be the blossoming of the 'fig tree' and the prophets foretold some very specific things that would take place in the Holy Land.

For nineteen hundred years, almost, the land of Palestine was as if smitten by a curse: The hills, once verdant and clothed in a mantle of forestation, became barren and dustblown, the olive groves gave way to treeless desert, the vineyards disappeared and the verdant valleys became swamps from which the stench stung the noses of passing travellers. The flocks disappeared, the fields became the wilderness and even the little rain there was came down polluted with the ever present dust of the desert. How different from the land flowing with milk and honey the children of Israel had entered and conquered. Historians are agreed that much of this decline was a direct cause of the conquerors of the land denuding it of it's pleasant environment for their own benefit. Indeed the 'abomination' had made the land of Palestine 'desolate'.

We have seen how the Jews were scattered among the nations exactly as the prophets had foretold, and how they suffered the catalogue of horrors foretold many thousands of years before.

The predictions of the dispersion and the making desolate of the Holy Land are so numerous that it would take a complete book to comment on them all, but I will quote a few which are fairly representative of the many.

Early on in the writings of the prophet Moses we find a warning of what would happen to the people of Israel:

> *And the Lord shall scatter thee among all people, from the one end of the earth, even unto the other; and there thou shalt serve other gods, which neither thou nor thy fathers have known, even wood and stone. And among these nations shalt thou find no ease, neither shall the sole of thy foot find rest ....*
>
> Book of Deuteronomy 28: 63-65

That prophecy was written over 3,500 years ago. We know it to be a fact that the Jews were scattered into almost every nation on earth. It is also quite literally true that among the nations the Jews found no ease nor did they find rest from their wanderings. Persecution after persecution kept them moving from one country to another only to find new outbreaks of anti-semitism wherever they went.

Here's another prophecy that foretells the dispersal of the people of Israel (all Israel) among the nations:

> *And if ye will not yet for all this hearken unto me ... I will destroy your high places, and cut down your images, and cast your carcasses upon the carcasses of your idols, and my soul shall abhor you.*
>
> *And I will make your cities waste, and bring your sanctuaries into desolation, and I will not smell the savor of your sweet odors.*
>
> *And I will bring the land into desolation: And your enemies who dwell therin shall be astonished at it.*
>
> *And I will scatter you among the nations, and will draw out a sword after you; and your land shall be desolate, and your cities waste.*
>
> The Book of Leviticus 26: 27-33

Then, in the 8th century B.C., the prophet Joel wrote:

> *Awake ye drunkards, and weep; and wail, all ye drinkers of wine, because of the new wine; for it is cut off from your mouth. For a nation is come upon my land, strong and without number, whose teeth are the teeth of a lion, and he hath the cheek teeth of a great lion.*
>
> *He hath laid my vine waste, and barked my fig tree; he hath made it completely bare, and cast it away; it's branches are made white. Lament like a virgin girdled with sackcloth for the husband of her youth.*
>
> *The meal offering and the drink offering are cut off from the house of the Lord; the priests, the Lord's ministers, mourn. The field is wasted, the land mourneth; for the grain is wasted; the new*

*wine is dried up, the oil languisheth.*
*Be ye ashamed, O ye farmers; wail, O ye vine-dressers, for the*
*wheat and for the barley, because the harvest of the field is*
*perished. The vine is dried up, and the fig tree languisheth; the*
*pomegranate tree, the palm tree also, and the apple tree, even all*
*the trees of the field are withered.*

The Prophet Joel 1: 5-12

Could the prophet have painted a more dramatic word picture of utter desolation than that? Reading those words one can almost feel the hot dust of the arid desert on one's face.

The fact is that when the prophet wrote those words all the things he wrote about were plentiful in the land of Israel, few of his hearers would be able to imagine the circumstances of which he spoke. The Holy Land had not been called 'A land that floweth with milk and honey' without cause. To those who listened to him then, the prophet's words must have sounded as the ravings of a fevered mind. Little did his hearers know that every word was to come true. Let us list the prognostications, in the two short passages I have taken at random from the many hundreds of dire warnings to the nation of Israel and the Jews:

1. They were to be scattered into ALL nations from one end of the earth to the other.
2. They were to find no ease and they would wander from nation to nation.
3. The 'high places' of the Holy Land were to be destroyed.
4. The cities were to be made waste.
5. The sanctuaries, the temples and the synagogues were to be made desolate and their sacrifices and ritual to cease.
6. The land was to be inhabited by foreigners.
7. They would be killed when they were among the nations.
8. The vineyards would be desolate and the wine dried up.
9. The land would not grow wheat, barley and farm products.
10. Fruits would cease to grow.
11. The trees would not grow.

Each of those prophecies was literally fulfilled. By 1917 and indeed long before, Palestine, as predicted, became a wilderness.

## BLESSED IS HE THAT WAITETH AND COMETH TO THE 1335 YEARS.

Two thousand five hundred and twenty years after Jerusalem had been trodden down by the Gentiles, Jerusalem was to be delivered from it's 'treading down' — it was. One thousand two hundred and sixty years after the setting up of the 'Abomination that maketh desolate' that desolation was to cease. That year 1260 was also in some extraordinary way to be connected with the year 1335. We have seen that the year 1917 was 2520 years after the beginning of the 'treading down' by Nebuchadnezzar and 1260 years after the Moslems entered upon the Temple site, it was also the year 1335 years in the Moslem calendar.

Until 1917 the prophets had foretold the 'desolation' and subjection of Palestine and Jerusalem. After 1917, they foretold, things would change — Jerusalem would enter a state of 'blessedness'. To put it in modern language, Jerusalem was to see a reversal of all the things which had happened to it and the land of Palestine during the 'captivity' years.

Let us read a prediction of this state of blessedness as foretold by one of the ancient seers:

*And I will multiply men upon you, all the House of Israel, even all of it, and the cities shall be inhabited, and the wastes shall be built; And I will multiply upon you man and beast, and they shall increase and bring fruit; and I will Settle you according to your old estate, and will do better unto you than at your beginnings ... For I will take you from among the nations, and gather you out of all countries and will bring you into your own land.*
Book of Ezekial Chapter 36: Parts of 36: 8-21

That prophecy was written about 550 B.C. and, if you read the whole chapter, you will see it reverses the conditions predicted in the book of Leviticus and the book of Joel. They spoke of the dispersion and the above chapter speaks of the regathering, one of the going and the other of the coming back. It applies equally to Judah and the House of Israel, but it is with it's implications for the former (the Jews) we deal here.

## IMMIGRATION.

In the year 1914 there were only 85,000 Jews living in Palestine. By 1939 that number had increased to 445,000. 1946 saw 678,000 living in Palestine and by 1981 more than 3,378,000 Jews lived in their own land: That number will increase to 4,180,000 by 1992.

Despite the wars, the hardness of the toil and inflation, immigration remains one of modern Israel's major problems. Jews from all over the world, young and old, continue to 'come home'. How did the prophet foresee all this 2,500 years before it happened?

## AGRICULTURAL PRODUCE.

The farmers of Israel do not have to hang their heads in shame now! By 1976 Israel was exporting 3000,000,000 dollars worth of exports, of this great total 330,000,000 dollars worth was agricultural produce. Israel has a problem — not only do they export, they have so much food they can't eat what they have left. Another prophet foretold that their vats would overflow. That is certainly true.

Here are the facts; Israel produced in 1976 the following:

|  | 1948 | 1976 |
|---|---|---|
|  | tons |  |
| Wheat | 21,200 | 301,400 |
| Barley | 20,900 | 32,800 |
| Grapes | 8,400 | 17,800 |
| Citrus fruit | 272,700 | 1,552,800 |
| Sugar beet | NONE | 248,500 |
| Other fruit | 7,200 | 206,600 |
| Vegetables, potatoes & melons | 11,900 | 806,800 |
| Poultry, meat | 5,040 | 142,100 |
| Acres under cultivation | 412,000 | 1,055,000 |

I say again: How did the prophet know? And why did it happen at exactly the time in earth's history that the prophets said it would happen? Chance or the moving of the 'invisible hand'?

## RELIGION AND THE JEWISH STATE OF ISRAEL.

*"I will ... bring your sanctuaries into desolation, and I will not smell the savour of your sweet odors."*

So had said the prophet and it became a fact. The ancient faith of Israel became something to be practised in the home, behind closed doors. The 'high places' of religious worship and veneration were outside Jewish control and for centuries the Jews were forbidden to worship at these places. Has the situation been reversed since 1917? I can do no better than quote at length from the publication 'Facts about Israel'.

*The great majority of Israel's inhabitants are of the Jewish faith. Here they can observe the injunctions of the Torah and celebrate the holy days in a Jewish environment in the historic Jewish Homeland. Bible and Talmud are studied throughout the educational system; Sabbath and festivals are part of the air __ at home, in school and out of doors: Purim, Shavuot and Simhat Torah celebrations overflow into the streets.*

*Supreme religious authority is vested in the Chief Rabbinate, made up of an Ashkenazi and a Shephardi Chief Rabbi and the*

*Supreme Rabbinical Council. It decides on the interpretation of the Jewish law, and supervises the rabbinical courts.*

*There are eight regional rabbinical courts, with a bench of 66 Jewish religious judges, and a Rabbinical Court of Appeal presided over by two Chief Rabbis.*

*Religious needs and services are provided by 179 religious councils and some 320 religious committees in smaller localities, financed jointly by the State and local authorities.*

*These are under the administrative control of the Ministry of Religious Affairs, but in matters of religion are subject to the authority of the Chief Rabbinate.*

*There are almost 6,000 synagogues, and 387 officially appointed rabbis.*

*Jewish dietry laws are observed in all Jewish defence units and in all Government and public institutions.*

*Jews are again free to pray at their most venerated Holy Places: the Western Wall of the Temple Court in Jerusalem, Rachel's Tomb, the Tombs of the Patriarchs in Hebron, and other centres of tradition and sanctity.*

*David's Tomb on Mount Zion in Jerusalem, the Cave of Elijah on Mount Carmel, and the tombs of the Maimonides, Rabbi Meir Ba'al Haness and Rabbi Shimon Bar Yohai are other places with Biblical and Talmudic associations.*          Pages 66-67

Exactly as prophecied over 2,750 years ago, the 'high places' have been returned to Judah-Israel.

## STREAMS IN THE DESERT.

Almost eight hundred years before Christ, the prophet Isaiah foretold the following:

*Thus saith the Lord ... Behold I will do a new thing; now it shall spring forth; shall ye not know it? I will even make a way in the wilderness, and the rivers in the desert.*
*The beast of the field shall honour me, the jackals and the ostriches, because I give waters in the wilderness, and rivers in the desert, to give drink to my people, my chosen.*
                    Book of the Prophet Isaiah 43: 19-20

That prophecy is remarkable because it foretells the desert will be irrigated but it is the more remarkable because the desert did not exist when Isaiah prophecied it. The land was then a verdant land and the prophet looks to, and past, the time when the desert would become a wilderness, and foretells that it will again be watered.

Today Israel has regional and national water systems and most of them are interconnected so that they form one large integrated water system. There were 410,000 acres of desert land under irrigation by 1967. The Kinneret-Negev project has a capacity of 320 million cubic metres and its rivers flow through the land out into the Negev Desert.

"Rivers in the desert" as the prophet said. The main conduit of the National Water Carrier IS a river and it does flow THROUGH THE DESERT.

From the very early days of Israel 'shooting forth', water had played an important part in her development. The prophets foresaw it being so, for on many occasions they linked the revival of Israel with predictions regarding the water supply. One of the very early examples of water causing the desert to flourish is to be seen in the development of Jaffa — Tel-Aviv. We cannot help thinking of the prophecy of Isaiah in his 35th chapter when we think of Tel-Aviv — he said: *"In the wilderness shall water break out, and streams in the desert. The parched ground shall become a pool, and the thirsty land springs water."*

In 1909 a Russian Jew named Dizengoff formed a company with a capital of sixty thousand francs. He purchased twenty acres of dunes just outside the city of Jaffa, just eight years before Jerusalem was delivered in 1917. Dizengoff decided to build a city on that land and by the year 1921 the city he built had a population of 14,000. Today that city has a population of over 400,000, it's name? Tel-Aviv.

By 1935 those sand dunes had flourished to the extent that three thousand athletes from forty countries competed in the Olympic Games there.

One of the major contributing factors to Tel-Aviv becoming the city it is today was the discovery of considerable amounts of pure water in the sub-strata.

A minute to midnight on the prophetic clock? Well, shall we say just a little more? The hands of the prophetic clock are approaching the midnight hour when the earth as we know it, according to the prophets, is to pass away.

Mankind is on the brink of events such as have never been experienced by mankind before, as we shall see in future chapters.

## TO RECAPITULATE.

★ Both Jesus and Daniel foretold the setting up of what they called the 'Abomination of the Desolation' on the site of the Temple.

★ From the time the Temple site was occupied to the deliverance of Jerusalem was to be 1260 years — it was.

★ The 1260 years expired in 1917 — the Moslem year 1335.

★ 1290 years after the occupation of the Temple site, thirty years after the deliverance of Jerusalem, another event was to take place of significance to the Jews. In 1948 the Jews proclaimed 'The Jewish State of Israel'.

★ All the afflictions of the 'dispersal' were to be reversed from 1917 on — they have been. The land has been repopulated, agricultural produce has increased sharply and the free practise of the Jewish faith has returned to the land.

★ Everything the prophets said would happen HAS happened and in the years that they predicted the events would take place.

Can we still believe that there is not an 'invisible hand' guiding earth's history and a silent voice pronouncing 'The Horoscope of the Nations'?

We are nearing the end of the age, of that there is no doubt, but more is to happen, predicted to take place by the ancient seers before THE MIDNIGHT HOUR CHIMES.

# 10.
# The Amazing Vision Seen by Dr.Theodore Herzl

Everyone who is acquainted with the history of the Zionist movement knows that Theodore Herzl was a man of vision but how literally he was 'A man of vision' is not often realised.

Theodore Herzl was born in the city of Budapest on 2nd May 1860. In 1884 he became a Doctor of Law after studying at the University of Vienna. As you would expect of someone of his calling, Theodore Herzl was an intellectual, not given to flights of fancy, yet he tells of a remarkable vision which spurred him on toward the great achievement of his life, the foundation of the Zionist movement.

Before we deal with Herzl's vision, however, for the benefit of those who have not had cause to study the history of Zionism let me give a brief outline of this political motivating force behind the establishment of the modern Jewish state of Israel.

Though, throughout the ages, the eyes of the Jews have been on the Holy Land, little was really achieved until the Zionist movement came into being. It was the Zionist movement which popularised initially, and brought about ultimately, the foundation of the Jewish State of Israel.

In 1886 Theodore Herzl became the literary editor of the Viennese newspaper "Neue Freie Presse" and in that same year published his now famous pamphlet Der Judenstaat (The Jewish State).

This pamphlet was the inspiration which led the 'fathers' of modern Israel, Weizman and Ben-Gurion, to fight for the establishment of a Jewish homeland.

The part played by Dr. Theodore Herzl in the conception of the modern state of Israel was acknowledged by Ben-Gurion and the State of Israel when the body of Herzl was flown from it's original resting place and buried in Tel-Aviv.

## TWIN DATES?

We have seen that 1917 was the Moslem year 1335 and I have mentioned that that, to the present, seems to be the only Moslem date of the three, 1260, 1290 and 1335. The thought occurred to me that each of these dates may be twin dates. Perhaps the end of the period 1335 is not just a date out of step but a dual date: Since the Christian and the Moslem are so inextricably linked in the 1917 deliverance perhaps the prophets predicted in both calendars, or there may even be a deeper reason which I will discuss in a future chapter. There has always been a school of prophecy which considers that many prophecies have a major and minor fulfilment so why should the prophet not express the things concerning the deliverance of Jerusalem in both the Mohammedan dates and the Christian dates? It was just a thought and for several months I thought no further about it. Then, one day I began to wonder why, Zionism playing as it has such a large part in the return of the Jews to Palestine, was not mentioned in the time periods given by Daniel. Undoubtedly, Zionism ranked in importance with the deliverance of Jerusalem and the date of the foundation of the State of Israel. With this in mind, I pursued the speculation about dual dates.

If 1917 was the Mohammedan year 1335, then the year 1290 would be 45 years earlier. 1335 minus 1290 equals 45. Forty Five A.D. years are 43½ Mohammedan years because a Mohammedan year is slightly shorter than an A.D. year. Forty three and a half from 1917 brings us to the year 1873.

Obviously some event of great importance should have taken place in that year if my speculation upon there being dual dates in Daniel's prophecy was correct. With Zionism in mind I turned the pages of the history books to find what had happened in that year. Had Theodore Herzl, the arch-prophet of Zionism, been ignored by the prophet? Had Zionism been ignored by the prophet? If so, why? The questions crowded in.

The date of Herzl's birth was not 1873. Herzl, in fact, passed from being twelve years of age to being thirteen years of age in that year. Nor was it the date of Herzl's death. It was not, of course, any date in the history of the Zionist movement because, as I have said, Herzl was only thirteen years of age and the Zionist movement had not commenced. It did turn out to be the birth year of several people who later occupied minor positions in the Zionist movement, but I discarded that as an avenue of enquiry because I could see no logical reason why the arch-prophet should be ignored and some minor official noted. There is, in fact, not one major international event in connection with the Jews or Jerusalem that took place in the year 1873 and I was certainly not going to 'scrape the bottom of the barrel' to find something insignificant that fitted the date. Then, when I had almost dismissed from my mind the proposition that the dates may be dual, and after I had consulted a number of students of prophecy regarding the date and asked them if they knew of anything that had happened appertaining to that date which might have affected Jerusalem or the Jews, I came upon a strange fact.

I was reading about Theodore Herzl when I came across a passage in which he described how he came to form the Zionist movement. Few people seem to have taken note of the fact, but just before he died Herzl told his friends that he was brought to pursue the cause of Zionism by a VISION HE HAD HAD OF THE MESSIAH. The Messiah had commissioned him to perform great wonders and deeds for his people — that was how the movement which led to the establishment of the present state of Israel came into being. When did Herzl have that vision? When he was twelve years of age, he said, in the year 1873!

As if that were not enough, Herzl had described the Messiah as being dressed in white linen. Just come back with me for a moment to the prophecy of Daniel:

> *Then I, Daniel, looked, and, behold, there stood two others, the one on this side of the bank of the river, and the other on that side of the bank of the river.*
> *And one said to the man CLOTHED IN LINEN, who was above the waters of the river, How long shall it be to the end of these wonders?*
> *And I heard the man clothed in linen, who was above the waters of the river, when he held up his right hand and his left hand unto heaven, and swore by him who liveth forever, that it shall be for a time, times and an half... And I heard but I understood not. Then said I, O my Lord, what shall be the end of these things?*

*And he said, Go thy way, Daniel; for the words are closed up and*
*sealed till the time of the end.*                    Daniel 12: 5-9

Daniel identifies the man in white linen as 'my Lord' or, in other words, the Messiah.

Did the apparition which appeared to Daniel and instructed that the book of prophecy should be closed, appear again to Dr. Theodore Herzl in 1873 and open up again the words of the prophecy? Is it coincidence that from that time onward a number of books such as that of Dr. Grattan Guiness' book "Light for the Last Days" began to pour from the presses alerting students of prophecy to the significance of the year 1917?

## THE TWIN DATE OF 1260.

Reason tells us that if the two dates in the same chapter have 'twin' dates then we should expect the third to also have a 'twin' fulfilment.

Let's try our sum again and see!

1335 minus 1260 = 75. The shorter Mohammedan year brings us to about 73 years. 1917 less 73 brings us to the year 1844 A.D.

1844 is an outstanding year in the history of Britain and the Jewish nation for it was in that year that Britain forced the Turks to issue the Edict of Religious Toleration which allowed the Jews freedom of worship once more. From that date forward the Turkish Empire went into decline (the drying up of the river Euphrates — a term I will explain later).

# 11.
# The
# Coming World
# Conflict

To the question "Will there be a Third World War?" the answer is: Yes!

Nothing is more consistently foretold by the prophets than the last great cataclysmic war of human history, the Battle of Armageddon.

Unfortunately the word has been misused over the years and the word 'Armageddon' has passed into common usage to describe any large-scale conflict. Some people spoke of the First World War as being "Armageddon", others have spoken of the Second World War in similar terms. Admittedly the word could not be bettered for descriptiveness, one only has to hear it and images are conjured of massive armies hurling themselves at one another.

However, the Armageddon foretold by the prophets is not just a descriptive word used to signify any war, nor even any large war, it is a specific term used to describe a specific war to take place at a specific time in earth's history in a specific location.

The prophet Ezekial, who wrote about 570 B.C., is but one of the prophets to foretell the coming conflict:

> *And the word of the Lord came unto me, saying, Son of man, set thy face against Gog, of the land of Magog, the chief prince of Meshech and Tubal, and prophesy against him.*
> *And say, Thus saith the Lord God: Behold, I am against thee, O Gog, the chief prince of Meshech and Tubal.*
> *And I will turn thee back, and put hooks into thy jaws, and I will bring thee forth, and all thine army, horses and horsemen, all of them clothed with all sorts of armour, even a great company with bucklers and shields, all of them handling swords: Persia, Ethiopia and Libya with them; all of them with shield and helmet; Gomer, and all it's hordes; the house of Togarmah of the north quarters, and all it's hordes; and many people with thee. Be thou prepared, and prepare for thyself, thou, and all thy company that are assembled unto thee, and be thou a guard unto them. After many days thou shalt be visited; in the latter years thou shalt come into the land that is brought back from the sword, and is gathered out of many peoples, against the mountains of Israel, which have been always waste; but it is brought forth out of the nations, and they shall dwell safely, all of them.*
> *Thou shalt ascend and come like a storm; thou shalt be like a cloud to cover the land, thou, and all thy hordes, and many people with thee.*

That is taken from the 38th chapter of the Prophecy of Ezekiel. The subject of his 36th chapter is the regathering of the people of Israel in Palestine. The 37th chapter deals with the 'Valley of Dry Bones' vision in which Ezekiel sees the whole nation of Israel coming out of the graves of history, being clothed with flesh and being made to live.

It is following these events that the inspirer of the prophet addresses himself to Gog.

I have said that when we study prophecy we should always be careful to find first to whom the prophecy refers. It would be wrong of me now to ignore that requirement. Both chapter 36 and chapter 37 refer to the re-establishment of the 'Whole House of Israel' and that, of course, refers to both the Jews and the ten tribed House of Israel. We have seen how the Jews have fulfilled the prophecies made to them and returned to the land of Palestine, but we have not yet seen the re-emergence of the House of Israel. There is, however, in the prognostications of the seers, a time given when the ten tribed House of Israel would be revived, there is foretold the place where they would be revived, and we shall examine these in our chapter "The Mystery of the Missing Millions".

Chapters 36 and 37, therefore, we know have been, or are in the process of being fulfilled: We know, therefore, that chronologically we stand very close to the Battle of Armageddon.

St. John the Divine had a vision of Armageddon six hundred and seventy years after Ezekiel's time, and he said:

> *And the sixth angel poured out his bowl upon the great river, Euphrates, and it's water was dried up, that the way of the kings of the east might be prepared.*
>
> *And I saw three unclean spirits, like frogs, come out of the mouth of the dragon, and out of the mouth of the beast, and out of the mouth of the false prophet.*
>
> *For they are the spirits of demons, working miracles, that go forth unto the kings of the earth and of the whole world, to gather them to the battle of that great day of God Almighty ... And he gathered them together into a place called in the Hebrew tongue Armageddon.*

Revelation 16: 12-16

The prophet Joel wrote a very short prophecy, just three chapters, and, looking down over 2,800 years to our day, foresaw the final battle of earth's history:

> *Proclaim this among the nations, Prepare war, wake up the mighty men, let all the men of war draw near; let them come up; Beat your ploughshares into swords, and your pruning hooks into spears; let the weak say, I am strong.*
>
> *Assemble yourselves, and come, all ye nations, and gather yourselves together round about; there cause they mighty ones to come down O Lord.*
>
> *Let the nations be awakened, and come up to the Valley of Jehoshaphat; for there will I sit to judge all the nations round about.*
>
> *Put in the sickle; for the harvest is ripe; come, get down; for the press is full, the vats overflow; for their wickedness is great.*
>
> *Multitudes, multitudes in the valley of decision; for the day of the Lord is near in the valley of decision.*
>
> *The sun and the moon shall be darkened, and the stars shall withdraw their shining.*
>
> *The Lord also shall roar out of Zion, and utter his voice from Jerusalem, and the heavens and the earth shall shake.*

Book of the Prophet Joel 3: 9-16

There are, of course, many other prophetic utterances referring to the battle of Armageddon, but I think the above from the prophets Ezekial, John and Joel will suffice. They tell us roughly when the battle will take place, they tell us where the battle will take place and they give us the names of the combatants.

## WHEN WILL ARMAGEDDON TAKE PLACE?

I have in my possession a book published in 1915 entitled "Is it Armageddon?" by Henry Sulley. The author is unknown to me, but the conclusions he draws from his studies of the writings of the ancient seers are truly astounding. It would have been so easy for him in those days, when the vast armies of Germany, her European allies, Russia, Turkey, the British Empire, France and Italy were hurling themselves at one another in deadly combat, to have answered in the affirmative. At the time, the word 'Armageddon' was being widely used as the world embarked upon the 'Great War' and what more natural than that that war should be identified with the great conflict foretold by the prophets.

Mr. Sulley, however, fell into no such trap, nor was he prepared to achieve a certain transitory fame by using his undoubted skill as an interpreter of the prophets in an opportunist manner. Not for him the technique so often employed by so-called students of prophecy, the hammering of the pieces of the jigsaw into place, the cutting of pieces of the jigsaw until they fit. If Mr. Sulley is still alive I must congratulate him on the faithfulness with which he treats his subject and his absolute commitment to not 'making things fit'. It is surprising how Nostradamus, who incidentally foretells very little which is specific, became so famous and people like Henry Sulley remain in relative obscurity.

I would like the reader to go back in mind to those days at the commencement of the Great War. Shed the hind-sight with which we can now view things and think, as far as is humanly possible, in the terms of a man living in 1915. Remember that the Holy Land is firmly in the hands of the Turks. Russia is still under the Tsar. Rasputin still lives. The sun never sets on the British Empire. Russia, France and the British Empire are in the grand alliance against Germany and her allies. Perhaps we should keep uppermost in our minds, though, that this was, in most people's minds, the war to end wars; the war from which everyone would return to begin the millenium of peace. It was almost heresy to consider the possibility of there being another conflict after Germany had been vanquished, something, it was anticipated each summer, which would happen 'before Christmas'. Men were still flocking to the colours 'for King and Country' in 1915 and a spirit of jubilation was everywhere. If the sun didn't set on the British Empire geographically, few had any doubt that it would ever set on the British Empire in time either. Men's main concern was that the war would be over before they could get to the battle front and 'have a go' at the Hun.

It is against this background that we must read the following quotation from Mr. Sulley's book "Is it Armageddon?". Under the heading "Summary" on page 82 of his book, he writes:

"The central theme of Armageddon is not Europe, but Palestine, when the land is invaded from northern Europe and Asia. The object of the present war is not the invasion of the Holy Land by a northern power coming against a PROSPEROUS Israelitish company there, but the subordination of Europe to a military power. Whether the present conflict will develop in the direction of Palestine in the terms of the prophecy is another matter.

All nations are to be gathered in the Armageddon debacle. At present only half the world is engaged in conflict, and that not in Palestine, or in the region of Megiddo, Jerusalem and Bazrah. The other half looks on, and for the present takes no part. Whether such a development will be the outcome of the war we must "wait and see", and that without discussing it's probabilities, which might hinder the wise use of the knowledge we now possess.

The premises show that at Armageddon RUSSIA AND BRITAIN WILL BE OPPOSED AND NOT, AS NOW, ACTING IN CONCERT. When the affliction of Armageddon comes, the Powers of Europe will not be grouped as they are at present. The unnatural alliance now subsisting between Russia, France and Britain, whose commercial and territorial interests clash, will have come to an end, while Italy and some Powers at present neutral will be in alliance with the northern confederacy and opposed to Britain, for "Libya and Ethiopia" are to be at the steps of the King of the North when he comes against the land of Palestine."

(Dan xi.43; Ezek.xxxviii.5).

Henry Sulley did not write with the benefit of hind-sight as I do when I refer to the return of the Jews to the Holy Land. He wrote BEFORE that had happened, but interpreted from the ancient prophets that before the Battle of Armageddon, there had to be a "prosperous Israelitish company there", that is, in Palestine. It is one thing to look back, as we can, and foresee Russia as a future protagonist but quite another to, as he did, foretell who would be allies in a future conflict, in a particular place. Can I say it again: Mr. Sulley's interpretation would appear to me to be more-up-to-date than tomorrow's newspaper.

Why, we must wonder, when we see how accurate the ancient seers were in their prognostications, are there still those among us who insist on forcing pieces of jigsaw to fit that patently do not fit? If there is one thing a reading of the writings of the prophetic interpreters shows, it is that those who have interpreted correctly are those who have accepted the writings of the prophets at their face value, and those who have failed in interpretation are those who have fallen into the trap of forcing predictions to fit contemporary history.

The plain fact is that Armageddon could not have taken place before 1948 because the circumstances under which the prophets foretold Armageddon would take place did not exist until then. A superficial reading of the prophecies makes it quite plain that Armageddon would be fought after Israel had been gathered out of the nations, returned to their own land and that land had been 'brought back from the sword'.

Though there is a certain amount of confidence in Israel, I would think that before Armageddon takes place Israel will have formed some very substantial treaty obligations with her Arab neighbours. Of course, that does not mean that Armageddon need be long delayed, for we know how quickly the international picture changes these days. Consider as one example the American relationship with the Chinese, a relationship one would hardly have thought possible fifteen years ago.

How the confidence will come about we do not know, but one thing is certain, Armageddon will not commence until Israel is dwelling safely or 'confidently'. That is sure to happen soon, for according to the prophetic clock it will not be long before Armageddon is to take place.

## THE DRYING UP OF THE RIVER EUPHRATES.

In breaking the code we noted that rivers in prophecy denote the power of the country they represent. Even today we speak of the Tiber as representing Rome, whilst no-one would doubt which city we meant if we spoke of the Thames. The Taff will immediately bring to mind the Welsh Valleys, and the Mississippi the Southern States of the United States of America. Who could doubt that we speak of India when we mention the Ganges or of Russia if we speak of the Volga?

If the Shannon is mentioned we bring into focus the Emerald Isles and the Seine will bring into mind the sophistication of Paris.

The river Euphrates in prophecy refers to the Turkish Empire, and the 'drying up' of the Euphrates is symbolic of the decline of the power of the Turkish Empire.

No-one could attack Palestine across the Euphrates whilst the Turks held their immense power in the Middle East. Let us remember that John was writing in A.D.95 when he foresaw the drying up of the great River Euphrates.

*And the sixth angel poured out his bowl upon the great river, Euphrates, and it's water was dried up, that the way of the Kings of the east might be prepared.*

Napoleon said "Constantinople is the key to the East" and he was right. Few of us today understand the immense power the Turks wielded in the Middle East prior to the First World War. Turkey was able to control virtually all intercourse between east and west. She held in her grip at one time a large part of Southern Europe and was supreme in Asia Minor, Syria, Mesopotamia and Egypt.

Today Turkey has little power, the great River Euphrates has dried up and the way of the Kings of the East has been prepared. How did the prophet foresee that this would happen, eighteen hundred years ago?

## WHERE WILL ARMAGEDDON BE FOUGHT?

The word Armageddon should be rendered Har-Magedon and it means the 'Mountains of Megiddo'. The mountains of Megiddo are less than 60 kilometres from the present Israel borders with Lebanon and Syria. Exactly the place one would expect the Israeli forces to meet an invasion from across the Euphrates: It all seems so obvious today as we study our modern maps and are familiar with Israeli battle plans in several recent wars. But let us remember, the prophet did not have the benefit of hindsight we have, yet his prognostication fits accurately modern history.

## WHO WILL BE THE COMBATANTS IN THE BATTLE OF ARMAGEDDON?

If you turn back to the commencement of this chapter and read again the prophecy of Ezekiel you will see the following as being the addressees of the prophecy. Not the House of Judah, nor the House of Israel, but nations with different names:

*Gog* • *Magog* • *Meshech* • *Tubal* • *Persia* • *Ethiopia* • *Libya* *Gomer* • *Togarmah*

Remember what we have said before: If we wish to understand the messages the seers wished to pass to us then we must first ask two questions: To whom was the prophecy addressed and when was it to be fulfilled?

The above is the list of countries the prophet foretold would attack Palestine at the battle of Armageddon. We will deal with them first, and then pass on to deal with the nations the prophet says will defend the Holy Land at the time of this attack.

There is little need, I think, for me to spend much time dealing with the three nations Persia, Ethiopia and Libya, for they are easily identifiable. However, we are then left with six names which cannot today be found on the map: *Gog, Magog, Meshech, Tubal, Gomer and Togarmah.*

Some time ago I came upon a book, published about 1940 by a

Dr. L. Sale-Harrison entitled "The Coming Great Northern Confederacy" and I must thank the publishers, Messrs. Pickering and Inglis Ltd., for allowing me to quote at length from it. The reason I am quoting at length is because I am left in some awe at the accuracy of Dr. Sale-Harrison's interpretation of the writings of the prophets.

We must remember that when he was writing this book the Second World War was just commencing — I suppose we were still at the 'phoney war' stage. The Soviet Union was yet to form it's infamous pact with Berlin — a pact conveniently forgotten now by socialists the world over. We were still a while away from the savage thrust to the heart which Hitler was to deliver to his 'ally'. British troops had not yet left the beaches of Dunkirk and the Battle of Britain had not then taken place in the skies above our land. As Dr. Sale-Harrison wrote, the Third Reich was at it's zenith, Austria, Czechoslovakia and Poland lay prostrate at the feet of an all-conquering Germany. We should not let ourselves forget, in our short review of the events of those days, how the Soviet Union savagely tore at the bleeding remains of the Polish nation as she lay bloodied and beaten at the feet of the Nazi's.

The book reads almost as history pre-written, so accurate is Dr. Sale-Harrison's interpretation. He says in his book that Russia would control part of Germany, that Germany and Austria would not remain one nation, and that ultimately Turkey would be in the Russian camp. The former two happenings seemed very unlikely in those dark days, but as we know, they took place. The latter is yet to take place. Because of the accuracy of his interpretation of the prophets, I thought I could do no better than to quote him when he writes regarding the 38th chapter of Ezekial:

## "THE NORTHERN CONFEDERACY".

"Verses 14 and 15 tell us that when the children of Israel dwell safely (confidently) in their own country, a great confederation of nations comes out of its place, that is, out of the north parts, to crush Israel in its fury. It is this confederation that we now wish to consider. The questions which are upon many minds are: Who are these nations, and when do they come against Israel? These questions can be very clearly answered from the Word of God. The prophecies which we desire to examine are in chapter 38. This chapter commences with the words: *And the word of the Lord came unto me saying, Son of man, set thy face against Gog, the land of Magog, the Prince of Rosh, Meshech, and Tubal, and prophesy against him.*

If one compares the translation of verses 1 and 2 as given above, with the reading of the Authorised Version, he will see the change of one word. The Authorised Version renders part of verse 2 as follows: *The Chief Prince of Rosh, Mesech and Tubal* but we have rendered it *The Prince of Rosh, Mesech and Tubal* which is in harmony with the language of the Revised Version.

In order to give the reason for this alteration, a few explanatory details are necessary. First, the Hebrew word for 'Chief' is 'Rosh'. Second, the Septuagint Version of the Old Testament usually signified by the Roman numerals LXX, which is a version translated into Greek by seventy (or seventy-two) Jewish scholars — from which it derives its name — at Alexandria, at the command of King Ptolemy Philadelphus, in the fourth century B.C. This Greek version, instead of translating the Hebrew word 'Rosh' into its Greek equivalent, leaves it untranslated; the translators of the Revised Version following the same course; therefore the Hebrew word 'Rosh' was not intended for its English equivalent 'Chief' but was used as a proper name. Hence the translation, *"The Prince of Rosh, Meshech and Tubal"*. But the Septuagint Version translates the two latter names 'Mosoch' and 'Thobol' as the Greek spelling for 'Meshech' and 'Tubal' so the Greek translation of this portion is 'The Prince of Rosh, Mosoch and Thobol'. In Ezekial 38, other names are mentioned, which are included in this great confederation, viz., Persia, Ethiopia, Libya, Gomer, and all his bands, and the house of Togarmah of the north quarters and all his bands. We must leave the consideration of Persia, Ethiopia and Libya, to a later publication, and only refer to Gomer and Togarmah in connection with our present book.

We will now endeavour to consider the questions already asked, viz., Who are these nations? and, When do they come against Israel? Can these questions be answered? Does the Word of God give definite information? Yes. The evidence is so clear and startling that it almost staggers one with its revelation.

## Chapter II.

## WHO ARE THESE NATIONS?

If we turn to Genesis 10, we will find that the origin of the names is given. This chapter indicates that Gomer, Magog, Meshech and Tubal are brothers, that Togarmah is the son of Gomer and a nephew of the latter three. Genesis 10:5 gives a clear and lucid statement showing that these names represent three things: (1) Different nations; (2) Different languages; (3) Settlement in different parts of the earth; also Genesis 10 closes with these words: *"These are the families of the sons of Noah, after their generations in their nations, and by these were the nations divided in the earth after the flood."*

The names in Ezekial 38, which we will now consider, are Magog, Rosh, Meshech, Tubal, Togarmah and Gomer.

## 1. MAGOG

Josephus says that the Greeks called the Scythians 'Magog'. They went from Asia Minor into the south of Russia having the Caucasian mountains as their southern boundary. It is interesting to note that the very word "Caucasus" means "God's Fort". "God" and "Chasan" (Fort) are two Oriental words from which it is derived. This becomes the setting of a very vivid picture of a nation migrating north, leaving as its southern protector a chain of mountain forts, in the name of which its people are inscribed.

## 2. ROSH

Bishop Lowther says "Rosh, taken as a proper name, in Ezekiel signifies the inhabitants of Scythia, from whom the modern Russians derived their name". It is significant that the Orientals called the people who dwelt upon the banks of the River Araxes, "Rhos" or "Rosh" and the Arabic name for that river was also called "Rosh", and the Scythian Tauri in the Crimea was called by the same name.

Now, Russia was called Muscovy, a name derived from Meshech, until Ivan IV, surnamed 'Ivan the Terrible'. He came to the Muscovite throne in 1533, and reigned until 1584. He was the first to assume the title of "Czar of Russia", "Czar" being derived from "Caesar". Though the Russian Empire was created by the Muscovite Princes, who were the first Grand Dukes of Moscow, yet it was Ivan who really consolidated and extended that great Empire, until it reached the White Sea in the north and the Caspian Sea in the south. It was henceforth called Russia. Why? Because God said it would be Rosh (or Russia).

## 3. MESHECH AND TUBAL

These are the progenitors of those who penetrated into South Russia, and then spread into the northern parts of the same great Empire.

The inhabitants of the Moshic Mountains, east of the Black Sea, are called Moschi. On the authority of Josephus and others we understand that the Moscheni were founded by Meshech, and the Thobelites by Tubal. We will now endeavour to show that Meshech and Tubal can be identified as Moscow and Tobolsk, the two great capital cities of East and West Russia. Let us carefully examine this supposed identification.

Moscow is derived from Muscovy, and Muscovy is derived from Meshech; and Tubal is the origin of Tobolsk. But we have already pointed out that the Greek spelling for "Meshech" and "Tubal", are "Mosoch" and "Thobol". In comparing the Russian pronunciation for these two cities, what do we find? A marvellous revelation. Compare the name "Mosoch" with "Moscow", and we find that the first syllable of each word is identical, and that the final letters "oc" are only reversed. Compare "Thobol" with "Tobolsk" and we discover that the first two syllables are practically identical, with only "sk" added to it. In "Moscow", the 'K' sound precedes the final vowel instead of following it, as in "Mosoch". In "Tobolsk" the final "sk" is added, which is a much-used Russian suffix. If you look on the map of Eastern Russia and Siberia, you will see that the majority of the important towns have the final ending "sk". Therefore, we can definitely say that the inhabitants have added their own peculiar ending to the original names. "Tobol" being a city of Eastern Russia is no exception to this rule. Without doubt the original Greek names "Mosoch" and "Thobol" are identical with Moscow and Tobolsk, the capitals of Western and Eastern Russia respectively, the change being entirely accounted for by the pronunciation and spelling peculiar to Russia. Therefore, "Mesech" and "Tubal" of Ezekial 38, are identical with the present-day cities of "Moscow" and "Tobolsk". This shows that the prophecy refers to Eastern and Western Russia of which these towns are representatives. I have sought earnestly and visited a number of libraries and studied many volumes, besides conversing with Consuls and others acquainted with the Russian language and history, and I have carefully verified this information. Here the identification is seen in the locality, in the past migrations of its inhabitants, and in its language. Surely this is scientific enough for any intelligent person.

## 4. TOGARMAH AND ALL HIS BANDS.

Who are these? Some identify them as those who possess the land of Armenia, but when Wolf visited the Tartar Hordes who live south of the sea of Aral and between that sea and the Caspian, he found that they called themselves "Togarmah".

The latter seems to be the most probable identification, though it matters little: for if "Togarmah" represents the people controlling Armenia, that is in the south of Russia, which is in the north of Palestine; and if it is representative of those living between the Sea of Aral and the Caspian Sea, that is, in the

Southern portion of Russia itself, which is also in the North of Palestine, then either of these would completely fulfil the prophecy, yet it must be said in favour of the former that the Black Sea, which is north-west of Armenia, is sometimes called Togarmah and sometimes Ripath, also Jewish writers call the Turks "Togarmah" and the Armenians are often called "The House of Targom". "

Appreciate that when that was written, Russia and her allies posed no threat to Palestine.

It is not possible, I think, to improve on what Dr. Sale-Harrison has written, certainly I can add nothing to it, so I will not comment on it.

There are several words used by the ancient seers which I would like to comment on and they add weight to the comments of Dr. Sale-Harrison.

Ezekiel, prophesying to Russia and her allies, writes "Be thou prepared, and prepare for thyself, thou, and all they company THAT ARE ASSEMBLED UNTO THEE, and be thou a GUARD unto them."

The word "Guard" is used to denote the relationship of the Russian instigator to the people who "gather themselves" to her. It is a very interesting word, for it is used in Genesis 42:19 to denote one who imprisons, a prison guard.

Someone once said to me that they could see no difference between Soviet Imperialism and British and American imperialism. I made the point that there is a profound difference, it can be seen at once if you will take a piece of paper, divide it down the centre and write at the head of one column "Countries vacated by the Red Army since 1945" and at the head of the other column "Countries vacated by the United States and British Armies since 1945". One column will be blank, but to complete the other column it will take much writing and much study. The fact is, and it is a fact, that the Red Army has never allowed any country it has 'protected' to get out of it's grasp. In contrast, the American and British armies have left the territories of other nations as soon as those nations have asked them to do so. A survey of Eastern Europe is a survey of a downtrodden, impoverished and enslaved people where the concentration camp is still the order of the day and even the psychiatric ward has been pressed into horrific service to destroy those who dare dissent.

The past years have seen a falling away in patriotic thinking and almost a complete reversal of the adage "My country right or wrong". Now the slogan would seem to be "My country's always wrong" and one wonders why, what influence is abroad which causes even eminent politicians to disregard the plain facts of history? We have recently had a leading British politician saying "I can never forget that the brave Russian armies fought to save our country, without them we would today be a slave state in Nazi Germany." He had disregarded the facts of history, and those facts are quite indisputable and to my knowledge have never been disputed outside the Soviet orbit, where, as we know, history is revised to order. The fact of history is that when this country stood alone, the Russians, with full knowledge of Hitler's racist doctrines, with full knowledge of Hitler's persecution of the Jews and with full knowledge of his imperialist and aggressive intent, made a pact with that foul murderer. They did not come to the aid of this or any other country, they were quite indifferent to the suffering of ordinary working people in Poland, Austria or Czechoslovakia, choosing rather, when Britain fought, to shake hands with the tyrant and aid him in his evil murderous designs. Not until Hitler attacked Russia did Russia suddenly decide it was expeditious to fight with us. Whatever we may think Russia did for us, was done by them for self preservation, not with the intent of saving either this country or the United States of America.

The contrary is true, for had Britain and the United States stood back and allowed Hitler to attack Russia with impunity, there is no doubt Russia would have been subjugated. Instead, Britain and America poured arms ashore on the Russian continent to assist the beleaguered Russian armies. When did the Russians send Britain or America one gun or one ounce of food? Respect for the undoubtedly magnificent fight the Soviet troops put up at Stalingrad and Moscow must be tempered with a solemn recognition that these men were none other than the murderers of the citizens of Finland, Poland, Hungary and Czechoslovakia. Russia is a nation which is a "guard" or "prison keeper" of millions of subjected people.

In the days before they were to descend on Palestine, and trigger off the last great battle of earth's history, the Russians were to be, in the Hebrew, a "mishmak" to her allies, a "prison guard".

There are one or two other words we should examine. The prophet speaks of "Gomer and all his hordes or bands"; the Hebrew word translated "Hordes or bands" is "Agappim" and carries the meaning "wings". The word translated "sword" in the passage is in the Hebrew "Baraq" and means "Destroying weapon" or "lightning". The word translated "safely" when the prophet speaks of Israel 'dwelling safely' at the time of Armageddon is the Hebrew "Betach" and bears the interpretation "in confidence".

The West must not underestimate the dire peril in which it stands, according to the prognostications of the prophets, peril which is the more acute because of the blindness which seems to afflict even the most reasonable people when they assess the Soviet posture on the international stage. There seems to be a willingness — I almost wrote 'an eagerness' — to grant the Soviet Union the benefit of the doubt however heinous her crimes.

One wonders why Soviet crimes are so exempt from positive action by the peoples of the world. We act quickly enough to stop our athletes competing in South Africa, but Soviet racism is 'overlooked' .. How many black soldiers serve in the Russian army? How many coloured immigrants are allowed into the Soviet Union? How many coloured players are there in Russian athletic or sports teams? How many blacks are in the Soviet government? How many blacks work in the Russian government service? How many blacks are in the Russian police force? How many Jews are oppressed because they ARE Jews — is that not racism?

Could this international madness which causes us to persecute our friends for committing crimes against humanity, whilst allowing crimes of greater gravity against humanity to go unchecked in our enemies, be caused by something beyond human influence?

One does hope that the future will see Britain and America giving succour to their friends and refusing to listen to a vocal minority of do-gooders, the fellow travellers, wittingly or unwittingly, of Communism, who exhort and cajole us into doing the Russian's bidding.

Do not take the Soviet threat lightly. Evil as it was, Hitler's Third Reich was a nothing compared to the threat that now hangs over mankind. Even today, more butchery takes place throughout the Communist world in one year than took place in Hitler's Germany throughout the whole existence of the Third Reich.

Little wonder the Russians, the Communist Party and the leftists who control much of the information fed to us through the media, like to keep us looking back to the events of the forties: It would indeed be a revelation to our nation if that amount of newspaper space were devoted to reporting, and analysing, the horrors being perpetrated in Communist countries TODAY.

## LIKE A CLOUD TO COVER THE LAND.

The prophet Ezekiel, writing of the Soviet Union, said:

*Thou shalt ascend and come like a storm; thou shalt be like a cloud to cover the land, thou, and all thy hordes, and many people with thee.*

How often we in the West are belaboured from political platform and pulpit alike for spending so much money on arms when people in the 'third world' are starving. "Much better" we are told, "to dismantle such defences as we have, and use the money to expand the social services in our own country, spend more on education and contribute more to foreign aid." It is to be wondered why those nations which spend the most on equipment of war and subscribe the least to the world's foreign aid programme are not the recipients of such advice. How any Marxist or any member of the Communist party has the gall to carry a banner through the streets of Britain or America calling for disarmament I do not know. The facts show, and they are FACTS, that despite the terrible deprivation in which many people in Russia and other Communist countries live, Russia spends more of her resources on arms than any nation on earth.

"Disarm", scream our British Marxist friends, "we are spending far too much on defence." In 1977 there were 340,000 people in the United Kingdom forces and there were 2,000,000 in the United States armed forces. Compared with those figures Russia had 3,500,000 men under arms. The Soviet Union had a million and a quarter more people in their armed services than Britain and America combined. I would say to any propagator of disarmament — unless you are prepared to carry your demonstrations on to the streets of Moscow you must face the charge of duplicity and insincerity.

"The Book of Numbers", an excellent statistical publication by Heron House Publishing Company, says, "The U.S.S.R. is the most military-minded nation in the world. It poured a staggering £72 thousand million into its 1976 defence budget. That's sabre-rattling on a grand scale". America spent £8 thousand million less, and the United Kingdom spent £65 million less — and the Marxist tells US to stop spending so much on arms.

There is not a Communist nation on earth that is not armed to the teeth, so if you REALLY believe in the 'Peace Movement', don't get involved with the Communists.

## THE CONFEDERACY.

Whatever may happen in the next few months, or maybe few years, the fact is that, according to the ancient seers, the Soviet Union, Ethiopia, Libya and Iran will be together at the Battle of Armageddon.

Only in the past few years has Libya entered the Soviet camp, 2,500 years after the prophet had foretold they would.

Ethiopia is now sustained by Cuban troops and Soviet 'advisers' and an obscene persecution has taken place in that land against those who will not conform to the Communist party line. Who would have thought, in the days of the late Haile Selassie, that Ethiopia would sever her links with the West? The ties that bound us together were so great that such an event was not foreseeable even twenty years ago, certainly in those days the Ethiopians had no love of the Soviet Union. One of the titles by which Haile Selassie called himself was "The Lion of the Tribe of Judah", Who could foresee? Many did because they had read the writings of the prophet Ezekiel and he said so 2500 years before it happened.

A few years ago the Shah of Persia was the most powerful reigning monarch in the Middle East, he had a sizeable modern army to back his power and the nations of the West guaranteed the security not only of his throne but of his nation. The Shah was committed to the West and was a bastion of Western policy in the Middle East: Surely the Americans would never allow him to be deposed for was he not an essential supporter of their policy in the area? In 1979 the 'impossible' happened, not only did the Americans allow the Shah to be deposed but it must be said that the American administrators of that time betrayed him. Who could have foreseen the Persians (Iranians) leaving the Western fold? Ezekiel did, 2500 years before it happened! Whatever American and British policy is from here on, though there may be a healing of wounds between America and Iran and the present Iranian government may be deposed, Iran will be in the Russian camp before the Battle of Armageddon. It seems unlikely that the present Islamic Shi'ite government would wish to support the atheistic regime of the Soviet Union — therefore we may expect a change of government in Iran.

Though, since the First World War, Turkey has been friendly to us and may still be counted an ally of the United States and Britain, she, like Persia, will be among the nations to come down to Palestine with the Soviet Union at the Battle of Armageddon.

## THE DEFENDERS.

We have seen the identity of the nations which will attack the land of Palestine, now let us look at what the prophet foretells about the people who will defend Palestine. It should be noted here that every nation on earth will be involved in this war, Armageddon, so the prophet does not give an exhaustive list of either the attackers or the defenders. The nations mentioned are the instigating nations around whom the other unnamed nations gather.

Here is the continuation of the prophecy of Ezekiel:

*It shall also come to pass that at that same time shall things come into thy mind, and thou shalt think an evil thought; And thou shalt say, I will go unto the land of unwalled villages; I will go to those who are at rest, who dwell safely, all of them dwelling without walls, and having neither bars nor gates, to take spoil and to take prey; to turn thy hand upon the desolate places THAT ARE NOW INHABITED, and upon the people that are gathered out of the nations, who have gotten cattle and goods, who dwell in the midst of the land.*

Book of the Prophet Ezekiel 38: 10-12

This fragment of the prophecy adds something to the return of the Jews to Palestine. Walls were erected in the time of the prophecy to keep invaders out, in times when no war was anticipated the walls were neglected and villages built without walls. Bars and gates also signify security against the enemy.

It is obvious from this prophecy that at the time the Soviet Union attacks Palestine the attack will be brought about by the defencelessness of the inhabitants of that land, and indeed of the nations who support them.

## WHY THE PEACE MOVEMENT WILL PROSPER.

Much as I dislike the thought, you can be quite sure that the so-called 'peace movements' of the world are about to have far reaching successes as our politicians, merely to advance their political careers, not because they regard disarmament as desirable, yield to the pressure brought upon them by well-meaning people who do not understand the aims of dictators nor grasp the dangers we face.

Even the Jewish State of Israel will yield to the pressures brought upon them by the 'peace movements' and their allies. We may therefore expect a dramatic change in Israeli policy in favour of the 'wets'. No doubt we shall all be 'softened up' by a show of Soviet allegience to the United Nations Organisation. There are yet to be olive branches proffered by the Soviet Union which will dupe people into believing that their intentions are honourable.

Israel is well armed at present, but before the Battle of Armageddon she is to be 'a land of unwalled villages', 'dwelling without gates or bars'.

It is this, the prophet says, that will encourage the Soviet Union to attack: *"I will go up to the land of unwalled villages"*.

I well remember how we vowed, after Neville Chamberlain had come back from Hitler with his worthless piece of paper proclaiming 'Peace in our time', never again to follow a policy of appeasement. History had taught us, we said, that no bully, no tyrant, no warmonger nor any international blackguard would ever be turned aside from his hell-bent pursuits by appeasement. Yet we still exchange and place our trust in equally worthless pieces of paper.

We sometimes forget we had a great disarmament movement in the days prior to World War II. Their argument was that if we set a good example to the dictators by disarming, they would follow our example. The result? We did — they didn't!

Perhaps the very young cannot understand why those of another generation do not accept their proposal that if we disarm it will encourage the Soviet Union to do the same. Well, I'll tell them the reason — WE'VE heard it all before. We've heard it many times, from many tyrants and IT'S NEVER WORKED. Bullies do not respond to weakness whether those bullies are individual or international.

Make no mistake! I say it with sorrow, for who can criticise a man who had such a love of peace as Neville Chamberlain and who wants to criticise young people, or older people for that matter, who so love peace they will get involved in trying to preserve it? THE SECOND WORLD WAR WAS BROUGHT ABOUT NOT BY WARMONGERS BUT BY PEACE—

MONGERS.MILLIONS OF JEWS DIED IN GAS CHAMBERS BECAUSE WE LISTENED TO THE 'DISARMERS'.

There are times when it is more disastrous to be sincerely wrong than insincerely right. Millions have died in Cambodia and Vietnam as a direct result of the peace marches staged in Britain and the United States during the war there. Millions more have been slaughtered as a result of the activities of the 'peace movements' of this world than have ever been killed by the warmongers of this world. The only answer to a demagogue is to confront him at the earliest possible time, with the firmest possible resolution and the greatest possible power. The Second World War started because Hitler had been allowed to continue long after his real character was recognised and long after he should have been stopped. People who said he should be stopped were labelled "warmongers". Churchill was even sent into the political wilderness because he preached the gospel of 'stop him now before it is too late'. The peacemen prevailed and millions of people died as a direct result of that well-intentioned foolishness. We are, unfortunately, about to do it again — WHEN WILL WE EVER LEARN?

As you watch the gradual disarmament of the Western nations and of the Jewish State of Israel, perhaps you would like to reflect on the fact that what you are seeing was foretold 2500 years ago by the prophet Ezekiel.

## WHO ARE SHEBA, DEDAN AND THE MERCHANTS OF TARSHISH?

Just as Poland became the 'last straw' to Britain in the last war, the invasion of Palestine will become the 'last straw' to countries the prophet calls "Sheba, Dedan and the Merchants of Tarshish" at the opening of the Battle of Armageddon. Here's what the prophet says will happen:

*Sheba, and Dedan, and the Merchants of Tarshish, with all it's young lions, shall say unto thee [Gog], Art thou come to take spoil? Hast thou gathered thy company to take prey, to carry away silver and gold, to take away cattle and goods, to take great spoil?*

The House of Judah will, of course, be at the battle because they will be occupying the land, the House of Israel will be fighting at that battle also because by that time there will be a unity between the House of Judah and the House of Israel amounting to federal government. We have yet, remember, to find the House of Israel.

Who are Sheba, Dedan, the Merchants of Tarshish and the young lions thereof?

TARSHISH is mentioned several times in prophecy. Referring to the return of the Jews to the Holy Land, the Prophet Isaiah foretells :

*Surely the isles shall wait for me, and the ships of Tarshish first,*
*to bring thy sons from far, their silver and their gold with them,*
*unto the name of the Lord thy God, and to the Holy One of Israel*
                                                            Isaiah 60:9

Tarshish is identified as dwelling in 'the isles'. From the prophets we can see there were two places spoken of as Tarshish and both of them are in the British Commonwealth of Nations.

In the Book of Kings we read:

*And King Solomon made a navy of ships in Ezion-Geber, which is beside Eloth, on the shore of the Red Sea, in the land of Edom. And Hiram sent in the navy his servants, shipment that had knowledge of the sea, with the servants of Solomon.*

Chapter 10 of the same book tells us that "the king had at sea a navy of Tarshish." Now we must ask the question: Why was a fleet of ships made on the shore of the Red Sea and crewed by specialist mariners, servants of Hiram and Solomon, referred to as 'a navy of Tarshish'?
The Second Book of Chronicles provides us with the answer when it says:

*For the kings ships went to Tarshish with the servants of Hiram; every three years once came the ships of Tarshish bringing gold, and silver, ivory and apes, and peacocks.*
                                                       II Chronicles 9:12

## EASTERN TARSHISH.

The ships of Tarshish were called by that name because they went to Tarshish, just as today we would speak of a British Airways plane going to New York as being 'the New York flight'.
For years the place called the 'Eastern Tarshish' was a mystery. Obviously it was between a year and eighteen months journey from the Holy Land. There was, of course, no Suez Canal in those days, so ships leaving the Red Sea would pass the straights of Bab-el-Mandeb and steer eastwards. The ships would then hug the coast of Arabia, they did not steer by compass in those days, and onward to Hindustan. A five thousand mile journey would take them to India and that could have been well accomplished in the three years given for the return journey.
Gold, silver, ivory, apes and peacocks were all obtainable in India. Nevertheless, controversy raged for many years about the identity of the Eastern Tarshish. We owe the resolution of the problem to the science of philology, and in particular to a French philologist who lived at the turn of

the century, M. Vinson.

The word 'Kangaroo' has come to our language from Australia and the word 'Khaki' from India, and when such words are found in a language they testify to intercourse between the two countries, the country that originated the word and the country which has absorbed the word into it's own language. We would not, for example, have the word 'cafe' in our language had we not had dealings with France.

Vinson realised that the Hebrew word for peacocks gave the key to exactly where the ships of Tarshish sailed. The Hebrew word is "thuciyyim", it was akin to the South Indian word "tokei". He also found that the word for ivory could be divided into two, the one the Hebrew signifying 'tooth' and the second the South Indian word for 'elephant'. Similarly the word for 'apes' was derived from the South Indian.

## WESTERN TARSHISH.

There was another Tarshish to which ships sailed from the Holy Land. In the Book of the Prophet Jonah (the Jonah of Jonah and the whale fame) written about 850 years before Christ, we read:

> *Jonah ... rose up to flee unto Tarshish, from the presence of the Lord, and went down to Joppa [Tel-Aviv]; and found a ship going to Tarshish: so he payed the fare thereof and went down into it.*
> Chapter 2:3

Obviously Jonah would not have embarked on the Mediterranean coast if he had intended to journey eastwards, neither indeed would the ship have been sailing from that coast to go eastwards.

The prophet Ezekiel mentions this 'Western Tarshish':

Tarshish was thy merchant by reason of a multitude of all kinds of riches; with silver, iron, tin and lead, they traded in thy fairs.

> *Tarshish was thy merchant by reason of a multitude of all kinds of riches; with silver, iron, tin and lead, they traded in thy fairs.*
> Ezekiel 27:12

None of the above merchandise was exported from India at the time that was written. So where was the Tarshish which exported silver, iron, tin and lead?

Encyclopaedia Brittanica records:

> "It is possible that they (the Phoenicians) reached the coasts of Britain, then called the Cassierides, or Tin Islands, in search of the tin of Cornwall;" Page 889. 1973 edit.

Another quotation from Brittanica tells us that these Phoenician ships were almost certainly the 'ships of Tarshish' spoken of in the Bible.

"Their fleets were divided into two types — 'long ships' or galleys, for speed and rapid manoeuvre, armed with a sharp ram at the bow and propelled by two or three banks of oarsmen (these are almost certainly what are called in the Bible the "ships of Tarshish")."                                   Page 890. 1973 edit.

The phrase the 'Merchants of Tarshish, with all it's young lions' is an unusual phrase but becomes understandable in view of the above quotations. Certainly there seems to have been no other place beyond the Straights of Gibraltar from which a continual trade in tin could have been carried on other than from the 'Tin Islands'.

## THE MERCHANT EMPIRE.

Britain is always depicted as a lion just as Russia is depicted as a bear. It is not, therefore, stretching the imagination too far to think of the countries of the Commonwealth as being the 'young lions thereof'.

Why, though, 'The Merchants of Tarshish'? Is it coincidence that commerce played so large a part in the birth of the 'young lions'? The East India 'Merchant' Company received it's charter from Queen Elizabeth I in 1600. India was governed by the 'Merchant' Company until the British Government took over. Similarly, Canada was 'brought up' under the Royal charter given to the Hudson Bay Company in the reign of Charles II. In 1889 the chartered South African Company was another example of commerce giving birth to a 'young lion'.

Today, despite all we hear about the disintegration of the British Commonwealth of Nations, it remains the largest community of nations in the world. There are 959,660,905 people who claim allegiance to this free association of peoples. That compares with a total population in the Soviet Union of 267,700,000 and a total population in China of 982,550,000.

Could it be that when the prophet foretold the Merchants of Tarshish, with all the young lions thereof, would withstand the Soviet Union when they invade Palestine he was also giving an indication of how the young lions would be 'born' i.e. through the old 'merchant' companies? It is an interesting point of speculation and depends very much for stronger evidence, on the writings we shall examine in our chapter "The Mystery of the Missing Millions".

Perhaps in identifying the 'Merchants' of Tarshish' we should also give due weight to the fact that it was the British Empire troops to whom fell the privilege fulfilling the prophecies regarding the deliverance of Jerusalem.

On the original shield of the East India Company there is a globe with a band around it, and two lions supporting a shield. Upon the shield are two lions and three full rigged ships.

## HENRY SULLEY FORESAW FEDERAL GOVERNMENT.

I make no apology for mentioning again the book "Is it Armageddon?" and it's author Mr. Henry Sulley. Writing in 1915 he could not quite understand the phrase "Tarshish with all the young lions thereof shall say unto thee", for of course the "young lions" in those days formed part of the British Empire and declaration of war was agreed by the King in Privy Council assembled. How then, he reasoned, can the "young lions" have anything to say regarding peace or war? Here in his own words is how he reasoned in 1915, basing his reasoning on the prognostication of the prophets:

"The words, "Tarshish with all the young lions thereof shall say unto thee" may be taken to imply some power "to say" vested in the "young lions" as an integral part of the Tarshish (British) political sphere. At the present the Colonies can scarcely be said to speak for peace or for war ... something more than the appointment of Colonial members of the Council seems necessary before the terms of the prophecy are completely fulfilled. The corresponding relation involved seems to require some form of representation more extensive in character and more directly connected with the central government that at present exists. This may be the meaning of the prophecy, and suggests the establishment of an Imperial Council of Empire dealing with Imperial questions."

Pages 62-63

We know today that he was quite correct in his interpretation, true the consultative procedure is not called an Imperial Council of Empire, but the 'young lions' are now able to make their own decisions as to whether they will go to war. We now have Commonwealth Conferences, a forum of free and willing members of this world-wide club.

In a foot-note, Henry Sulley puts forward the proposition that the Empire exists under a form of Federation of the Empire. It's a view that ought to be canvassed widely today, for then the British Commonwealth of Nations would be the most powerful force in the world. There seems to me to be no reason why even the United States of America could not be part of such an organisation, for they have the most successful system of Federal Government in the world. Acting in concert, such a widespread people could ensure that no decisive attack could be launched upon them and thus they would ensure nuclear weapons would not be used. No-one will ever launch a nuclear attack unless they stand a substantial chance of not receiving a mortal wound themselves.

## THE GATHERING OF THE NATIONS.

As I have said, the combatants in the First World War believed that war to be the war to end wars. One would have thought that to be a reasonable enough idea, for, has mankind not become very knowledgeable indeed in these past years? Could we not have expected that mankind would eschew war as a method of settling international differences? Yes, indeed, we could have expected it, and yet, as I write, the whole world is as an armed camp. Never has there been greater preparation for war and never has there been so many potential 'powder kegs'. If only we could identify the philosophies for which people are supposed to be fighting, or preparing to fight, it would be some consolation but even that is not possible. No sooner does a revolution start than it splits within itself and those two split again — multiplication by division!

The Prophet John wrote:

> *And the sixth angel poured out his bowl upon the great river, Euphrates, and it's water was dried up, that the way of the kings of the east might be prepared.*
> *And I saw three unclean spirits, like frogs, come out of the mouth of the dragon, and out of the mouth of the beast, and out of the mouth of the false prophet.*
> *For they are the spirits of demons, working miracles, that go forth unto the kings of the earth and of the whole world, to gather them to battle of that great day of God Almighty....*
> *And he gathered them together into a place called in the Hebrew tongue Armageddon.*
>
> Revelation 16: 12-16

I have repeated that prophecy because, if you read a book in the way I read a book, you will not trouble to turn back to a previous page and re-read it.

John saw three unclean spirits like frogs and that the 'unclean spirits' had a job to do, that job was to gather the nations of the world together to the Battle of Armageddon.

We need not, as some have, trouble ourselves with the word 'frogs' for the seer does not say that the 'unclean spirits' are frogs but that they are LIKE frogs. Frogs were particularly repulsive to the Israelite, because, of course, a plague of frogs was one of the punishments on the Egyptians before the Exodus, though no reference to that is intended by the seer. The seer is indicating here how the 'unclean spirits' work to gather the nations together to that great battle. Frogs are evasive and elusive, they hop and leap hither and thither and there is no way of knowing 'which way they will jump'. They seem not to have an aim, they seem to follow no sense of direction, one never knows what they are going to do next. I personally cannot say I find frogs unattractive, but I think in general it is true to say that people find them loathsome and ugly.

The important words to which I wish to draw your attention are the words 'unclean spirits' for it is they that gather the nations together to the Battle of Armageddon.

'Unclean' is translated from the Greek word 'Akarthartus' and it is the same Greek word translated throughout the gospels to denote the state of devil possession.

'Spirit' is from the Greek word 'Pneuma' and is the same word used when the 'spirit' is said to have descended 'like a dove' on Jesus at his baptism. It denotes a supernatural spirit not a human spirit.

Some have tried to interpret the three 'unclean spirits' as being influences coming from personages mentioned, and emanating from within them. The view has been widely held that they represent nothing more than evil intent on behalf of certain nations, but the original does not bear that interpretation. The original words chosen by the prophet were meant to emphasise the supernatural origin of the 'spirits'.

If you, my reader, do not accept the existence of supernatural forces, then of course you will reject what I write and you will dismiss the seers vision at once. I do hope if you do that you will never again refuse to walk under a ladder, nor throw a pinch of salt over your shoulder, both of which actions attest to a belief in something existing and ordering our lives which is beyond our ken.

I, however, make no apology for saying that the plain teaching of the prophet is that it is no human agency which gathers the world together to that great battle, but forces from outside this world. The plain teaching of the prophets is that the real battle is not between men and men but between principalities and powers. The problems on earth, they say, do not commence on earth but in a realm of which human beings know very little, a realm in which the whole of our future is dictated.

Perhaps the prophet will have done us a service for is there a better way of understanding the madness of the nations than attributing it to some form of 'devil possession'?

The Battle of Armageddon, the prophets say, will not only be a titanic clash between the nations of the world, it will be nothing less than the culmination of the age-long spiritual battle for the Adamic Race.

Is all pre-ordained? In practical terms it makes very little difference to mankind whether the things of which the prophets spoke are pre-ordained or merely foreseen. Either way, it would appear, they are going to happen.

# THE DEFEAT OF THE SOVIET UNION AT ARMAGEDDON.

The prophet Ezekiel describes in horrific detail the complete destruction of the Soviet Forces at Armageddon. I think I need do little other than to quote the prophet:

> *Therefore, thou son of man, prophesy against Gog, and say, Thus saith the Lord God: Behold, I am against thee, O Gog, the chief prince of Meshech and Tubal,*
>
> *And I will turn thee back, and leave but a sixth part of thee, and will cause thee to come up from the north parts, and will bring thee upon the mountains of Israel.*
>
> *And I will smite thy bow out of thy left hand, and will cause thine arrows to fall out of thy right hand.*
>
> *Thou shalt fall upon the mountains of Israel, thou, and all thy hordes, and the people that are with thee; I will give thee unto the ravenous birds of every sort, and to the beasts of the field to be devoured.*
>
> *Thou shalt fall upon the open field; for I have spoken it, saith the Lord God.*
>
> *And I will send fire on Magog, and among those who dwell securely in the isles; and they shall know that I am the Lord.*
>
> *So I will make my Holy name known in the midst of my people, Israel ... And they that dwelt in the cities of Israel shall go forth, and shall set on fire and burn the weapons, and the handspikes, and the spears, and they shall burn them with fire seven years ...*
>
> *And it shall come to pass in that day, that I will give unto Gog a place there of graves in Israel, the valley of the travellers on the east of the sea; and it shall stop the noses of the travellers, and there shall they bury Gog and all his multitudes; and they shall call it the Valley of Hamon-Gog.*
>
> *And seven months shall the house of Israel be burying them, that they may cleanse the land.*
>
> Book of the Prophet Ezekiel 39: 1-12

"And I will send fire on Magog" would indicate that the land of Magog is referred to, thus it would seem there will be destruction in the Russian homeland as well as on the battlefield.

## SUMMARY.

The ancient seers foretell:

1. There will be a Third World War.
2. That war was to be fought after the Jews had returned to Palestine.

3. It was to be fought after Turkish rule along the Euphrates was 'dried up'.
4. The war would be fought between the Soviet Union, Libya, Ethiopia, Iran and their allies on the one hand and the British Commonwealth of Nations, the United States of America, the Jewish State of Israel and the House of Israel on the other.
5. There is a strong possibility that there will be some form of Federal Government of Anglo-Saxon people prior to the battle.
6. The peace movements of the western world will have outstanding successes leading to the disarmament of the Western Powers. The Jewish State of Israel will also feel confident enough to drop her guard, probably because of seemingly 'copper-bottom' guarantees by Arab States, the United Nations and the Western Allies.
7. The battle will not be fought in Europe but in Palestine with it's prime battle at Megiddo.
8. Iran will change it's present regine for a left-wing government or the Soviet Union will subjugate Iran.
9. The whole world will be 'gathered together' to this battle by supernatural forces working through three earthly agencies.
10. The war will end with the complete defeat of the Soviet Union and her allies.

# 12.
# The Mark
# of the Beast
# – 666

That we are about to witness some of the most traumatic political events the civilised world has seen is clear from the writings of the ancient seers.

Within a few years, according to the prophets, the economy of the civilised world will be operable only by the consent of, and on the terms laid down by, an Islamic Empire which will rule a large part of the earth's surface.

The oil producing nations will be swept by a wave of religious fervour such as has not been seen since the Prophet Mohammed himself inspired the great upsurge of religious, political and militant Islam.

Iran is already an Islamic Republic and we are all aware of the extraordinary scenes of religious fervour that take place in that country and which appear regularly on our television screens. The old faith is being resurrected, and people are accepting disciplines one would not have expected to be revived in this twentieth century.

It is, however, Iraq not Iran which, according to the ancient seers, will be ·the centre of this world-wide empire, and it will probably not be Baghdad which will be the capital city of the empire but that ancient site, now deserted but perhaps soon rebuilt, Babylon.

The empire will stretch to the Punjab and include, by either consent or conquest, the Arab states, Turkey, Armenia to the Caucasus Mountains, Egypt, Libya, Tunisia, Morrocco and a part of Spain. There will also be incursions into mainland France.

This rise to power will be sudden and be achieved as a result of the economic power as well as the military power the revived Muslim Empire will wield. It will succeed in the short term, because of the policy of appeasement nations of the world will pursue.

Though swift and spectacular, the triumphs of Islam will be short-lived, for they will be undermined by the political philosophy of dialectical materialism. Power and wealth, the conquering armies will soon realise, means nothing in our modern age if the fruits of that power and wealth are not shared by the people.

The nature of the Islamic revival will change as Marxism gains the ascendancy and the final great union of earth's history will be formed in preparation for it's plunge to Armageddon and destruction.

It will be interesting to read carefully the columns of our newspapers as we see these things beginning to come to pass.

## THE MYSTERIOUS BEASTS OF THE ANCIENT SEERS.

There can be few who have not heard of the 'Beast' of the Apocalypse. His, or it's, identity has fascinated mankind for almost 1900 years. The beast of the vision of the prophet John, which he saw when he was banished to labour in the marble quarries on the small island of Pafmos, has recently become big 'box office' at cinemas throughout the world and on television.

The 'Omen' films have earned millions of dollars for their makers. Who could have credited that a vision seen in 96 A.D. would hold such a fascination for space-age man? The films were, in fact, based upon a partial misconception of what John wrote, but, in fairness to the makers of the films, it must be said that many of their misconceptions are shared by theologians: We recognise, too, that film-makers seek to entertain, not to provide us with a theologically accurate discourse.

It is remarkable how 'popular' the 'Beast' has been throughout the ages. Almost every nation, into whose language the Apocalypse has been translated, has had those who have speculated as to the identity of the

'Beast'. Every generation, too, for 1900 years or so, has sought to identify the 'Beast' — usually the unfortunate recipient of the dishonourable title has been someone with whose way of life contemporary society has not agreed.

Some numerologists identified Nero as being the 'Beast', despite having to mis-spell his name to make it's numerological value add up to the required number — 666. Antiochus Epiphenes, too, was thus identified. The number 666 has kept preachers and numerologists busy for years and anyone whose name could be construed to approximate to the numeric 666, even if that name had to be spelt backwards, frontwards, sideways or inside-out, has been in danger of being identified as that supremely evil person.

Napoleon was identified as being the Beast, as were Stalin, Hitler, Mussolini, a succession of Popes, Henry Kissinger and, I am told, even issues of credit cards!

Despite the nonsense which has surrounded identification of the 'Beast', the fact is that the prophets DO predict a political entity they call 'The Beast' will exist in the world during the last days of this dispensation, and immediately prior to the Battle of Armageddon. Foolish guesses there have been, but the prophets are quite emphatic, that the 'Beast' will arise and the quest to find his identity has lost neither it's fascination nor momentum.

*And I stood upon the sand of the sea, and saw a beast rise up out of the sea, having seven heads and ten horns, and upon his horns ten crowns, and upon his heads the name of blasphemy.*

*And the beast which I saw was like a leopard, and his feet were like the feet of a bear, and his mouth like the mouth of a lion; and the dragon gave him his power, and his throne, and great authority.*

*And I saw one of his heads as though it were wounded to death; and his deadly wound was healed, and all the world wondered after the beast.*

*And they worshipped the dragon who gave power unto the beast; and they worshipped the beast, saying, Who is like the beast? Who is able to make war with him?*

*And there was given unto him a mouth speaking great things and blasphemies, and power was given unto him to continue forty and two months. And he opened his mouth in blasphemy against God, to blaspheme his name, and his tabernacle, and them that dwell in heaven.*

*And it was given unto him to make war with the saints, and to overcome them; and power was given him over all kindreds, and tongues, and nations. And all that dwell upon the earth shall worship him, whose names are not written in the book of life of*

*the Lamb slain from the foundation of the world.*
*If any man have an ear, let him hear.*
*He that leadeth into captivity shall go into captivity; he that killeth with the sword must be killed with the sword. Here is the patience and the faith of the saints.*
*And I beheld another beast coming up out of the earth; and he had two horns like a lamb, and he spoke like a dragon.*
*And he exerciseth all the power of the first beast before him, and causeth the earth and them who dwell on it to worship the first beast, whose deadly wound was healed.*
*And he doeth great wonders, so that he maketh fire come down from heaven on the earth in the sight of men.*
*And deceiveth them that dwell on the earth by the means of those miracles which he had power to do in the sight of the beast, saying to them that dwell on the earth, that they should make an image to the beast, that had the wound by a sword, and did live.*
*And he hath power to give life unto the image of the beast, that the image of the beast should both speak, and cause that as many as would not worship the image of the beast should be killed. And he causeth all, both small and great, rich and poor, free and enslaved, to receive a mark in their right hand or in their foreheads. And that no man might buy, or sell, except he that had the mark, or the name of the beast, or the number of his name. Here is wisdom. Let him that hath understanding count the number of the beast; for it is the number of a man; and his number is six hundred three score and six.*

Book of Revelation. Chapter 13: 1-8

You will see that the prophet John did not write of one beast but of two. Of the first he says *"And I stood upon the sand of the sea, and saw a beast rise up out of the sea"*, and later, in verse 11 he writes, *"And I beheld ANOTHER beast coming up out of the earth."*

The imagery is baffling until we turn back the pages of prophetic utterance some seven hundred years to the writing of the prophet Daniel. Daniel wrote of four 'Beasts', gave their various characteristics and acquainted us with the time the first of his four beasts would appear on earth.

It is only possible to arrive at a clear understanding of the meaning and identities of the two 'Beasts' of John in the Apocalypse, when we are familiar with the identities of the four beasts of Daniel. It is one of the prime arguments for the supernormal knowledge of the prophets that their prophecies are inextricably intertwined.

The words "and power was given to him to continue forty and two months" is very significant. We have seen how years are years of days.

1 year – 365 days. Thus one 'year' in prophecy is one year of days or 365 years.

This rule applies also to the word "month" when used prophetically.

1 month – 30 days.
42 months – 1250 days or years.

The ancient seer when he says that the first 'Beast' was given power to continue "forty and two months" is telling us that the period of 1250 years will be very significant in the existence of the 'Beast', indeed so significant as to positively identify him.

Is it therefore not of the utmost significance that:

From the Babylonian captivity of the Jews to the Islamic subjugation of Jerusalem was                                                               1250 years.

From the Islamic subjugation of Jerusalem to the expulsion of the Turks by the British army was                                                      1250 years.

Allowing for the fact that a mistake of four years was made in the computation of the A.D. dates by Dionysius and the birth date of Jesus being B.C.7 and not A.D.1 as is commonly supposed, is it not significant that Omar took Jerusalem for Islam 666 years after the birth of Jesus?

We may see some significance also in the fact that the Dome of the Rock which stands on the Temple site is the oldest surviving Mosque in Islam.

The identity of the Beast 666 has been the subject of considerable speculation but when the predictions of Daniel and John are compared there is little doubt as to its identity. See flip page overleaf.

# DANIEL     INTERPRETATION     REVELATION

## DANIEL

**604-535**

7 In the first year of Belshaz'zar, king of Babylon, Daniel had a dream and visions of his head upon his bed then he wrote the dream, and fold the sum of the matters

2 Daniel spoke and said, I saw in my vision by night, and, behold, the four winds of the heaven strove upon the great sea

3 **And four great beasts came up from the sea, diverse one from another**

*First world empire. Babylon (cp 2:37-38)*

4 The first *was* like a lion, and had eagle's wings; I beheld till the wings were plucked, and it was lifted up from the earth, and made stand upon the feet as a man, and a man's heart was given to it.

*Second world empire: Medo-Persia (cp 2 39, 8 20)*

5 And behold another beast, a leopard like a bear and it raised up itself on one side and it had three ribs in the mouth of it between its teeth; and they said thus unto it, Arise, devour much flesh.

*Third world empire: Greece (cp. 2:39; 8:21-22; 10:20; 11:2-4)*

6 After this I beheld, and, lo, another, like a leopard, which had upon its back four wings of a fowl; the beast had also four heads, and dominion was given to it.

*Fourth world empire: Rome (cp. vv. 23-24; 2:40-43; 9:26)*

7 After this I saw in the night visions, and, behold, a fourth beast, dreadful and terrible, and strong exceedingly, and it had great iron teeth; it devoured and broke in pieces, and stamped the residue with its feet; and it **was diverse from all the beasts that were** before it, and it had ten horns.

*Rome: final form of fourth world empire, the ten kings and the little horn (vv. 24-27; see v. 14, note)*

8 I considered the horns, and, behold, there came up among them **another little horn,** before which there were three of the first horns plucked up by the roots; and, behold, in this horn *were* eyes like the eyes of man, and a mouth speaking great things.

## INTERPRETATION

*The interpretation of beast vision*

15 I, Daniel, was grieved in my spirit in the midst of *my* body, and the visions of my head troubled me.

16 I came near unto one of them that stood by, and asked him the truth of all this. So he told me, and made me know the interpretation of the things.

17 These great beasts, which are four, *are* four kings, *who* shall arise out of the earth.

18 But the saints of the Most High shall take the kingdom, and possess the kingdom forever, even forever and ever.

19 Then I would know the truth of the fourth beast, which was diverse from all the others, exceedingly dreadful, whose teeth *were of* iron, and its nails *of* bronze; *which* devoured, broke in pieces, and stamped the residue with his feet;

20 And of the ten horns that *were* in its head, and of the other which came up, and before whom three fell; even of that horn that had eyes, and a mouth that spoke very great things, whose look *was* more stout than its fellows.

## REVELATION

**96 - 100 B.C.**

10 And there are seven kings five are fallen, and one is, *and* the other is not yet come, and when he cometh, he must continue a short space.

11 And the beast **that was,** and is not, even he is the eighth, and is of the seven, and goeth into perdition.

12 And the ten horns which thou sawest are ten kings, who have received no kingdom as yet, but receive power as kings one hour with the beast.

13 These have one mind, and shall give their power and strength unto the beast.

**The Beast, the eigth king existed before 96 A.D. Did not exist in 96 A.D. Would exist after 96 A.D.**

*The beast out of the sea the deadly world healed*

13 **And I stood upon the sand of the sea,** and saw a beast rise up out of the sea, having seven heads and **ten horns,** and upon his horns ten crowns, and upon his heads the name of blasphemy.

2 And **the beast which I saw was like a leopard,** and his feet were like *the feet of* **a bear,** and his mouth like the **mouth of a** lion, and the dragon gave him his power, and his throne and great authority.

3 And I saw one of his heads as *though* it were wounded to death, and his deadly wound was healed, and all the world wondered after the beast.

4 And they worshiped the dragon who gave power unto the beast; and they worshiped the beast, saying, Who *is* like

## (Date column)

604-535

Babylon 603 B.C.

Medo-Persia Iranian Troplis took Babylon 541 B.C.

Greece 330 B.C. 63 B.C.

Rome 63 B.C.

Byzantine 1453

Mohammedon Empire 636 A.D.

## DANIEL (continued)

the beast? Who is able to make war with him?

5 And there was given unto him a mouth speaking great things and blasphemies, and **power was given him to continue forty** *and* **two months.**

6 And he opened his mouth in blasphemy against God, to blaspheme his name, and his tabernacle, and them that dwell in heaven.

7 And it was given unto him to make war with the saints, and to overcome them; and power was given him over all kindreds, and tongues, and nations.

8 And all that dwell upon the earth shall worship him, whose names are not written in the book of life of the Lamb slain from the foundation of the world.

9 If any man have an ear, let him hear.

10 He that leadeth into captivity shall go into captivity; he that killeth with the sword must be killed with the sword. Here is the patience and the faith of the saints.

*The beast out of the land: the number of a man, 666*

11 And I beheld another beast coming up out of the earth; and he had two horns like a lamb, and he spoke like a dragon.

12 And he exerciseth all the power of the first beast before him, and causeth the earth and them who dwell on it to worship the first beast, whose deadly wound was healed.

13 And he doeth great wonders, so that he maketh fire come down from heaven on the earth in the sight of men,

14 And deceiveth them that dwell on the earth by *the means* of those miracles which he had power to do in the sight of the beast, saying to them that dwell on the earth, that they should make an **image** to the beast, that had the wound by a sword, and did live.

15 And he hath power to give life unto the image of the beast, that the image of the beast should both speak, and cause that as many as would not worship the image of the beast should be killed.

16 And he causeth all, both small and great, rich and poor, free and enslaved, to receive a mark in their right hand, or in their foreheads,

17 And that no man might buy or sell, save he that had the mark, or the name of the beast, or the number of his name.

18 Here is wisdom. Let him that hath understanding count the number of the beast; for it is the number of a man; and his number *is* six hundred three-score *and* six.

Daniel writes of four 'Beasts' but in his interpretation he, very significantly, only deals at length with one of them — the fourth.

There have been many fanciful theories as to who or what is meant by the prophetic usage of the word 'Beast'. There is really no need for such speculation— Daniel quite plainly tells us and we need not speculate further.

> *I, Daniel, was grieved in my spirit in the midst of my body, and the visions of my head troubled me.*
> *I came near unto one of them that stood by, and asked him the truth of all this. So he told me, and made me know the interpretation of the things. THESE GREAT BEASTS, WHICH ARE FOUR, ARE FOUR KINGS, WHO SHALL ARISE OUT OF THE EARTH.*

So 'Beasts' in prophecy stand for kingdoms or nations.

However, let me remind you again of our previously mentioned criteria. The ancient seers did not view the centre of the stage of history as being in either Europe or America, as many of our commentators are wont to do. There were many kings and kingdoms on earth during and after the time of Daniel, but the ancient seer was concerned only with those that afflicted Jerusalem, Palestine and the Jews. Even the House of Israel was outside of that sphere which we may regard as the main hand on the prophetic clock.

It is of the utmost importance that we realise that the four 'Beasts' of Daniel and the two 'Beasts' of the Apocalypse exist in relationship to Palestine, Jerusalem and the Jews.

So what empires were represented by the four 'Beasts' of Daniel and the two 'Beasts' of John in the Apocalypse?

When Daniel wrote, Babylon had reduced the Jews to servitude. Babylon was to be followed in 541 B.C. by the Medo-Persian Empire (the people we'd now call Iranians). In 330 B.C. the Greeks unseated the Medo-Persians and in 63 B.C. the Roman Empire subdued the Greeks.

So there we have the four beasts of Daniel:

> Babylon to 541 B.C.
> Medo-Persia to 330 B.C.
> Grecian to 63 B C.
> Roman to 63 A.D.

But how was Daniel able to look down six hundred years of history and predict the coming empires so accurately?

## THE PASSING OF THE BABYLONIAN EMPIRE.

Daniel lived during the reign of the first beast and there are many interesting facts about the passing of the Babylonian Empire which I would like to comment upon but space forbids. However, I cannot resist just two facts which I am sure you will find as fascinating as I.

Remember that Babylon, being the first of the succession of Gentile world empires to afflict Palestine, is the corporate name given by the ancient seers to all those empires who are successors in title to ancient Babylon. Succession passed from one to the other by conquest of Jerusalem.

If, then, we wish to trace the succession of the beasts until we arrive at the beast of our day (666), we must trace those empires who passed to each other by conquest that title deed of succession, Palestine.

It would be wrong, I think, to pass over Babylon and it's defeat by the Medo-Persians without mentioning just two of the many mysterious happenings which surrounded that conquest.

You will remember that the "Times of the Gentiles" or the time which Jerusalem was to be 'trodden down of the Gentiles' was to be 'seven times' which equalled 2520 years — just keep that in your mind for a moment!

## BELSHAZZAR'S FEAST.

We have seen how seemingly impregnable mighty Babylon was. Come with me for a moment to this impregnable city into a room some 60ft wide by 172ft long — we know the size because archaeologists have identified the remains. Nebuchadnezzar, who had boasted "Is not this the mighty Babylon that I have built?" has, like the transient beings even the mightiest humans are, died and his son's son, Belshazzar, is on the throne.

Undoubtedly Belshazzar feels confident this night, surrounded by the mighty defences of the city. In the banqueting hall Belshazzar's feast is in full swing — a drunken orgy attended by the king's concubines, his wives and the princes of the kingdom. They drink and the laughter becomes louder, the behaviour more lewd, the jokes more bawdy, until they see the licentious goings-on through a blurred mist of intoxication.

On the table are the gold and silver cups looted from the Temple at Jerusalem: We can only imagine the feelings of Daniel the Jew as he watches the sacred cups from his beloved temple being put to such a use.

Suddenly the laughter ceases and the action 'freezes'. Cups halfway to the lips tipple and fall to the floor. Drink-gorged faces drain of colour and reeling brains sober. All eyes turn in fear and horror in the same direction — I cannot tell it better than the historic narrative:

*In the same hour came forth the fingers of a man's hand, and wrote over against the lampstand upon the plaster of the wall of the king's palace; and the king saw the part of the hand that wrote. Then the king's countenance was changed, and his thoughts troubled him, so that the joints of his loins were loosed, and his knees smote one against another.*

Daniel 5: 5,6

You can imagine the scene, can't you? One moment ribald laughter and debauchery and the next a horrified silence as the ghostly hand wrote upon the plaster wall deliberately, ominously and irrevocably " MENE, MENE, TEKEL, UPHARSIN" (Daniel 5:25)
The narrative tells us what happened next:

*Now the queen, by reason of the words of the king and his lords, came into the banqueting house; and the queen spoke and said, O king, live forever; let not thy thoughts trouble thee, nor let thy countenance be changed. There is a man in thy kingdom, in whom is the spirit of the holy gods ... he will show the interpretation.*
Parts of Daniel 5: 10-12

If the queen thought the interpretation would be such that it would do anything to cheer the king, she was mistaken for the interpretation announced the end of the kingdom of Babylon:

*God hath numbered thy kingdom ... Thou art weighed in the balances and found wanting ... Thy kingdom is divided and given to the Medes and Persians.*
Parts of Daniel 5: 26, 27, 28

Within hours Belshazzar the king of the Chaldeans was killed and sixty-two year old Darius the Mede took Babylon — the second of the four beasts had arrived.
Perhaps you have always thought of the 'writing on the wall' as being a rather fanciful ghost story. If so, look again at the words the hand wrote — only the research of recent years has brought to light their real significance — MENE, MENE, TEKEL, UPHARSIN.
Remember that the writing on the wall was Aramic, and Daniel, the interpreter, was a Hebrew.

"Mene" is the Aramaic equivalent of the Hebrew "Mina".
"Tekel" is the Aramaic equivalent of the Hebrew "Shekel".
"Parsin" is the plural of "Peres" (note the difference in Daniel's interpretation in verse 28).

The interpretation, therefore, of the writing on the wall at Belshazzar's feast was "A mina, a mina, a shekel and half-a-mina."
The International Encyclopaedia tells us that the smallest unit of weight is a Gerah. One thousand Gerahs equal one gold Mina.

| HEBREW | ARAMAIC | GERAHS |
|--------|---------|--------|
| MINA | MENE | 1,000 |
| MINA | MENE | 1,000 |
| SHEKEL | TEKEL | 20 |
| HALF MINA | UPHARSIN-PERES | 500 |

|  |  | 2,520 |

Do you remember that the 'times of the gentiles' were to run for 2520 years or 'seven times'? Is it not more than coincidence that enshrined in the writing on the wall at Belshazzar's feast was the exact number of years the gentile nations were to exercise domination over Jerusalem? I ask you solemnly — ghost story or supernatural intervention in the affairs of mankind?

But let us go back to Belshazzar's feast for a few moments. Possibly the feast was a gesture of defiance to the Medo-Persian enemy threatening the city, for the garrison had twenty years supply of food and drink, or perhaps it was just an orgy of self-satisfaction on Belshazzar's behalf that Babylon was safe from invasion. Certainly confidence abounded, for we are given to understand that over a thousand nobles were gathered at the feast.

Belshazzar could not have known, of course, because he was not addicted to reading the ancient Hebrew prophets, that two hundred years before the feast a Jewish prophet by the name of Isaiah had foretold the downfall of Babylon in the following words:

*Thus saith the Lord to his annointed, to Cyrus, whose right hand I have holden, to subdue nations before him; and I will loose the loins of kings, to open before him two leaved gates; and the gates shall not be shut.*
The Book of the prophet Isaiah. Chapter 45:1

That fateful night, the night of Belshazzar's feast, two hundred years after that prophecy had been uttered, as Belshazzar and his court drank and desecrated the vessels of the Temple which they had looted, the Medo-Persian army were busy outside the city.

As Belshazzar roared his songs of merriment, shovels were digging an alternative channel for the River Euphrates to divert it from running through the city. Soon the river was diverted into it's old bed, which by-passed the city, and the river bed which ran through the city was dry.

Yet there should have been two mighty leaved gates to stop the invading army, but, history tells us, ON THAT NIGHT THE LEAVED GATES

WERE LEFT OPEN, EXACTLY AS THE PROPHET ISAIAH HAD
FORETOLD TWO HUNDRED YEARS BEFORE!

Babylon fell in exactly the way the prophet had foretold centuries
before. Coincidence or supernatural intervention?

Who was the commander of the invading army? Why, Cyrus, of course
— the very name the prophet had given two hundred years before.

So the first beast of Daniel passed into history and the second 'Beast'
thundered onto the world stage.

## THE SECOND BEAST OF DANIEL –
## THE MEDO-PERSIAN EMPIRE.

Because the prophet Daniel does not take much space in dealing with the
second and third 'Beasts' neither shall I.

The Medo-Persian Empire lasted for a little over two hundred years
before being defeated by the Greeks. It's end came when Alexander the
Great, with some 50,000 men, defeated a Persian army of over 1,000,000
men.

## THE THIRD BEAST OF DANIEL – THE GRECIAN EMPIRE.

History attests the military prowess of Alexander the Great, but he, too,
had his frailties. He died a drunkard's death and his government was
thrown into confusion.

On the death of Alexander, the Grecian kingdom was divided. The one
part of the kingdom was lost when Philip V was defeated at Pydna in 168
B.C. and the other part of the kingdom lost when Corinth was destroyed
by Mummius in 146 B.C.

It is significant that, albeit unconsciously, Alexander the Great
confirmed that he was in the great succession of Babylonian world powers
by making his home in Babylon.

## THE FOURTH BEAST OF DANIEL – THE ROMAN EMPIRE.

We shall see that the fourth Beast of Daniel and the first Beast of John
in the Apocalypse, are one and the same.

I have remarked that Daniel does not lay much emphasis on the second
and third beasts, rather as though they were mere interludes in history
between two mighty events. Daniel regarded the fourth beast or fourth
empire as being the most important of all for he devotes much space to a
vivid description of it and to the interpretation of what it represents. Here
is what he says about the fourth beast:

*Then I would know the truth of the fourth beast, which was*
*diverse from all the others, exceedingly dreadful, whose teeth*

*were of iron, and it's nails of bronze, which devoured, broke in pieces, and stamped the residue with it's feet. And of the ten horns that were in it's head, and of the other which came up, and before whom three fell; even of that horn that had eyes, and a mouth that spoke very great things, whose look was more stout than it's fellows.*

Now let us compare the fourth beast of Daniel with the first beast of the Apocalypse, always remembering that the two men wrote separated by seven hundred years.

## THE FIRST BEAST OF THE APOCALYPSE.

I will summarise the vision of the two beasts which John had on the Isle of Patmos.

He saw a beast coming out of the sea — Daniel's four beasts came out of the sea.

The first beast of John had a 'mouth like a lion' and Daniel described his first beast as being 'like a lion'.

John's first beast had the 'feet of a bear' and Daniel describes his second beast as being 'like a bear'.

The first beast of John is described by him as being 'like a leopard' and Daniel's third beast was said by Daniel to be 'like a leopard'.

John's first beast had 'ten horns' and Daniel's fourth beast also had 'ten horns'.

It is impossible to escape the conclusion that the first beast of John was, in fact, nothing less than the embodiment of all the four beasts of Daniel.

Compare carefully the beasts of Daniel and the first beast of John in our comparison chart on page and you will be in no doubt that John's beast is the culmination of all that had gone before.

There can be absolutely no doubt, therefore, that the first beast of the Apocalypse is nothing less than the embodiment of the gentile world empires which had afflicted the land of Palestine, the Jewish people and Jerusalem from the time of Daniel to 96 A.D. when John wrote.

We can therefore be quite certain that what John saw was the gentile world system to HIS TIME. However, in A.D. 96 the beast had yet a long time to live and was to undergo several transformations. The beast of John's Apocalypse was AT THAT TIME the Roman Empire.

## WHY IS THAT OF INTEREST TO US TODAY?

Because the beast was to live on to the end of our age and we are all to be affected by his existence. Both Daniel and John foretell that the beast will have world-wide influence immediately prior to the Battle of Armageddon.

I repeat again what the prophet John said about the years preceding the last great battle of earth's history — a battle which we have seen is about to take place.

*And I saw three unclean spirits, like frogs, come out of the mouth of the dragon and out of the mouth of the beast, and out of the mouth of the false prophet. For they are the spirits of demons, working miracles, that go forth unto the kings of the earth and of the WHOLE WORLD, to gather them to the battle of that great day of God Almighty.*

The Book of Revelation 16: 13, 14

Though the identity of the beast must be judged by it's relationship to the Jews, Palestine and Jerusalem, there is no nation on earth whose people can afford to be disinterested in the identity of the beast for it's existence will have a profound effect on all our lives.

The beast is, in these 'last days', to be one of the agencies instrumental in gathering the nations of the world together for the Third World War, that great conflict, which according to the prophets will be fought in Palestine on the plains of Meggido.

## WHO IS THE BEAST – 666?

There are two answers beloved of students of the prognostications of the ancient seers, many of whom will agree with my reasoning so far. Few, however, will agree with my conclusions from here on.

It is often believed that the second beast of the Apocalypse, which is to arise in the 'last days', is to be a 'revival' of the fourth beast of Daniel and the first beast of the Apocalypse.

There is a modicum of truth in that view. I cannot subscribe, however, to the view that the succession of the beast is to be expected to appear in Europe in the 'last days'. The theory has it that pagan Rome was succeeded by the Holy Roman Empire and that it therefore follows that either the Papacy must be the beast or there will be a revival of the Holy Roman Empire in Europe in the 'last days'.

This faulty exegesis arises because European man finds it unthinkable that any other part of the world than Europe should be the centre of political power.

The beast in all it's manifestations for over 2500 years has always existed in connection with Palestine, the Jews and Jerusalem and there seems to me to be no good reason why that should not continue to be so.

Much is made of the phrase "And his (the beast's) deadly wound was healed", but to assume from that that the beast was ever to be wounded to death is to wrench the text from it's context. It was only 'one of it's heads' which was wounded not the beast itself. The beast itself has never gone out of existence, a brief look at the history of Jerusalem shows that the beast was there carrying out his function until 1917 when the 'times of the gentiles' were fulfilled.

The false view that the old Holy Roman Empire would be revived has sidetracked many into accepting the theory that the European Community is, in fact, the revived Roman Empire. The fact that it is founded on the Treaty of Rome has, perhaps justifiably, misled some into accepting that view. Once having accepted the premise, it then becomes inevitable that the Papacy comes under suspicion as being either part of the beastly function or Babylon or both.

To maintain that the beast is either the Roman Catholic Church or the nations of Europe as a revived Holy Roman Empire is to ignore entirely the fact that Palestine was, is and always will be the centre of prophecy. The beast has nothing to do with Europe, except to the extent it will involve the whole world in conflict.

More important even than the aforementioned arguments, is that the view that the beast is to be a European revival of the Holy Roman Empire is historically untenable, for the Holy Roman Empire in Europe did not inherit the beastly succession historically.

## THE DIVISION OF THE ANCIENT ROMAN EMPIRE.

We are agreed, I think, to the point where we can identify the beast as being the Roman Empire at the time of the writing of the Apocalypse in 96 A.D.

We have to agree, too, because history is plain on the point, that the beastly succession of power passed from one empire to the next by the conquest of Palestine. There seems no logical reason why the method of succession should be changed in the case of either the first or second beasts of the Apocalypse.

Who followed Rome as conqueror of Jerusalem? The answer to that question gives us irrefutable evidence as to who continued the beastly succession after Rome.

"The Times Atlas of World History" gives a very clear account of the division of the Roman Empire. Commenting on the division of the Roman Empire into eastern and western, it says:

"The centre of gravity was shifted eastwards: hence Constantine established a new capital and a Christian city at Byzantium, renamed Constantinople (330), while a new taxation system resulted in an economic revival. But further decline was merely postponed, not overcome. Although theoretically governed by joint rulers, the Empire gradually broke into an eastern and western half, and outlying provinces fell to barbarian invaders. Rome itself was sacked by the Visigoth Alaric (410) and the

Vandal Gaeseric (455); and in 493 an Ostrogothic kingdom was established in Italy. THE WESTERN EMPIRE HAD FALLEN TO THE INVADERS, while Justinians attempt in the mid-sixth century to reunite the two halves led to no permanent reunion. YET IN THE EAST THE BYZANTINE EMPIRE SURVIVED FOR ANOTHER THOUSAND YEARS, UNTIL THE CAPTURE OF CONSTANTINOPLE BY THE TURKS IN 1453."

Even judged by the standard of secular history, the succession of the Roman Empire did not reside in Europe.

The Roman Empire divided into two parts, the western and the eastern empires: Much confusion has arisen among interpreters of the ancient seers because they have not taken this fact into account. Following the Roman Empire in the conquest of Palestine was the BYZANTINE EMPIRE. Thus the 'title deed' passed not to the western Roman Empire but to the BYZANTINE EMPIRE.

Under Byzantine rule Palestine was divided into three parts — Palaestina Prima, Secunda and Tertia.

Though the Byzantine Empire endured for a thousand years after the western Roman Empire had disintegrated, it did not endure in it's 'beastly' succession for nearly that long.

Jerusalem fell to Islam in 634 B.C. and from 660 B.C. onwards Palestine was ruled by the Omayyad dynasty. There followed rule by various Muslim dynasties and thus the gentile beast continued it's control of Palestine.

In 1099 the crusaders swept into the land, slaughtering most of the Moslems and Jews who were living there in the process. Though the crusaders' rule was interspersed with periods of challenge and counter-challenge it was not until 1291 A.D. the rule of the crusaders came to an end.

Subsequently a cast of ex-slaves came to power in Egypt. The military-minded "Mamelukes", for such they styled themselves, drove the crusaders out of the Holy Land and took control.

In 1516 Palestine was conquered by the Ottoman (Turkish) Emperor Selim I. From that time until the fateful year 1917 the Turks ruled Jerusalem.

The history of Jerusalem and it's various conquerors is long and fascinating and I feel it such a pity that space forbids that I give no more than this brief outline. I think, however, that what I have said will be sufficient to show the unerring accuracy of the ancient seers and the unique place Jerusalem has in the history of mankind.

You will remember that the four beasts of Daniel and the first beast of John in the Apocalypse were to exist for 2520 years. It was exactly 2520 years from the time Nebuchadnezzar, that great Babylonian beast of Daniel, entered Jerusalem to the year the British army drove the Turks from the Holy City.

Both Daniel and John had said that the beast would have ten horns but only seven heads upon which those horns would grow:

*And I saw a beast rise up out of the sea, having SEVEN HEADS and TEN HORNS.*

Revelation 13:1

In verse 12 of Chapter 17 of the Book of Revelation, we are told what the 'horns' represent:

*And the ten horns which thou sawest are ten kings.*

Is it coincidence that the empires which controlled Palestine from the time of King Nebuchadnessar to the deliverance by the British army in 1917 were exactly ten?

| Babylon | Medo-Persia | Greece | Rome | Byzantine |
|---------|-------------|-----------|-----------|-----------|
| Moslem | Holy Roman | Crusaders | Mameluke | Turkish |

Exactly ten, the number of 'kings' or leaders the prophet saw symbolised by the horns of the beast. The beast, however, only had seven 'heads' out of which the horns grew.

Babylon     Medo-Persia     Greece     are three separate heads.
Rome     Byzantine     Holy Roman Empire     are out of one head.
Moslem     one head.
Turks     are one head.
Mameluke     is one head.

Is it again coincidence that though the horns were ten they actually grew out of seven different 'heads'?

## THE BEAST OF THE LAST DAYS.

We have seen that the first beast of the Apocalypse was finally destroyed in 1917, exactly 2520 years after it had first afflicted Palestine and the Jews.

The prophet John, however, foresaw a second beast which would come upon the political scene in the 'last days' and cause the power of the first beast to be revived.

You will recollect that John said of the first beast:

*And I saw ONE of his heads as though it were wounded to death;*
*and his deadly wound was healed, and all the world wondered*
*after the beast.*

The Book of Revelation 13:3

We have seen that the last form of the first beast of the Apocalypse was not Roman but Turkish. The 'horn' was Turkish but the 'head' upon which it grew was Moslem.

The head which was wounded to death is therefore Islam.

We have already witnessed in amazement a revival in Islam. It is quite true to say that the world has witnessed this phenomenon in wonder.

Come back with me to the turn of the century, the First World War is yet fourteen years in the future, oil is not in great demand and the European powers virtually control the world. The Islamic world is disspirited and, apart from the Turks, unarmed. Those eighty years ago it seemed as though Islam had been wounded to death — certainly a far cry from the heady days when Islam, having subdued the whole of the Mediterranean African coast, swept into Spain and France.

The world has wondered at the recent Islamic revival but the world will wonder the more in the near future, for the prophets predict that we are about to see a revival in Islam which will cause the whole world to 'wonder'.

Listen to how the prophet John describes this coming political event:

*And I beheld another beast coming up out of the earth; and he*
*had two horns like a lamb, and he spoke like a dragon.*
*AND HE EXERCISETH ALL THE POWER OF THE FIRST*
*BEAST BEFORE HIM, and causeth the earth and them that*
*dwell on it to worship the first beast, whose deadly wound was*
*healed ... And he hath power to give life unto the image of the*
*beast, that the image of the beast should both speak, and cause*
*that as many as would not worship the image of the beast should*
*be killed. And he causeth all, both small and great, rich and poor,*
*free and enslaved, to receive a mark in their right hand, or in their*
*foreheads. And that no man might buy or sell, except he that had*
*the mark, or the name of the beast, or the number of his name.*
*Here is wisdom. Let him that hath understanding count the*
*number of the beast; for it is the number of a man; and his*
*number is six hundred, three score and six [666].*

The Book of Revelation 13: 11,12,15,16,17 & 18.

Some commentators have spent much time in looking for various marks which may be interpreted as being "The Mark of the Beast". There is really no justification for assuming that people are actually going to have a brand mark or a tattoo mark on their right hand or their forehead.

I would say to students of the prophets who insist upon the mark of the beast being a literal mark, that, to be consistent, they must expect Christians to have "Jehovah" marked or branded on their foreheads for does not John say iń chapter 14:

*And I looked, and, lo, a Lamb stood on Mount Zion and with him an hundred forty and four thousand, having his Father's name WRITTEN IN THEIR FOREHEADS.*

Why WILL people always miss the point? The point the prophet is making is that the beast will have world-wide economic power, he will sit astride world trade.

The whole world will wonder after the beast whose deadly wound was healed! We ARE beginning to wonder! When the oil producing nations speak the world holds it's breath. Since the Second World War every civilised nation on earth has become totally dependant on oil. Without oil the great war machines of the super-powers would become inoperable, world industry would suffer a complete collapse and commerce would be thrown into confusion.

In his book "The Unholy War", Marius Baar writes:

"Financial analysts estimate that Middle East oil nations may amass $500 billion of investment money in the next five years. This sum would have BOUGHT EVERY SHARE TRADED ON THE NEW YORK STOCK EXCHANGE IN 1978 AND 1979."

Let us make no mistake; Islam is about to become the most powerful empire the world has EVER SEEN — I do not use those words lightly. The day is coming, according to the ancient seers, and very soon, according to the signs of the times, when the whole world will be unable to carry on trade and commerce except to the extent they do so by permission of Islam

And the power of the Islamic world is not only in their oil. They now hold considerable amounts of property, shares, gold and currency. It is frightening to think what would happen if every Arab nation withdrew the money it has invested in the West.

We have, of late, seen the commencement of this predicted period when men will be able to neither buy nor sell without having the mark of the beast in their hands or in their foreheads; The age of subservience to the beast has commenced.

When the Iranian revolution unseated the Shah, who would have thought that the United States of America and Britain would behave as they did? I do not defend the Shah but, whether rightly or wrongly, the West had encouraged him to think of himself as an ally. Ultimately, to placate Islamic feeling, the West abandoned him. Many world leaders must now wonder if it is really very sensible to depend on the power of either Britain or America for their defence.

It is to the eternal credit of the much maligned President Richard Nixon that he went to Egypt to publicly pay his last respects to his former ally.

Would Britain and America have cared what Iran thought of their actions fifteen years ago? No! That is just one small sign of the many which show how the balance of world power is changing.

The American hostage issue was another indication of how the West fears the ability of the Islamic countries to bring our economy to a grinding halt. Let's not forget that we live in early days yet, the fear will deepen in the years to come.

On British television a while ago there appeared a film entitled "The Death of a Princess" in which there were scenes which offended the Saudi-Arabians. Would one not think that the British Government would make it plain to foreign governments that we have a tradition of free speech? No-one complains when rather blasphemous stuff, from a Christian point of view, is shown. However, when the Arabs speak it seems our most cherished traditions are open for discussion. The British Foreign Secretary went to Saudi-Arabia and actually apologised for the film having been shown — such already is the power of a threatened trade boycott by Arab nations.

## THE SECOND BEAST GIVING LIFE TO THE FIRST BEAST.

At the time the second beast appears on earth the prophet John sees the first beast as an 'image'. We all know what an image is, it is a likeness of someone which has no life in it.

There could not be a more accurate description of Islam from the time of it's decline, 'the deadly wound', until the recent Islamic revival began. Islam is no longer a lifeless 'image', it now both moves and speaks.

The great Islamic revival has started and if anyone thinks we are witnessing a purely Iranian phenomenon they are sadly mistaken. The prophet foretells that the second beast will exercise "All the power of the first beast before him". Well may we contemplate that mighty surge of religious fervour which took Islam to world conquest.

Islam is returning to it's old doctrines and it's people back to their old loyalties. That which was stone-like and dead is coming back to life. The new leaders of Islam have already caused a major miracle to happen but what has happened is as nothing to that which is to happen.

## THE NEW WORLD ISLAMIC MAP IS ALREADY IN PRODUCTION.

There are many moderate forces in Islam, one thinks of the late President Sadat and of men of the ilk of Sheik Yamani. According to the ancient seers, however, such men are not to be in the ascendancy. The

Ayatollah Khomeini, or a person of similar persuasions, is to be the kind of Muslim to whom the Islamic world will turn for it's salvation.

Viewed from the West, Islam looks to be a rather insignificant religious sect and probably the predictions of the ancient seers seem, even now, to be something of an exaggeration. That Islam should wield such world-wide power, even given the fact that they have oil, still does not seem possible.

Let the West be warned, Islam is no insignificant sect. The military power of Islam will, within a very few years, make the power of the Axis forces in the Second World War look as a toy army. There are 800 million Muslims in the world, many of them at the moment paying token homage to their religion, but a great awakening is coming such as the awakening that swept the Muslim armies through the Mediterranean coasts of Africa, into Spain and France.

While Britain, America, Europe, the Soviet Union and her satellites, wallow in the troughs of economic confusion, the Islamic nations stash away their almost uncountable billions of oil revenue. They have the manpower, they have the money, and soon, they will have the arms — what then?

On Sunday 7th February 1982 the "Sunday Times' published an article from which the following is taken:

## "HOW THE MULLAHS EXPORT REVOLUTION"

### by Amir Taheri

"A NEW WORLD MAP, published in Tehran and dedicated to Ayatollah Khomeini, divides the planet into three zones: black for 'Grand Satan America and it's colonies,' red for 'Heathen Russia and it's dominions', and green for 'the universal Islamic Republic representing the will of Allah'.

The map, published on the third anniversary of the republic, defines the Islamic world from Indonesia to Morocco. It includes the Muslim republics of the USSR, Albania and Muslim inhabited parts of Yugoslavia as a single entity under the "Imam".

The creation of an Islamic world power is central to Khomeini's scenario for universal salvation ..."

World domination is the aim of the revolutionary leaders in Islam, as yet they have had startling but limited success, soon however they will become all powerful.

# THE MYSTERIOUS WORLD DICTATOR – THE BEAST 666.

We have seen that the four beasts of Daniel and the two beasts of John were in fact a succession of nations which afflicted the land of Palestine and the city of Jerusalem throughout the ages.

As we have followed the history of Palestine and the nations which have trodden down that afflicted country, we have seen that the last in the line of succession were the Turks in 1917.

In that year the world entered into the final phase of it's history as we know it. The 'run-in' to the day of that great culminating battle of earth's history began as General Allenby pronounced those historic words "I have come not as conqueror but as deliverer." That Jerusalem had ceased to be trodden down was confirmed later in the same fateful year when Lord Balfour declared that there should be a national home for the Jews in Palestine.

We are, as prophesied, seeing the re-appearance of the 'head' of the beast, the deadly wound of which was healed. There is good news for Islam in the prognostications of the ancient seers and there is bad news.

If we take the good news first, it is that the new Islamic Empire is destined to become an empire of such power and magnificence that the whole world will stand in awe and wonder. This mighty empire will sit astride the means of economic survival of the nations of the world, will demand, and obtain, their allegiance in return for sustaining their economic well-being. In the words of the prophet, the nations of the world will neither be able to buy nor sell unless they have the mark (the Assent) of the beast.

Make no mistake about this fact — not Babylon, nor Greece, nor Rome at the height of their glory, will have had the might that the latter day Islamic Empire will have at the zenith of it's power.

The bad news for the leaders of Islam, however, is that there is in existence a power which will become head of their mighty empire and so transform it that it will not be recognisable as the Islam they have known. The prophet John speaks of "The dragon who gave power unto the beast."

You will remember that in that Apocalyptic vision of the personages responsible for gathering the world together to the Battle of Armageddon, there were three — the beast, the dragon and the false prophet.

## THE WAR OF THE WORLDS.

It is central to the teachings of the ancient seers that there are powerful forces in existence which, though unseen by man, seek to control planet earth. This war of the 'spirit world' is obviously beyond the ken of twentieth century man, and we could discount the possibility of it existing at all were not the ancient seers accurate in so many of their predictions. We should consider though, that mankind has no proof of the non-existence of such supernatural combatants other than the fact that they cannot be seen — but then neither can the force of gravity be seen.

Twentieth century man has reduced the notion of a contest between 'good' and 'evil' — a concept which exists in almost all of earth's religions — to a mere philosophical concept. To the ancient seers, however, 'God' and the 'Devil' were no simple personifications of certain qualities. The 'spirit world' was very real to them and they regarded it as having very real power to control and influence the affairs of men. The great battle for supremacy which raged throughout, what we shall call for the want of a more precise term 'the heavens' was the battle of battles — the battle of which all earthly battles were merely symptomatic.

## THE BEAST PERSONIFIED.

The four beasts of Daniel and the two beasts of John were to be national systems but in the last of the two beasts of John the spirit that had motivated the whole of the gentile world system was to become incarnate. The final beast is not only to be a national system, it is to be — A MAN. About this fact John is quite emphatic.

*And here is wisdom. Let him that hath understanding count the number of the beast; for it is the number of A MAN; and HIS number is six hundred three score and six.*
                                    The Book of Revelation 13:18

Prophetic commentators have often made a mistake which has badly misled them in their attempts to identify the last beast, they have assumed that the beast will be a united entity. They seem to have missed completely the plain historic fact that none of the succession of beasts have had very much in common, nor have they been nations united or in formal alliances. The one function they have ALL performed is that of treading down Palestine and Jerusalem, but apart from that function they have had little love one for the other. One only has to read the history of Babylon, Medo-Persia, Greece and Rome to realise that they engaged ferociously in both internal and external conflict.

That the final beast will also be both united in it's role as persecutor of the Jews and invader of Palestine and torn within itself by strife is plain. It is plain, too, that this final beast will have a further function, one not performed by the previous beasts. In addition to it's function as persecutor of the Jews (the House of Judah), it will also be at enmity with the House of Israel. The reason none of the previous beasts fulfilled this task is because the House of Israel was 'lost' and unknown to them during their existence.

# A VITAL CLUE TO THE MYSTERY MAN – 666.

In his book "The 'Age of Uncertainty'', Professor J. K. Galbraith writes:

"If we agree that the Bible is a work of collective authorship, only Mohammed rivals Marx in the number of professed and devoted followers recruited by a single author. And the competition is not really very close. The followers of Marx now far outnumber the sons of the Prophet."

Of course, Professor Galbraith makes an altogether unsubstantiated assumption regarding the number of "professed and devoted" Marxists there are. Who can possibly know? No country which embraces the Marxist philosophy has ever had a general election. Until such a time as the Marxist masters of the Communist nations see fit to allow properly supervised secret ballots, we shall not know how many Marxists there are in the world.

The Professor is correct, however, if we substitute his words "professed and devoted followers" the words "subjected human beings". Whilst every Communist country has to enforce, often with the death penalty, emigration controls, I cannot myself accept that there are nearly as many enthusiastic Marxists as Professor Galbraith would have us believe. Perhaps living in a Marxist society is a cure for Marxism.

It may be that Professor Galbraith did not realise that, writing that paragraph, he was confirming very much what the prophet John had predicted some nineteen hundred years before.

Marxism cannot, of course, be ignored in any discussion of the modern or, for that matter, historic, political scene. More people are enslaved by Marxist governments than have been enslaved by any dictatorial regime in the history of mankind.

Of the several remarkable things about Marx, one is that such an intellectual lightweight should have affected the history of the world so profoundly. It is remarkable too, that as his life-style testified, since he had no real convictions or concern regarding the plight of the poor or even his own family for that matter, people should have given him a credence after his death which was withheld from him during his lifetime.

Marx was, during his life, no grand and glorious revolutionary as some would have us believe, but rather the possessor of a fevered mind with a self-assessment which at times bordered on paranoia.

He followed in a family tradition of opportunism and treachery, constantly seeking power at the expense of principle, even then not finding it. His father had betrayed his Judaism because it was politically and commercially expedient to do so, and embraced Christianity only for as long as that was useful to him. Karl Marx, too, at one time wrote evangelical discourses that would have done credit to Billy Graham. So it was that the family proceeded from Judaism to Christianity and onward toward whatever bright horizon beckoned at the time.

A biography of Marx which should be read by everyone who has an interest in the politics of our day is "Marx" by Robert Payne. Mr. Payne's work does not suffer from the prejudice of political commitment, his subject has been thoroughly researched and he brings to us the man behind the legend. I quote from his introduction:

> "The man described in these pages has very little in common with the infallible oracle worshipped by the Communists. He (Marx) was human and vulnerable, only too vulnerable. He was far from being a paragon of Communist Virtues. He went on monumental pub crawls, speculated on the stock exchange, seduced his maidservant, fathered an illegitimate child, dallied with aristocratic young women, and enjoyed his visits to expensive watering places, where he would consort with the wealthy and the privileged. Bakunin accused him of being a police spy, but this was an understatement, for he delivered the documents of the International into the hands of the British Home Secretary, the head of the police. He exploited everyone around him — his wife, his children, his mistress and his friends — with a ruthlessness which was all the more terrible because it was deliberate and calculating. His tastes were those of a feudal aristocrat."

As Mr. Payne points out: "We live in the age of Marx. A thousand million people, nearly half the world, are ruled by governments which claim to be practising his teachings ..."

## THE NUMBER OF A MAN.

I have said that the number 666 has been variously interpreted and applied to numerous personages throughout the ages. As I mentioned in an earlier chapter, every number in the writings of the ancient seers has a significance.

Number six is the number of man, the number which depicts the limit of the extent of human achievement, the number of materialism.

If we have to look for the identity of that which bears the number of man, or materialism, and came to fruition in the year 1917 we have no further to look than Marxism.

## DIALETICAL MATERIALISM.

Materialism is the central theme of Marxism. Man is seen by him as master of his own destiny. Half the people living on this planet have, in the past 65 years, been brought under a political system which is quite literally

666 — man first, man last, and anything inbetween man again.

In the article on "Dialectical Materialism" in Encyclopaedia Britannica, the following point is made:

"Marx and Engels understood materialism as the opposite to 'idealism' by which they meant any theory which treats matter as dependent on mind or spirit, or mind or spirit as capable of existing independent of matter. For them, the materialistic and idealistic views were irreconcilably opposed, throughout the historical development of philosophy. They adopted a thorough going MATERIALISTIC approach, holding that any attempt to combine or reconcile materialism with idealism must lead to confusion and inconsistency. Stressing the priority of matter and the secondary or derivative character of mind and ideas, they denied the possibility of supernatural or transcendental reality."

Karl Marx was contradiction personified: A man who taught that man had no need of spirituality or God and was indeed master of his own destiny, and yet a man who in his early years was an evangelical Christian and was NEVER an atheist.

MARXISM, however, is purely man orientated. Man, the great SIX of the ancient seers and the numerologist, is the very element of which Marxism is composed. Never in any philosophy has the saying of Jesus "Man cannot live by bread alone" been so completely denied. Marxism is the greatest materialistic dogma of our time — all but forbidding religious instruction to half the people of this earth.

*And here is wisdom ... count the number of the beast ... it is the number of a man ... six hundred, three score and six.*

Nothing from the beginning to the end of the personified beast was to have any other quality, the whole thing was to be man centred. The only worship was to be on the altar of materialism.

We must differentiate between Marx and Marxism. Marx is dead — Marxism is very much alive. Marx was no atheist as he claimed — Marxism is an absolutely atheistic philosophy.

An 'agnostic' is one who professes not to know whether God exists — a doubter. An 'atheist' affirms there is no God as a statement of belief. Karl Marx was a profound believer in the existence of God and the Devil to his dying day. So the great contradiction between Marx and his teaching remains.

Is it not a vindication of the prognostication of John in the Apocalypse that a philosophy of materialism should swamp half of mankind, commencing in the very year (1917) the prophet had foretold the beast with the mark 666 — the mark of materialism — would arise?

## THE WORLD SCENARIO FROM HERE ON.

I will now sum up this chapter, though I have more to say about Karl Marx in the next chapter.

1. Daniel the prophet, writing about 540 B.C. foresaw that four beasts (nations) would afflict Palestine — they did exactly as he foresaw.
2. Over 600 years later, the prophet John foresaw that the fourth beast of Daniel would have 'seven heads' and 'ten horns'.
3. Daniel, Jesus of Nazareth and John foresaw the 'Times of the Gentiles' lasting for 2520 years which expired in 1917.
4. By the time the British came to capture Jerusalem from the Turks, from the time of Daniel there had been exactly 'ten horns' or conquerors but they arose from seven 'heads' or sources.
5. We have traced the succession of beasts through history and found that Islam was the last form of Daniel's fourth beast and John's first beast. Islam was the head of this beast which was 'wounded to death'.
6. John foresaw this 'deadly wound' being healed in the last days and the beast reviving to such a degree that the whole world 'wondered after the beast'.
7. The beast was to receive it's power from a mysterious being called 'the dragon' and was to be ruled by 'A MAN' whose number would be the number of 'man' or 'materialism' 666. We have identified that as being Marxism or the doctrine of "Dialectical Materialism".
8. The man 666 set up his centre of power in the very nation Gog and Magog that the prophet Ezekial said would descend on Palestine in the 'last days' to the Battle of Armageddon. The Soviet Union is the centre and despensor of the doctrine of materialism (666.
9. We are about to witness a mighty and almost unbelievable upsurge in Islam. Though we see the first signs of an Islamic revival, that revival has a long way to go but it's going to go that 'long way' very quickly.
10. The personification of the beast will, however, take control of the revived Islamic Empire.

We shall see how Islam will be conquered by the beast 666 in a later chapter.

# 13.
# The
# Great
# Dragon

I have touched upon the fact that the ancient seers saw human history as being an extension of the "War of the Worlds". That they taught the absolute opposite view from Marxism is plain.

Though the ancient seers did not teach a "God of the Golden Throne" existed, nor that there was a Devil, with horns, forever poking an eternal fire — they did teach that powerful unseen forces were, and are, battling for supremacy and that human history reflected that spiritual battle.

The 'Beast' of the last days was to be powered by a being which John, in the Apocalypse, describes as the 'Dragon'. There is, in fact, no mystery about the identity of the dragon, for the prophet John made it's identity quite plain:

*And I saw an angel come down from heaven, having the key of the bottomless pit and a great chain in his hand. And he laid hold on the dragon, that old serpent, who is the Devil and Satan, and bound him a thousand years.*

Book of Revelation 20:2

We commenced our enquiry into the prognostications of the ancient seers by asking if there is an 'it' out there, or up there. The ancient seers are emphatic that there is not only an 'it' but several 'its' fighting for supremacy.

Those of a 'science fiction' turn of mind often speculate upon whether there is life on other planets. The ancient seers, I fear, have nothing to say on that subject but they put it beyond doubt their view was that there exists conscious, intelligent and powerful life in the universe around us. A life that is without form, as we know form, and yet has the ability not only to influence events on earth, but also to inhabit individuals and nations.

The prophet Paul developed this theme when he wrote:

*We wrestle not against flesh and blood, but against principalities, against powers, against the rulers of the darkness of this world, against spiritual wickedness in high places.*

Ephesians 6:12

I do not propose in this chapter to discourse upon the nature of the existence of 'God' and the 'Devil'. My purpose is to show that the seers did teach of this spiritual battle, and teach of it both consistently and emphatically.

Twenty years ago one would have been thought eccentric, to say the least, if one professed belief in an actual 'Devil'. The 'Devil' had been banished not only from our society but also from our pulpits. Man, it seemed, had had second thoughts about the existence of such a being — we began, quite irrationally, to believe in only those things we could see.

Today, however, there are signs that the 'Devil' is making a comeback. There are signs that there is a movement of opinion toward a belief in a phenomenon which had been discounted as being of a purely psychological origin — devil possession. Belief in the existence of a 'Devil' or 'Evil being' has emerged from the confines of the fringe religion and is now discussed quite openly and seriously among fairly traditionally thinking people. We often read in the press of the activities of 'Poltergeists' and the 'casting out of evil spirits' has become almost too common to report in any but local of papers. Not only the Church of England and the Roman Catholic Church, but the non-conformist denominations now are seen to, once again, take 'Devil possession' seriously.

I must ask you in all seriousness to consider, in the light of the accuracy of the prophets' prognostications, whether earth's history is moving forward under the guidance of an invisible hand, or of one or more pairs of invisible hands. Are there 'beings' 'out there' which may be within the comprehension of our faith but outside the comprehension of our intellect?

## THE DRAGON IN HISTORY SINCE 1917.

"The dragon which gave power to the beast." The prophet makes it plain that there is to be a unity between the 'dragon' or 'Devil' and the personalised beast 666.

The question we must ask is: Has the political system produced by 666 (Marxism) got roots in Satanism? If not, then it does not fit the bill. The beast 666, though MATERIALISTIC, must, according to the ancient seers, be rooted in Satanism.

I now make a startling claim — Karl Marx was not an atheist nor was he an agnostic, he was — A SATANIST!

The application of the political philosophy Marx propounded, though claiming to be atheistic, was and is Demonistic. I contend that the prophet who wrote the Apocalypse has been proved quite literally accurate when he wrote of the 'Devil' giving power to the beast. Marxism is a demonic philosophy.

If you remind me of the seemingly humanitarian objectives of the early Marxists I will remind you of the prophet John's description of the last beast who had *"Horns like a LAMB and spake like a DRAGON."*

Communism has followed it's founder well in it's ability to speak in one way and act in a way diametrically opposed to it's utterances. Was it not George Orwell, himself a convinced socialist, who, looking through satirical eyes at the Soviet system coined the phrase "double-think" and "newspeak"?

The chapter in Robert Payne's book "Marx", entitled "The Demons" commences: "There were times when Marx seemed to be possessed by demons, when rage overflowed in him and became poison, and he seemed to enter into a nightmare."

Certainly all that thinking men have ever associated with 'the works of the devil' have followed the teaching of Marxism, just as catastrophe followed him during his lifetime.

Of Marx' six children, two daughters committed suicide and two others died of malnutrition. One of Marx' sons-in-law also committed suicide. Marx' mother too, exhibited strange powers, foretelling the very day and hour of her own death fifty years previously.

It is, of course, part of the Satanic tradition to invert words and phrases — thus at the Satanic Mass is the Lord's Prayer recited backwards. Having been an evangelical Christian, Marx knew well the sanctity of the word "Emmanuel" meaning "God with us." Yet he chose to invert the word and write "Oulanem", a drama written by Marx which Communists are careful to suppress:

"Till I go mad and my heart is utterly changed, See this sword —
THE PRINCE OF DARKNESS SOLD IT TO ME."

Karl Marx

A colleague of Marx, Georg Jung wrote of him "Marx will surely chase God from his heaven and will even sue him, Marx calls Christian religion one of the most immoral of religions."

That doesn't sound very much like atheism, does it? You cannot chase someone who does not exist — it's like saying 'there's no dog there, I'll kick it'.

The Satanist, Moses Hess, introduced Karl Marx into the so-called "League of the Just" and wrote "Dr. Marx, my idol, will give the last kick to medieval religion and politics."

Edgar Bauer, describing various members of the club to which he and Marx belonged, wrote of Marx:

"Who comes rushing in, impetuous and wild —
Dark fellow from Trier, in fury raging,
Nor walks nor skips, but leaps upon his prey
In tearing rage, as one who leaps to grasp
Broad spaces of the sky and drag them down to earth,
Stretching his arms wide open to the heavens.
His evil fist is clenched, he roars interminably
AS THOUGH TEN THOUSAND DEVILS HAD HIM BY THE
HAIR."

Neither was the First International without it's Satanist connotations. Bakunin, an associate of Marx in the First International, wrote: "Satan is the first free-thinker and saviour of the world. He frees Adam and impresses the seal of humanity and liberty on his forehead, by making him disobedient."

I quote from a book by Don E. Stanton "Mystery 666":

"According to Bakunin, another early Communist was Proudhon, who also worshipped Satan, and wore the same hairstyle (as Marx). Proudhon wrote:
'We reach knowledge in spite of him (God), we reach society in spite of him. Every step forward is a victory in which we overcome the Divine.' He exclaims. 'God is stupidity and cowardice; God is hypocrisy and falsehood; God is tyranny and poverty; God is evil .... I swear, God, with my hands stretched out towards the

heavens, that you are nothing more than the executioner of my reason, the sceptre of my conscience ... God is essentially anti-civilised, anti-liberal, anti-human.' The link between Satanism and Communism is not coincidence but can be detected in many ways. Bukharin who was secretary-general of the Communist International, revealed that as early as twelve years of age, after reading the Book of Revelation, he longed to become the Anti-Christ. And realising that the Beast is the son of 'great whore' he insisted his mother confess to having been a harlot.

The same Bukharin wrote of his associate, Joseph Stalin, 'He is not a man, but a devil.' Is it coincidence that the first pseudonymn under which Stalin wrote was "Demonoshwile" which means "Demoniac"?"

None of the foregoing is consistent with Marx or the Communist party holding an atheistic position. How can there be such hatred of the non-existent?

Through the years the signs of a supernatural force in the affairs of Communism have become increasingly apparent. Whilst one cannot always accept what the press reports about conditions inside a country, the fact remains that we do not have to rely on press reports for the facts about the appalling brutality of Soviet oppression.

I say again, the human tragedy which is Communism is testified to by the millions of people willing to risk their all, including their lives, to get out of countries controlled by Marxism. To see, as I saw, the refugees from Cuba landing in the United States of America and to hear the stories of life in that country is harrowing in the extreme.

However, a mystery remains. It is, in fact, the same kind of mystery which surrounds the rise of Hitler to power — why, despite the human oppression and the economic failure of the whole Marxist system are there so-called intellectual people who are persuaded to infiltrate it into our colleges? Do they not realise that were they to bring Marxist government to Britain and America, they would be subjecting their own children to the very kind of society from which millions of men and women are trying to escape?

Why do men follow failure, for failure Marxism has certainly proved to be? It is incongruous but true that the Soviet block could not exist today without the constant financial assistance of the capitalist world. We must be out of our minds in the West, to lend money to Soviet industry at LESSER rates of interest than our banks will lend money to either British or American industry. Britain and America continue to bolster the economy of the Soviet Union and her imprisoned countries, we continue to feed the Russian millions who, as a direct result of the failure of the Marxism economic theory cannot feed themselves. Meanwhile the Soviets divert the resources we send them to build massive weaponry systems to use against us. One feels that such insanity cannot exist even among that admittedly unbalanced section of our community — politicians. Why, then, does it happen? Is it because there is some 'power' permeating the world as the ancient seers foretold there would be?

## HITLER WAS A SOCIALIST.

Of course, Karl Marx did not only spawn the Soviet Union, he was also 'father' of Hitler's Germany.

Socialism has played a trick on the world in coining the phrases 'left' and 'right' to classify political beliefs. Masters of the techniques of propaganda, the socialists have gradually infiltrated their interpretation of history into our minds via their control of the classroom, university campus and media, until they can brainwash most of us into believing exactly what they want us to believe.

The Marxist Socialist will always be prepared to describe any police action designed to protect the innocent as being "Gestapo tactics", whereupon there is a 'Public Enquiry' and some old dodderer, having swallowed the bait, shackles the police and brings the day of revolution a stage nearer.

The 'rights of man' and 'civil rights' are phrases which trip very lightly off the tongue of our Marxist activist but we should always be aware that the only right a Marxist wants is the right for Marxism to take control of society. After that 'democratic right' has been achieved, the tables are turned and there must then be no right of opposition, because that would be called by an emotive name — 'revisionism'.

In a Marxist society man has only one right — the right to do as he is ordered. Trade unions do not exist as a bargaining entity, but rather as an instrument by which workers can be controlled and as an exercise in pseudo-democracy. One is therefore inclined to wonder why Marxists in the Trade Unions of free countries wish to destroy the rights their members have by aiding the election of Marxist governments.

Cut through all the nonsense talked by Marxist Socialists and you have a system which differs not one jot or tittle from the system operated by Hitler in Nazi Germany and Mussolini in Fascist Italy.

True 'Internationalism' is widely propagated but it is the same kind of 'internationalism' Hitler envisaged. The Polish worker is not autonomous, the internationalism of Moscow extends only to allowing the captive states within their orbit to do their bidding.

The Marxist Socialist international has absolved itself in the eyes of the world from the happenings of the Second World War by creating these artificial distinctions 'left' and 'right'.

It may be claimed that Hitler connived with capitalism to obtain and retain power, and so he did, but the Soviet Union and the Communist block are STILL conniving with capitalism to retain power, for without capitalist money, and capitalist-provided food, there would not be a Soviet block.

## HITLER WAS ALSO A SATANIST.

Who has ever explained in a satisfactory manner, how a whole race of civilised people could be led to such horrific acts by a person whom historians have seen fit to label as a 'madman'?

Gerald Suster, in his thoroughly researched work "Hitler and the Age of Horus" has made a very important contribution to the understanding of a phenomenon which many of us witnessed in our lifetime.

Nothing, I think, in human history and outside of the Soviet Union, has happened on the scale of that which happened in Nazi Germany during the years 1933-45. Even now many of us, our minds finding the events of those years beyond comprehension, still feel the years of the holocaust have the quality of a nightmare. Certainly nobody would have thought for a moment that civilised man could have descended to such depths. Of course, there are always those in a nation capable of dastardly acts, but a whole nation suddenly going berserk has to have a deeper explanation than 'mass hysteria'.

There is a point, a point of revulsion, beyond which the majority of human beings will not go. None of the biographers of Hitler have been able to comprehend why an unimpressive, semi-literate drop-out should suddenly galvanise a nation into the most appalling behaviour. In physique, the man was unimpressive, and yet he had a power which forced people to obey his will and to follow him, often to the death.

## THE ORDER OF THE GREEN DRAGON.

Marx and Hitler shared a bitter hatred of both the Russians and the Jews, both were racists of the worst order. It is surprising to see how Marx, the German, influenced the history of Russia and how one, George Ivanovitch Gurdjieff, was to affect the history of Germany.

Gurdjieff became a Tibetan lama, and took the name Dorjeff. After initiation into the various occult mysteries in Asia, following his period as a lama, he gave instruction in esoteric subjects in St. Petersburgh, Russia. The declared nature of his teachings was: "My way to develop the hidden potentialities of man; a way that is against Nature and against God."

Among Gurdjieff's pupils was one Karl Haushofer — one of Karl Haushofer's pupils was to be ADOLF HITLER.

Haushofer became a member of the esoteric society of the Green Dragon. There is every possibility that Rasputin was also a member of this secret order for his gift to the Russian Tsarina of a pair of green dragons is a matter of history — they were found sewn into her bodice in 1918.

It is no secret that Hitler believed in astrology, for we are accustomed to reading of the impatience of his generals because he often made decisions based upon astrological forecasts rather than military considerations.

## THE SATANIST DIETRICH ECKHART.

In the final paragraph of "Mein Kampf", Adolf Hitler gives a clue to his Satanism:

"I wish at the end of the second volume to remind the supporters and champions of our doctrine of those eighteen heroes, to whom I have dedicated the first volume of my work, those heroes who sacrificed themselves for us all with the clearest consciousness. They must forever recall the wavering and the weak to the fulfillment of his duty, a duty which they themselves in the best faith carried to it's final consequence. And among them I want also to count that man, one of the best, who devoted his life to the awakening of his, our people, in his writings and his thoughts and finally in his deeds: DIETRICH ECKHART."

Were it not for the work of Gerald Suster (and I commend a reading of "Hitler and the Age of Horus" to those who are still baffled by Hitler's astounding success in persuading people to do his will) the name of Dietrich Eckhart might well have remained unnoticed at the conclusion of Mein Kampf. I quote from Mr. Suster's book:

"Who was Dietrich Eckhart, why was he 'one of the best', what were his writings, thoughts and deeds, and why was Hitler so impressed by him? According to Konrad Heiden, 'Eckhart undertook the spiritual formation of Adolf Hitler', and it is hence necessary that we inspect this teacher. Dietrich Eckhart, was an admirer of Schopenauer and Nietzsche and a dedicated occultist ... Eckhart believed that he was destined to prepare the way for his leader, and he spoke of this belief to his friends in the Thule Group ... He met Hitler at some time during 1919 and the two men with so many interests in common developed an instantaneous rapport. If Hitler had been unaware of the Thule Group and it's activities prior to joining the German Worker's Party, he soon learned, and Eckhart said of him to the Thulists: 'Here is the one for whom I was but the prophet and forerunner'"

Is there not something of an eerie similarity between that final sentence and that spoken by John the Baptist of his relationship to Jesus of Nazareth? We must wonder whether the similarity was intentional on Eckhart's part or perhaps indicative of some spiritual power attempting a counterfeit.

# THE POWER OF THULISM.

Suster quotes Pauwels and Bergier in their explanation of the beliefs of the Thulists:

"(Thule) ... was supposed to be an island that disappeared somewhere in the extreme North. Off Greenland? or Labrador? Like Atlantis, Thule was thought to have been the magic centre of a vanished civilisation. Eckhart and his friends believed that not all the secrets of Thule had perished. Beings intermediate between Man and other intelligent Beings from Beyond, would place at the disposal of the Initiates a reservoir of forces which could be drawn upon to enable Germany to dominate the world again and be the cradle of Supermen which would result from mutations of the human species. One day her legions would set out to annihilate everything that had stood in the way of the spiritual destiny of the Earth, and their leaders would be men who knew everything, deriving their strength from the very fountainhead of energy and guided by the great ones of the ancient world. Such were the myths on which the Aryan doctrine of Eckhart and Rosenberg was founded and which these 'prophets' of a MAGIC FORM OF SOCIALISM had instilled in the mediumistic mind of Hitler."

Gerald Suster comments "Suddenly under the tutelage of Eckhart, the ex-dropout and ex-corporal began to display extraordinary talents." Is it coincidence that Marx and Hitler, both socialists and both Satanists, should find their fulfilment in the very generation when the 'Dragon' was to aid the Beast in "going forth unto the kings of the earth and of the whole world to gather them together to the battle of that great day"? Was it coincidence that Hitler received his vision of a greater Germany in — 1917?

## MUSSOLINI – SOCIALIST AND SATANIST.

Mention 'Fascism' or Mussolini and the Marxist Socialist will talk about the 'right wing' — not a bit of it! Mussolini was as socialist as they come.

Marx is the 'father' of Fascism too! Though not as harsh a dictatorship as those of Russia and Germany, Stalin and Hitler, the Mussolini dictatorship was nevertheless warmongering and totally undemocratic.

To deny that Fascism sprang from Marxism because there were differences of opinion among fellow socialists, one would have to deny that Chinese Communism sprang from Marxism because Chairman Mao changed it's complexion and quarelled with Russia.

Mussolini's father was, within the extent of his limited education, a Marxist. He wrote articles for various Socialist journals and took every opportunity to persuade his fellow men of the benefits of socialism. His children, too, were required to endure readings at bedtime from political works rather than from the more usual children's night-time fare.

Benito Mussolini received his Christian name because of his father's admiration for the Mexican revolutionary Benito Juarez. Benito had another name, Andrea, which he received because of his father's admiration for Andrea Costa, a founder of the Italian Socialist Party.

Mussolini often contributed to the left wing L'Avvenire del Lavoratore.

In "Mussolini" by Christopher Hibbert, we read:

"For he (Mussolini) had by now recognised himself as the leader in chrysalis. Prompted by ideas, still largely uncorrelated and not always understood, picked out of Nietzsche, and Schopenhauer, Blanqui, Hegel and Sorel and borrowed from the RUSSIAN BOLSHEVIKS, he was coming to the belief that was soon to dominate his life — that the existing order must be overthrown by an elite of revolutionaries acting in the name of the people, and that this elite must be led by himself."

## THE SCUM OF THE POLITICAL WORLD.

The fact is that Marxist Socialism has spawned the scum of the political world ever since that fateful year 1917.

What we must guard against is that in the highest political circles in our land the same tired old political phrases are being churned out, and the same ideas propagated. Little do our wet-behind-the-ears students realise that when they chant their 'revolutionary' slogans they are doing exactly what some well meaning people were doing seventy-five years ago. The 'revolution' produced Stalin, Hitler and Mussolini — I would beg of our Marxist politicians and our Marxist camp-followers to think again. When you have fought your fight, which you may be fighting in all sincerity, for there are great injustices in society, will you be discarded as the early 'revolutionaries' were discarded and find you have built a nation led by the lineal successor of Stalin, Hitler or Mussolini? Remember, oh, do remember, they all started by saying they were going to change society, give the people freedom, stop war. They did none of those things — quite the opposite. The only way you can live in anything like a free society is by adopting, with all it's faults, our system of one person one vote, and the minority accepting the decision of the majority.

## · MUSSOLINI AND SATANISM.

Most people would accept readily that Mussolini was a buffoon and a very destructive dictator, but there has never been quite the hatred of him, even among those who fought in the last war, there was of Hitler. Mussolini's lifestyle, however, would indicate that Mussolini was a Satanist and one of the latter day leaders to be inspired by the 'Dragon'. It is, of course, indicative of the Satanist that he cannot tolerate the worship of God. We find the first indications that Mussolini may have been a Satanist in the early pages of the book "Mussolini". Writing of Mussolini's childhood, Hibbert says:

"He would never stay long in church. The smell of the incense would make him feel sick, he said, while the colours of the vestments, the light of the candles, the singing and the noise of the organ, all upset him profoundly."

Mussolini viewed the church as an absolutely unnecessary organisation, was in constant conflict with the Popes of his time and described God as 'a spook' and 'vindictive, cruel and tyrannical'. On other occasions he would insist 'God does not exist'.

"Who was Christ?", Mussolini was given to asking. "A small mean man who in two years converted a few villages and whose disciples were a dozen ignorant vagabonds, the scum of Palestine"

His lifestyle would certainly support the view that he was Satanic. Early in life he contracted syphilis and was a self-confessed rapist. To be blunt, the man was in the tradition of his Marxist revolutionary friends — a thug. He did not hesitate to show the utmost brutality to the women he 'took' and should they demure from any of his excessive behaviour he would stab them with a knife he always carried. According to his socialist companions he was blasphemous in the extreme, even by their standards.

Of his standards of personal behaviour, so much has been written that a full account would require a book on it's own. I will therefore confine myself to one more quotation from "Mussolini":

"Still compulsively sexual he assaulted the various women who came to the room he took in a hotel ... he ravished them as a conquering warlord might ravish his captured slaves, and seems to have enjoyed the process whoever his companion might be. Totally uninhibited and wholly egocentric,he gave little thought to his lover's comfort or their pleasure, often choosing the floor in preference to the bed, removing neither his trousers nor his shoes. The whole uncontrolled process was usually over in a minute or two."

## THE DEVILS BELIEVE AND TREMBLE.

It would appear from what we have seen, that the so-called atheist Marx believed in God with a fervour matched by few Christians. Certainly the movement which followed and purported to implement his teachings did not show so much the signs of atheism as of Satanism. Early on in the history of the Bolshevik government of Russia, we find what can only be described as a national paranoia about things Christian and Jewish. It is notable that the Moslems in the Soviet Union have remained relatively undisturbed. The target is not, therefore, religion in general, but Christianity and Judaism, the religions of Israel, in particular.

The Russians do not either seem to have any distrust of, or emnity towards, the paranormal or the occult — a fact that would naturally follow if their society was Satanically inspired. In "The New Soviet Psychic Discoveries" by Henry Gris and William Dick, there is considerable documentary evidence to show that the Russian government does not object, indeed on occasions gives considerable help, to the investigation of the supernatural and supernormal. Why then this absolute hatred of Christianity and Judaism — especially as Karl Marx was a Jew?

From the beginning, when one would have expected the emerging nation to be more concerned with economic progress than religion — hunting, the Soviets show this hatred of things Christian which, as I have said, amounts to a national paranoia.

Here's a quotation from very early on in the history of Bolshevism in Russia:

"The Bolshevists mobilised the Komosmoltsi, of Youthful Communists, to divert the Christmas celebrations into anti-religious channels; but, according to explanations which are appearing in the press (about 1930) in order to prevent these young ruffians from turning this exalted movement, as on previous occasions, into a mere riot of crude obscenities which disgust rather than persuade, they authorised older and more experienced agitators in all big centres to guide the celebrations into more promising avenues. Zinovieff issued an anti-religious appeal in which he declared that, although the anti-religious campaign had failed hitherto, owing to faulty methods, the Communists were undaunted. He said:

'We will grapple with the Lord God in due season. We shall vanquish Him in His highest heaven and wherever He seeks refuge, and we shall subdue Him forever.... But we must be cautious – much, much more cautious than hitherto!' "

I ask you, in all reason, does that sound like atheism or something quite different — Satanism?

That all this has come to the fore at exactly the time given by the prophet — 1917 — is surely significant.

# A WORD ABOUT SOCIALISM.

I cannot close this chapter leaving my reader with the impression that the ancient seers had no vision of a world in which there would be far more justice than hitherto. This chapter has not been about socialism — it has been about a kind of socialism.

My early life was spent in what would today be called "A deprived inner-city area". I witnessed many crimes against humanity and against the dignity of man, and I would not want to be associated with a society which perpetuated those awful conditions.

I want society put right! The history of the past sixty-five years tells us that wherever it holds sway, Marxism makes society 'wrong'. We must strive for a better world for all our people but we must never think that because a system promises a better society that system either intends to keep it's promises, or is capable of keeping it's promises.

As I write, we have in excess of three million unemployed people in Britain, and everyone agrees that that is totally unacceptable. Every one of those unemployed people, however, is better off in monetary terms, and in terms of their standard of living, than the average worker in the Soviet Union.

## WORKERS UPRISING PREDICTED 2000 YEARS AGO

Nevertheless, the prophets forecast the rise of socialism two thousand years ago. A prophet, James, wrote in A.D. 45 of what would happen on the political scene in the 'last days':

*Come now, ye rich men, weep and howl for your miseries that shall come upon you. Your riches are corrupted and your garments are motheaten. Your gold and silver are cankered, and the rust of them shall be witness against you, and shall eat your flesh as it were fire. Ye have heaped treasure together FOR THE LAST DAYS.*
*Behold, the hire of the labourers who have reaped down your fields, which is of you kept back by FRAUD, crieth; and the cries of them that have reaped have reached into the ears of the Lord of Saboath.*

Book of James 5: 1-4

As we shall see in our chapter on "Babylon the Great — the Harlot of World Commerce", the ancient seers foresee a lot of disruption in the comfortable world of big business in the last days.

Isn't that prophecy of James, a really amazing prophecy? What a warning, given almost two thousand years ago, about the rise of the workers in the 'last days'. Who can deny that we have seen happen exactly what James foresaw, in one country after another, in our lifetime?

The prophet tells us that the 'cries' of the oppressed are 'heard' in that great spirit world. Marxism is NOT the way but neither is the present world order of commerce.

I reject Marxism on the grounds of consistent, proven failure.

# 14.
# The Greatest
# Economic Upheaval
# of all Times

We have seen that the ancient seers foretold the rise of Islam in the 'last days' and that Russia would infiltrate the Marxist philosophy into the Islamic revival, thus changing it's character dramatically, if not bringing it to an end.

In awesome wonder we have observed, through the eyes of the prophet, the rise of the great 'Beast' which would have such economic power over the nations of the earth that they would be able neither to buy nor sell without it's 'mark' or 'authority'.

The centre of world economic power is soon to move from the present Western financial centres of the world and be centred in an Islamic centre, very probably Iraq.

I would like to refer you to a vision of the prophet John which is to be found in the Apocalypse and written about 96 A.D.

> *Come here; I will show unto thee the judgement of the great harlot that sitteth upon many waters; With whom the kings of the earth have committed fornication, and the inhabitants of the earth have made drunk with the wine of her fornication.*
>
> *So he carried me away in the Spirit into the wilderness and I saw a woman sit upon a scarlet coloured beast, full of names of blasphemy, having seven heads and ten horns.*
>
> *And the woman was arrayed in purple and scarlet colour, and bedecked with gold and precious stones and pearls, having a golden cup in her hand, full of abominations and filthiness of her fornication.*
>
> *And upon her forehead was a name written, MYSTERY, BABYLON THE GREAT, THE MOTHER OF HARLOTS AND ABOMINATIONS OF THE EARTH.*
>
> *And I saw the woman drunk with the blood of saints, and with the blood of the martyrs of Jesus; and when I saw her, I wondered with great wonder ... And after these things I saw another angel come down from heaven, having great power, and the earth was made bright with his glory.*
>
> *And he cried mightily with a strong voice, saying, Babylon the great is fallen, is fallen, and is become the habitation of demons, and the hold of every foul spirit, and a cage of every unclean and hateful bird.*
>
> *For all nations have drunk of the wine of the wrath of her fornication, and the kings of the earth have committed fornication with her, and the merchants of the earth have grown rich through the abundance of her delicacies.*
>
> *And I heard another voice from heaven, saying, Come out of her, my people, that ye be not partakers of her sins, and that ye receive not of her plagues ...*
>
> *And the kings of the earth, who have committed fornication and lived luxuriously with her, shall bewail her, and lament for her, when they shall see the smoke of her burning.*
>
> *Standing afar off for the fear of her torment, saying, Alas, alas, that great city, Babylon, that mighty city! For in one hour is thy judgement come.*
>
> *And the merchants of the earth shall weep and mourn over her; for no man buyeth their merchandise any more:*
>
> *The merchandise of gold, and silver, and precious stones, and pearls, and fine linen, and purple, and silk, and scarlet, and all thyine wood, and all kinds of vessels of ivory, and all kinds of*

*vessels of most precious wood, and of bronze, and iron, and marble.*
*And cinnamon, and incense, and ointments, and frankincense, and wine, and oil, and fine flour, and wheat, and cattle, and sheep, and horses, and chariots, and slaves, and souls of men ...*
*The merchants of these things, who were made rich by her, shall stand afar off for the fear of her torment, weeping and wailing ...*
*And every shipmaster, and all the company in ships, and sailors, and as many as trade by the sea, stood afar off,*
*And they cried when they saw the smoke of her burning, saying,*
*What city is like unto this great city?*
*And they cast dust on their heads, and cried, weeping and wailing.*
The Book of Revelation. Parts of Chapters 17 & 18

I would point out that this prediction does not refer to the first Babylon the Great, for that city's glories had long since disappeared when John wrote the prophecy. In any case, a careful reading of the context shows that the events of the prophecy are to take place at the time of the Battle of Armageddon at the 'end of the age'.

## BABYLON NOT THE CATHOLIC CHURCH

Protestant commentators are almost unanimous in their identification of the Roman Catholic Church as 'Babylon the Great', this belief is so deeply held among some students of the prophets that what I am about to say will be counted among them as akin to heresy.

Babylon the Great is NOT the Roman Catholic Church!

Of course, if one wishes to use prophecy as a weapon against any religion one does not like, then it is possible to make some sort of case for identifying the Roman Catholic Church with Babylon the Great. The Roman Catholic Church, however, simply does not fit the prophecy.

Identification of the Roman Catholic Church, by Protestant theologians, as being the 'Babylon' of the Apocalypse follows quite naturally from the false exegesis that the Western Roman Empire was the last in the succession of powers which were the 'Beasts' of Daniel and Revelation. It is of course inevitable, having commenced at a wrong premise one is then committed to reaching a false conclusion.

The prophet says he saw "a woman sitting on a scarlet covered beast." There can be no doubt that this beast, from the prophet's description of it, is none other than the Beast (666). If one follows the line of thought which contends there is to be a revival of the old Roman Empire in the last days (which there is not), then one is inevitably led to the conclusion that the 'woman' is someone closely connected to the revived Roman Empire. What institution is more closely connected with Rome than the Church of Rome? We have seen, however, that the line of succession of the 'Beast' was with an Islamic power, NOT Rome, therefore the woman, Babylon, must be connected not with Rome but with Islam. It is hardly likely that an Islamic 'Beast' would support the Church of Rome.

In the identification, by Protestant commentators, of Rome with the Babylon of the Apocalypse, we have an example of how religious vindictiveness can cloud a true interpretation of the writings of the ancient seers, and an example of 'cutting' the pieces of the prophetic jigsaw to 'make them fit somewhere'. The pieces may fit but the resulting picture is crazy.

Two statements of the prophet, it is alleged, identify the Roman Catholic Church as being 'Babylon' — (i) That the 'woman' sits on 'seven hills' and (ii) "I saw the woman drunk with the blood of saints and with the blood of the martyrs of Jesus".

It is often said that Rome is built on seven hills and this, therefore, identifies Rome as being the 'woman' who is, in the prophecy, seen to be sitting on seven hills. I suppose a case can be made for many cities in the world being built on seven hills, providing one is selective enough in one's definition of what exactly constitutes a 'hill'. When, for example, does a rise in the ground qualify for the description 'hill'? How large has a 'hill' to be before it is described as a mountain?

We have seen in the chapter "Breaking the Code" that 'mountains' represent kingdoms and 'hills' represent nations of somewhat lesser prestige. We know the 'woman' in the prediction to be symbolic of Babylon, that much is clear from the context: We also know the 'Beast' to be symbolic of a succession of empires which afflicted Palestine, so it would seem perfectly reasonable to assume the 'hills' upon which the symbolic 'woman' sits also to be symbolic. The prediction does not refer to seven actual hills, but rather to the 'woman' Babylon being upheld by seven nations which will not rank with the great nations or 'mountains' of the world.

"I saw the woman drunk with the blood of saints and with the blood of the martyrs of Jesus". It is true that the Roman Catholic Church has a history, a history of which many of it's present clergy are not at all proud, of bloody persecution in the name of religion. It is perhaps fortunate for the Protestant movement, that it has split into so many parts, that each part has the convenient let out of being able to reply "Not us", when the charge of religious blood-letting in past generations is laid at it's door.

My view is, that though the phrase "drunk with the blood of saints" is certainly applicable to the Roman Catholic Church in a certain period of it's history, the same description can be equally well applied to sections of the Protestant Church. Persecution has never been, and is not today, the preserve of any one religion. The prophetic description certainly indicates Islam, which as a matter of policy has, through the centuries, been 'drunk' with the blood of Christians.

While discussing the Protestant view of Roman Catholicism in prophecy, I would observe that the Roman Church has variously been identified as the 'Beast', the 'False Prophet', 'Babylon' and the Pope himself often as the 'Anti-Christ'.

Having seen the Roman Catholic Church cannot be identified as the 'Beast', in passing I would like to say there is no basis for the assumption that the Pope is the 'Anti-Christ'.

The prophet-apostle John made it plain that 'The spirit of anti-Christ' was abroad in his time. There was then no Pope in Rome, in his day Rome was yet pagan.

Far from identifying the Pope as 'Anti-Christ' the prophet defined the doctrine of anti-Christ so clearly that he COULD NOT BE THE POPE.

*Who is a liar but he that denieth Jesus is the Christ [Messiah-God]? He is anti-Christ.*

1 John 2:22

I know of no Pope of Rome who had denied that Jesus is God incarnate — Rome has always been insistent on the doctrine of the Deity and Divinity of Christ. There are few, if any, even in this world where modernist thought abounds, Roman Catholic priests who would deny either the divinity or deity of Jesus Christ. Ironically, it is often the Protestant sects which brand the Pope as being the 'Anti-Christ', who themselves bear the identifying mark of the anti-Christ as given by the prophet — a disbelief in the doctrine, held so firmly by the early church, that Jesus of Nazareth was 'God incarnate'.

## WHO OR WHAT IS 'BABYLON THE GREAT' WHICH IS TO 'FALL' IN THE LAST DAYS?

Babylon was, to the ancient seers, much more than a political empire, it was a way of life and a method of government which was the antithesis of the Israelite way of life and method of government.

It is unfortunate that generations of theologians have left their people with the impression that the ten commandments and the prohibition of the eating of bacon and shellfish is the whole of the law as expressed by the prophets. Consequently there is little appreciation that the ancient seers laid down a comprehensive code of conduct for the individual, the family and the nation — a code which covered all aspects of moral conduct, representation of the people, the law and judiciary, national taxation, including how and what percentage of income should be collected, safety at home and work, social welfare, third party liability, immigration law and, of course, the practise of religion. There is much, much more to the laws of the ancients than "Thou shalt not commit adultery".

To mention that the ancient seers were concerned with economics is to seek derision from most people, yet such is the case. The economic laws they pronounced ensured there were no very rich and no very poor people. The seers emphasised duties and performance of these duties was expected of all sections of the community. There were rights, too, and these were accorded to all sections of the community. Benefits were to be gained from living an industrious life and those who would not work suffered the penalty of their idleness. They did not have the conception of there being 'public enemies'; those who offended against the people offended against 'the Lord' and punishment was predictable, just and severe. Had the nation continued to follow the precepts laid down by the seers the land would have remained fertile for they taught an intelligent agricultural policy. The nation would have been purged of vandalism and violence, for they believed that 'civil rights' were the property of the innocent and they didn't listen to nonsense questions such as 'Who are the innocent?' Life was not a 'divine right' but a 'divine privilege' and those who withdrew life from others sacrificed their right to life themselves.

Yes, people lived in fear — people still live in fear. Then, though, it was the GUILTY who lived in fear. Now it is the innocent who live in fear! Today we are so concerned about the 'civil rights' of the criminal that we forget the vast majority of law-abiding citizens have lost their 'civil rights' to walk the streets in peace and safety, to leave their homes without fear of having them broken into, and to live out their lives in the tranquillity we all have a right to expect. The administration of the Lord was a little short on understanding criminals, but that was more than compensated for by the fact that the criminals certainly UNDERSTAND the administration.

People, land and property all belonged to 'the Lord' so that men were free as long as they obeyed the law. No vast accumulations of wealth occurred for land and property were 'the Lord's' and belonged to a person as a tenant of the Lord for as long as that person lived. A person had incentive, because he could work hard on the land and make a good living, or not work at all, and starve. There was a national system of aid for those who COULD NOT WORK, but none for those who WOULD NOT work. If such starved their fate was met with complete indifference.

Accumulated wealth passing from generation to generation was not possible but, as long as the system was obeyed it was also unnecessary to accumulate wealth beyond a lifetime for the coming generation would have their portion of the land and, by their own efforts, were able to become prosperous or otherwise in their lifetime.

Industry not speculation was the road to success.

## MONEY, MONEY EVERYWHERE BUT NOT A BITE TO EAT.

The Babylonian system was quite different, being based upon the 'gold standard'. Far from being forbidden, usury, the lending and borrowing of money for interest, was considered to be a virtue. Money became a commodity which had worth in itself because it's value was tied to that most useless of all metals — gold.

There were other aspects of Babylonian life which were repulsive to the Israelites, their idolatry, their sexual license, their dictatorial system of government and their disposition to spend money on prestigious national projects rather than providing for the under-privileged in their society. It was, however, when Nebuchadnezzar erected the golden idol, and caused the finance ministers of the surrounding nations to bow to it, that the three Israelites, led by Daniel, refused even when faced with the threat of death in the fiery furnace, to bow down. Israel had no place for the false and vulnerable economic processes of Babylon.

We are exhorted to return to a system of barter by many unthinking people: All very well but if you happen to trade in elephants it gets a little difficult to pay your fare on the bus! The ancient seers saw nothing inherently wrong with money providing it was regarded as a convenient method of exchange. Economic disaster looms when money is dealt with as a commodity in it's own right.

Today fortunes are made, and lost, speculating in currency. A million pounds transferred from sterling to dollars can produce a considerable profit in a few days. The same money can then be put into yens and result in another profit. That million pounds has not been used to erect a factory, develop a housing estate, produce work or feed hungry mouths, it has been used as a commodity for buying and selling.

Vast amounts of money are slushing about the world causing economic distress and, in the future, ultimate disaster.

In the light of what I have written, read the extract from the Book of Revelation again and you will see that Babylon the Great, described as 'THE MOTHER OF HARLOTS', has nothing to do with religion but has to do with economics. Note the words:

*the kings of the earth have committed fornication with her*
*the merchants of the earth have grown rich through the abundance of her delicacies*
*the merchants of the earth shall weep and mourn over her for no-one buyeth their merchandise any more*
*the merchants of these things, who were made rich by her shall stand afar off … weeping and wailing*
*and every shipmaster, and all the company in ships, and sailors, and as many as trade by sea … cried when they saw the smoke of her burning*

None of the above can possibly refer to the Church of Rome; were the Roman Catholic Church to disappear tomorrow the impact on world trade would be minimal. Certainly the merchants of the earth would not wail — not unless they were Catholics, that is.

## THE COMING GREAT ECONOMIC DISASTER.

The prediction of the fall of Babylon the Great is the prediction of a coming world economic catastrophe. I think I cannot better the graphic description of the ancient seer in conveying the anguish of the international 'merchant' community when this, the greatest economic upheaval mankind has ever known, takes place.

On October 29th 1929, the Wall Street crash occurred and an era of financial euphoria came to an end. It all happened as the bursting of an over-inflated balloon. There has been an accurate assessment of how much money was lost but the gravity of the 'crash' can be judged by the fact that on that day there were 16,410,030 share transactions compared with less than 6,000,000 on a normal trading day.

Instability was inherent in the monetary system but it was a fairly inconsequential happening in London that provided the 'pinprick' which burst the balloon. A certain Clarence Hatry, a London banker, was arrested for a forgery of stock certificates and this started a wave of selling which spread to New York. Panic begat panic.

Such a relatively minor event as Hatry's forgeries would have done little to affect a healthy economic situation but the economic dominoes had been so placed that when the first was flipped they all fell.

## THE 'MAKE-BELIEVE' WORLD ECONOMY.

The real weakness which afflicted the economic world in those days exists today — make-believe in economic affairs. Industry is being continually bolstered by sales to nations who cannot afford to pay for the goods. Loans are made to those nations in the full knowledge that they will not be able to repay. Further loans are made so that the nations can pay the interest on the first loan and further loans are made to enable them to purchase more goods. Thus is the world descending into the economic abyss. Ultimately the financiers 'restructure' repayment periods but that is just another form of financial chicanery doomed to ultimate failure. Why do the experts not know? They do! The only choice left to them is to continue the suicidal process and suffer later, or stop it and suffer now. They elect to suffer later than sooner. World finance is caught in the Babylonian economic trap.

### DEBT TABLE

Dollars in Billions

| | |
|---|---|
| Brazil | 94.9 |
| Mexico | 91.0 |
| Argentina | 41.8 |

| | |
|---|---|
| Korea | 40.7 |
| Venezuela | 31.6 |
| Indonesia | 26.2 |
| Turkey | 23.6 |
| Philippines | 22.5 |
| Chile | 18.3 |

Unless money, the convenient form of exchange, reflects reality and real worth, not financial manipulation, then disaster must follow. At the basis of the whole unsoundness is the one word which was to the ancient seers anathema — 'usury'.

Socialists used to tell a now hoary old yarn to illustrate the unreality of our monetary system. There were two people shipwrecked on a desert island on which there was no food. One of the people had an orange and the other a thousand pounds. Who was the richer? The story puts into perspective where real value resides, not in the symbol, money, but in the reality, products.

International debts are increasing at an alarming rate, economically mankind is in a 'cleft stick'. A large section of the world have not enough to eat while another section of the world have to cut back on food production because there is no market. The same is so of many commodities.

The economic apple is rotten within, money has become a commodity, no longer merely a method of exchange but a vehicle of manipulation. Money is not now representing wealth nor creating wealth. Fictitious figures in bank computers represent nothing more than paper debts which cannot be recovered.

One of the many functions of a bank, even an international bank, is to borrow money from people who wish to lend it and lend money to people who can use it. There is one element in banking without which no bank can survive, it is — confidence. When those who lend money to a bank lose confidence in that bank they try to withdraw their money but often the people to whom the bank has lent money have not got it to repay. There are, at present, a dozen or so nations in the world deeply in debt to the banking community. A large amount of the money those nations have borrowed has been loaned to the banks by the Arab countries.

It is not difficult to see the scenario developing, is it? Ever more money is deposited with Western banks and loaned by them to countries who, if there was a crisis of confidence, could not repay. Thus the power of the Arab countries will increase. The monetary power of the Arab and Islamic countries is already so great that if all the money deposited by them in Western banks was withdrawn there would be international economic chaos.

At present, Britain and America are not tied to the Gold Standard, but the economic problems which lie ahead are, according to the ancient seers, so acute that a return to the Gold Standard may be contemplated. Babylon will once again hold the centre of the world stage economically. This will last, however, for a very short time before the whole world economy, including those of the Islamic and Arab countries, will crash in ruins.

If the ancient seers are right in their prognostications, from the ruins of the old will emerge a new world economic order based not on gold, nor usury, nor speculation, but on justice.

# 15.
# Peace –
# Then Sudden
# Destruction!

In the chapter "The Coming World Conflict", I mentioned the present, and growing, trend toward appeasement. It is not a surprising trend to those who have studied the prognostications of the ancient seers, for one of the signs they gave that the 'end time' had come was that there would be a feverish and naive working for peace.

I have said previously that one of the failings of the 'peace movements' is that they do not address their protests against war to the right quarter; their protests are wasted in Trafalgar Square or Times Square, they should be heard in Red Square. It is understandable of course, that they should choose the easy option because in Britain and America no harm is liable to befall them as they demonstrate. In the Soviet Union, however, they would soon learn that people who chant about peace, unless that chant is orchestrated by the State, are not very popular.

Unfortunately, and I strongly object to this, the 'peace movement' people would have it believed that they and they alone have the monopoly of seeking peace. Let me make it plain, there is not a sane man, woman or child in the Western world who does not want peace. Consider the efforts Britain made to avoid conflict with Hitler! Think for a moment, that immediately after the war the United States had the nuclear power to destroy absolutely the Soviet Union and she didn't use it. Why, then, should we want war now?

No, we who support re-armament believe that war is brought about when one country decides there is the possibility of winning the conflict, and when they believe that the other side has not got the means, or the will, to effectively defend itself. Afghanistan was not a well armed country but it is occupied by the Soviet Union. Despite considerable provocation, however, the Soviet Union has not invaded China — China is capable of defending herself.

It is well to remember that the only country which has suffered attack by atomic weapons DID NOT HAVE THE ATOMIC WEAPON AT THE TIME. Can you imagine that America would have dropped atomic bombs on Japan if Japan had had the capability of atomising New York?

I would have little to say about the 'peace Movements' if they were harmless, but they are not. We have all read the heart-rendering stories of the boat people of Vietnam. They have drowned in their hundreds of thousands escaping in unseaworthy craft. Many of those who survived have had to suffer rape, starvation and deprivation. Every anti-Vietnam war demonstrator, every member of the media in the free world, every politician of influence in Britain and America, every silly little film actress who vilified the United States of America for her part in that war, is personally responsible for the millions of deaths which have occurred in Vietnam and Cambodia in exactly the same way they would have been responsible if they had stopped the war against Hitler and allowed the Jewish race to be further decimated. No guard in a Nazi concentration camp bears a greater personal responsibility for death than they.

## PEACE – THEN SUDDEN DESTRUCTION.

The prophet Ezekiel foretold the final peace movement. It was, he foretold, to be a movement which would bring the nation of Israel to the brink of destruction: Ezekiel addresses his prophecy 'against the prophets of Isrel' or, in other words 'The leaders of Israel', both religious and political.

*Son of man, prophesy against the prophets of Israel that prophesy, and say unto them that they prophesy out of their OWN HEARTS, Hear ye the word of the Lord.*

*Thus saith the Lord God: Woe unto the foolish prophets, THAT FOLLOW THEIR OWN SPIRIT, and have seen nothing!*

*O Israel, thy prophets are like the foxes in the deserts. Ye have not gone up into the gaps, neither made up the hedge FOR THE HOUSE OF ISRAEL TO STAND IN THE BATTLE OF THE DAY OF THE LORD.*

*They have seen vanity and lying divination, saying, The Lord saith, and the Lord hath not sent them; and they have made others to hope that they would confirm the word ..... Because, even because they have seduced my people, saying, Peace; and there is no peace; and one built up a wall and the other daubed it with untempered mortar;*

*Say unto them who daub it with untempered mortar, that it shall fall; there shall be an overflowing shower; and ye, O great hailstones, shall fall; and a stormy wind shall break it .... the prophets of Israel who prophesy concerning Jerusalem, and see visions of peace for her, and there is no peace.*

The Book of the prophet Ezekiel 13:2-16 (Parts)

Firstly we should note that the prophet speaks of the time immediately preceding the Battle of Armageddon for he speaks of the 'battle in the day of the Lord'. We have already seen how we live in the days immediately preceding that time. The events described should, therefore, be happening today if Armageddon is as near as we think it is.

You will notice that the prophet says the leaders will
(a) Prophesy out of their own hearts and
(b) Follow their own spirit.

There are two kinds of spiritual leader, those who say the things they would like to be true and the things they think people would like to hear — always very popular folk! The others are those who teach that there are certain realities in life and no amount of wishing will alter the facts — very unpopular chaps!

One simple fact, I think, with which everyone will agree is that once something has been discovered it will never be 'undiscovered'. Nuclear weapons are with us for as long as this old earth of ours exists. Certainly, we may persuade the leaders of our land to stop making the bomb and to stop possessing it, but that will not stop other countries having it and using it.

I have heard it said that if we did not have the bomb it would not be used on us — a false bit of reasoning if ever I heard one.

Mussolini used poison gas on the Abyssinians, not because they had it but because they didn't have it. Mussolini did not use poison gas on

225

Britain and France not because we did not have it but because we did have it. I have no doubt that Mussolini would not have used poison gas on Abyssinia had the Abyssinians had the capability of saturating Rome with the stuff.

The United States of America and Britain, let's not forget Britain's responsibility in this, did not drop the atom bomb on Japan because Japan had the atom bomb but because Japan did not have the atom bomb.

How popular it is to don one's dog-collar and windcheater, tell people that Christianity stands for peace and that all we have to do is sit back, and as quoth the little boy who pulled out the plum, say "what a good boy am I". I can but express shock that these men, who are supposed to be students of the prophets, are not acquainting the people with what the prophets taught. Certainly they say 'prophesy' what is in their hearts, the things they would like to see, but, equally certainly, they do not 'prophesy' or tell the people the things revealed by the prophets.

Some of the prognostications of the prophets are so awful, that if they are not accurate ministers of the church would be better going on a 'Ban the Bible' march than a 'Ban the Bomb' march. Their prognostications are either true or untrue, if true then men of the cloth should be alerting the leaders of Britain and the President of the United States of America to the problems which face us in the coming years. If untrue, these predictions are so evil that there is a good case for burning the lot. As we shall see in another chapter, the prophets of Israel were not 'wets' nor 'doves' — they were realists.

## THE WALL OF UNTEMPERED MORTAR.

Ezekiel predicts a latter day conspiracy in which leaders both political and religious will conspire to gain popularity by telling the people what they wish to hear rather than unpalatable truths. He sees the building of an insecure wall and he sees that wall being daubed to conceal the cracks, with untempered mortar. The phrase 'untempered mortar' may equally well be spoken of as 'whitewash'. The word 'daub' carries the connotation of something which is done in haste and without any real intent of success.

We have seen that in olden times the walls around villages, in Palestine, were the means of defence. Hedges were the farmer's defence against wild animals, the destruction caused by the winds and erosion.

The 'wall of untempered mortar' spoken of by the ancient seer is therefore a defence system which is incapable of meeting an attack. The daubing of that wall with 'untempered mortar' represents an attempt to conceal the instability of the wall from those who depend upon it for their safety. The prophet is saying that, in the last days, there will be gaps in the defences of the Jewish State of Israel, of the United States of America and of the British Commonwealth of Nations brought about by the neglect of our politicians to tell us the truth and the neglect of our religious leaders to proclaim the prognostications of the ancient seers regarding Armageddon. It cannot be said that there are gaps in the defences of Israel brought about by neglect. The fact that the Jewish State of Israel launched a pre-emptive strike against the Iraqi nuclear plant testifies to the fact that they, at least, are on their guard. There is then, inherent in the prediction, the foretelling of the fall of the present form of government in the Jewish State of Israel. The 'doves' will gain the ascendancy in even that enlightened country. Note that in your diary, for the disarmament of the Jewish State of Israel does not seem to be probable as I write, but it will happen and in the not too distant future.

Not only is there to be neglect of real defences but there is to be a great deal of effort in the last days put into building a 'wall', the purpose of which is to do nothing other than reassure. 'Let's keep the public quiet by doing something'. The public does have to be kept quiet because they normally have so much more sense and foresight than their leaders.

Sincere people sought peace in the years before the Second World War and none more determinedly than our own Prime Minister, Neville Chamberlain — their efforts failed. There is always a deep divide between the facts of life and wishful thinking. Millions of lives could have been saved had our leaders faced the facts rather than following 'their own spirits'. It is never sensible to attribute to animals the same thought processes as one attributes to human beings, similarly it is always unsafe to assume that the dictators of this world respect law or think and behave in the same way we do. To Hitler, people were fodder for his ambitions and untruths the tools of his trade. Today, to the Communist, people are pawns in an international game and poorism is a tool of his ambition.

If I remember aright, it was that very popular singer Vera Lynn who used to sing "Wishing Will Make It So". Unfortunately, it will not in the case of war and peace. Whatever the spirit which emanates from the ladies and gentlemen of the peace movements, it is sure not to find a response in the spirit of conquest which now pervades the Eastern Block.

We have seen that the prophecy concerning the building of the 'wall of untempered mortar' was to take place prior to the battle of 'that great day of the Lord' or Armageddon. We have seen, too, that the 'end time' commenced in 1917 with the end of the times of the Gentiles. The question we must now ask is: Has anything happened since 1917 which we may legitimately say is a fulfillment of the prophecy? There have always been people in every generation campaigning hopelessly for peace and, of course, if they are very young they will feel they are saying something new.

The fact is that never before in human history has there been such an intense organising for peace. Never has there been so much 'building of walls with untempered mortar'. Let us note carefully that the prophet did not say the nations would have no walls, he said they would have false walls, insecure walls. Builders of walls know very well that to daub them with untempered mortar will not hold the wall together. The building of a wall daubed with untempered mortar is a public display of 'doing something', a fool's effort to deceive his fellow men and perhaps an attempt to deceive himself also. Did the builder but think, his experience would tell him that the thing would not hold together when it came under stress, that he was engaged in a useless exercise. Thought does not enter into the activity of building walls of untempered mortar, the exercise is one of placating the people, giving them a false sense of security.

## POLITICAL QUACKERY.

I knew of a person who went to his doctor and the doctor had to tell him he was suffering from a terminal illness. He consulted an unqualified person who told him that by taking a potion prepared from certain fungi he would be restored to health. The patient spoke ill of the doctor and his 'lack of skill' and praised the unqualified person to his DYING day. Yes, he died, he died in the manner the doctor had foreseen from his examinations of the patient, and very much within the time the doctor had said. In the meanwhile, however, the patient had encouraged many people to foresake the 'negative' doctor and place their faith in the 'positive' quack. We all like to hear the things we want to hear, and we all dislike hearing the things we don't want to hear. In the above instance no harm was done, the patient died under the quack in exactly the same way as he would have died being treated by the doctor. But what a tragedy had he had an illness that could have been cured and he had forsaken the stark reality of the doctor's diagnosis for the easy remedy, only to find it ineffectual.

As long as there are elections to be won and lost, there will be politicians who will encourage the building of 'walls of untempered mortar'. "Tell the people what they want to hear" is the order of the day. Placate and appease the tyrant, pretend that everything is alright, carry on daubing the walls of untempered mortar lest by telling the stark truth people will cry 'warmonger'.

When the First World War came to it's inconclusive end the world was convinced that war had become so horrific that nations would never again resort to conflict to solve their differences. So it came about that within eighteen months of the 'times of the Gentiles' being fulfilled the prognostication of the ancient seer regarding 'walls of untempered mortar' began to be fulfilled. In January 1919 the text of the covenant of the League of Nations was agreed.

That the League of Nations was an entity unique in human history may be seen from Encyclopaedia Britannica 1973 edition page 851.

"The central, basic idea of the movement (the League of Nations) was that aggressive war is a crime not only against the immediate victim but against the whole human community; that accordingly it is the right and duty of all states to join in preventing it; and that if it is certain that they will so act; no aggression is likely to take place. SUCH AFFIRMATIONS MIGHT BE FOUND IN THE WRITINGS OF THE PHILOSOPHERS OR MORALISTS, BUT HAD NEVER BEFORE EMERGED ONTO THE PLANE OF PRACTICAL POLITICS.''

## THE LEAGUE OF NATIONS A
## 'WALL OF UNTEMPERED MORTAR'

Perhaps the supreme irony was the part played by the United States of America in the grand farce which was The League of Nations. A former President of the United States, William H. Taft, was crusading for the formation of a League of Nations as early as 1915. President Woodrow Wilson can, I think, be said to have been THE motivating force behind it's formation. Wilson was on firm political ground for in 1916 both the large parties, Republican and Democrat, had fought the election on the United States of America joining the organisation when it was formed. Despite the enthusiasm of the American people, the deep involvement in the setting out of articles of the American government, and the absolute dedication to the idea of the President of the United States — America didn't join!

Having proposed, organised, and arguably, brought into being the 'wall of untempered mortar' which was the League of Nations, the most powerful nation in the world refused to seek safety within the wall, choosing rather to withdraw into another 'wall of untempered mortar' — isolationism. We all know how long that 'wall' lasted. The 'untempered wall' of isolationism lasted just as long as it took the Japanese to build their forces to launch their infamous attack on Pearl Harbour. America recognised the 'gaps' spoken of by the prophet on that day. Millions of Americans died, not as a result of arming but as a direct result of disarming.

To appreciate how well founded the League of Nations was, it is necessary to realise how comprehensive was it's membership. Today most people have a vague idea it existed as a mainly European club, that is not so. If ever a 'peace movement' had impressive credentials it was the League of Nations. The members were:

| | |
|---|---|
| Afghanistan | Canada |
| Albania | Chile |
| Argentina | China |
| Austria | Columbia |
| Belgium | Costa Rica |
| Bolivia | Cuba |
| Brazil | Czechoslovakia |
| Bulgaria | Denmark |

| | |
|---|---|
| Dominican Republic | Mexico |
| Ecuador | Netherlands |
| Egypt | New Zealand |
| El Salvador | Nicaragua |
| Estonia | Norway |
| Ethiopia | Panama |
| Finland | Paraguay |
| France | Persia |
| Germany | Peru |
| Greece | Poland |
| Guatemala | Portugal |
| Haiti | Rumania |
| Honduras | Siam |
| Hungary | Spain |
| India | Sweden |
| Iraq | Switzerland |
| Ireland | Turkey |
| Italy | South Africa |
| Japan | U.S.S.R. |
| Latvia | United Kingdom |
| Liberia | Uruguay |
| Lithuania | Venezuela |
| Luxembourg | Yugoslavia |

Such was the world-wide 'support' for the concept of peace. Excuse me if I use modern parlance but today, with hindsight, it looks more like a 'hit list' for war.

Trouble was not long delayed. In 1923 a group of Italian officers were killed on Greek soil and Mussolini occupied Corfu in order to force the Greeks to pay compensation.The same year the French occupied the Ruhr.

In 1931 the Japanese launched their attack on Manchuria and a long series of debates ensued. To read those debates is akin to reading a debate of the United Nations when one member aggresses against another today. Japan was to suffer dire consequences if she did not withdraw, the nations of the world left her in no doubt that they disapproved. They told Japan not to be naughty and please stop it and Japan promised her troops would bè withdrawn as soon as their mission had been accomplished. The Japanese did not withdraw and the League of Nations was left muttering futile and puerile threats.

Mussolini's attack on Ethiopia took place towards the end of 1935. Economic sanctions followed the attack but did not prevent him from occupying the country he had bombed and gassed into submission. The sanctions ended in 1936 and Italy remained a member of the League of Nations and THE CONTROLLER OF ETHIOPIA.

I rarely criticise Sir Winston Churchill but I have to remark on one statement he made "Jaw, jaw is better than war, war." It's quoted often even today. What a clever little saying, isn't it? It's one of those sayings which make us wish we'd said it. Unfortunately it is more witty than true. What would have happened if the League of Nations had cut short Mussolini's imperial aspirations by confronting him over Corfu? Would he then have had the stomach for gassing Ethiopians? Or what if the League of Nations had thrown him out of Ethiopia? Would he then have had the stomach for the Second World War? The answer is most certainly no. Unfortunately the world got used to 'Jaw, jaw' and Hitler, nor Mussolini, nor Stalin worried over-much that the world called them naughty boys. They soon realised that the wall was of 'untempered mortar'.

In 1934 Hitler gained control of Austria after the Nazi assassination of the Austrian Chancellor. The League of Nations response? 'Jaw, jaw', of course. Was 'Jaw, jaw' better than 'war, war'? Hardly, for at that time Germany could have been defeated in a matter of weeks and had we gone to 'war, war' instead of 'jaw, jaw' millions of Jews and millions of German and Allied fighting men would have been saved from death, the world would never have known the holocaust. Hitler launched the Second World War but it was the doctrine of 'Jaw, jaw' which was responsible for it. The wall of 'untempered mortar' had failed again.

It was to be expected that after seeing France get away with her adventure in the Ruhr, Mussolini with his in Corfu and Ethiopia, and Hitler with his adventure in Austria, the demagogues were in great heart. The punishment for aggression was established, there was now plenty of case law, "Stop it, don't do it again, the League will be very annoyed with you .... you bad, bad boys."

The League of Nations solemnly talked throughout 1936 whilst Hitler re-militarised the Rhineland and civil war broke out in Spain. In 1937 Japan invaded China and the League of Nations continued to 'Jaw, jaw'. The League left Japan in no doubt they were annoyed. JAPAN STAYED IN CHINA!

In December 1939 the last stone fell out of the 'wall of untempered mortar'. Finland appealed for help to the League of Nations when she was savagely invaded by the Soviet Union. Poor Finland, I wonder what she really expected, anything better than all the other nations who had believed the myth? Of course, nothing happened, no-one came to her aid, but they did expel the Soviet Union from the 'club'. So the Soviet Union goes into history as the naughtiest boy of them all — the only nation to have been expelled from the League of Nations.

1939 was the year, too, when Hitler annexed Bohemia and Moravia, Lithuania ceded Memel to Germany, Germany invaded Czechoslovakia and Poland. Ultimately 'War, war' saved Europe where 'jaw, jaw' had failed. And what a terribly savage war it was compared with the war we would have had to fight had the League of Nations not been a 'wall of untempered mortar'. Just five years prior to the outbreak of war in 1939 the dictators were weak, bluff and a reliance upon the 'doves' in the League of Nations being the only cards of any worth in their hands. Never has a game of poker been played for such high stakes or with such success. "Ah", you may say, "but they didn't win in the end.": No they didn't, but if you recollect, that was no thanks to 'peace movements', 'jaw, jaw' or the 'wall of untempered mortar'.

## THE UNITED NATIONS ORGANISATION.

There are many things which the United Nations Organisation has done which are admirable — keeping the peace and preventing aggression is not among them. The United Nations Organisation is, in fact, the second generation 'wall of untempered mortar'.

The United Nations formally came into existence on October 24th, 1945, and there are today 154 member states. This vast organisation had a budget for the years 1980-81 of $1,247,793,200.

One of the many amusing activities of the United Nations Organisations is to put 'peace keeping' forces into places where it is thought war may break out, then, when war does not break out, to withdraw the 'peace keeping force' and allow the two sides to solve the problem in the traditional way, the way they would have done had the United Nations kept out of it in the first place.

It is not, I think, over-facetious to say that were there adequate and internationally understood Latin translations of 'stop it' and 'tut, tut' they could very well become the motto's of the General Assembly of the United Nations and the Security Council.

I must resist the temptation to discuss the United Nations Organisation at length and in general, and discipline myself to keeping to the subject which is the United Nations as a wall of 'untempered mortar'.

It should by now have dawned on any thinking politician that no nation on earth can rely on the Security Council for it's security. The failures of the Security Council to secure, have been so prolific and consistent as to make it impossible to comment fully in this volume. I therefore propose to mention a few episodes which are fairly typical of the ineffectiveness of the organisation.

After President Nassar of Egypt announced that his country had nationalised the Suez Canal, an international waterway by convention, Israel launched a full scale attack on Egypt. Britain and France intervened and demanded that the combatants withdraw their forces to a distance of ten miles from the canal.

The United Nations Organisation agreed to put a 'peace-keeping' force between the combatants if Britain and France would withdraw. The matter was agreed and the United Nations Emergency Force arrived. Egypt agreed to allow the United Nations to clear the Suez Canal of obstructions.

A sigh of relief went around the world, the Jews especially appreciated the 'buffer' between them and their Egyptian neighbours. Still Egypt continued to arm and so did Israel. Then some eleven years later the unbelievable happened. The whole world knew that the Jews and the Arabs were prepared to plunge their teeth into each others' throats. On May 19th 1967 the 'peace-keeping' force was withdrawn at the request of President Nassar, war ensued within the month. Fortunately for them, the leaders of Israel had not depended for their security on the assurances of the United Nations.

In October and November 1956 an uprising in Hungary was ruthlessly suppressed by Soviet troops and armour. The Soviet Union vetoed attempts to deal with the matter through the Security Council. When the question was raised at the General Assembly and the nations of the world passed a resolution telling Russia to cease military operations, leave the country and allow free elections in Hungary, the Soviet Union merely ignored the resolution, and today, 25 years after that resolution, Hungary is still under the heel of the Soviet Union and there are even now no free elections held in Hungary. How's that for a 'wall of untempered mortar'?

Why is the United Nations a 'wall of untempered mortar'? Why can't it work as a world peace-keeping force? For the simple reason any resolution of the Security Council can be vetoed by one vote. The Security Council has become largely a centre for the maintenance of self-interest. By the time events are debated at the General Assembly, the matter is often a fait accompli. The large powers can safely ignore resolutions of either the Security Council or the General Assembly. The whole thing depends upon common agreement, and of course, wars do not happen when there is agreement, they happen when there is disagreement. The United Nations cannot keep the peace simply because when the nations do not agree they cannot act.

Another failure of the United Nations is in respect of the Afghanistan affair. Once again, the Soviet Union has chosen to ignore an instruction of the United Nations to 'get out' of that tortured country.

## N.A.T.O. – WALL OF UNTEMPERED MORTAR.

As I write there is a great debate among British politicians as to whether Britain should withdraw from N.A.T.O. There is a considerable debate in Europe, too, about many aspects of the N.A.T.O. alliance.

The characteristic of untempered mortar is that it has no cohesion, it doesn't 'stick together'. There are elements in N.A.T.O. which, according to the prophets, will be on different sides at the Battle of Armageddon. Far from being the defence system it was devised to be, N.A.T.O. may well prove to be the 'fifth column' within the Western World.

N.A.T.O. forces have joint exercises and, of course, the various armed forces are subject to their own governments. At the time of writing, France has two Communist members in it's cabinet: The West seems not to be concerned but, what would we have said if the United Kingdom had had two Nazis in the war cabinet during the Second World War?

The free nations took no effective action either through N.A.T.O., the United Nations or any other of it's so-called organisations when the Russians invaded Afghanistan and they have taken no effective action in the Polish crisis.

It is indeed saddening to realise that the West's answer to the Polish crisis rests primarily in the President of the United States asking Americans to light a candle in their window over Christmas. You will no doubt remember Jimmy Carter issuing the dire threat to Iran during the hostage crisis that he would not light the lights on the Christmas tree in Washington if the Iranians did not release the hostages. Must we not conclude that the leaders of the West have absolutely no insight into the mind of dictators? Have we really become so naive that we believe either the Soviet Union the Polish government or the Iranian government give a twopenny duece about whether we light the lights on our Christmas trees or whether we burn so many candles we drown in our own candle grease?

One can understand why the United States government is reluctant to initiate effective action against the Soviet Union for they received little enough support from their 'allies' during the Vietnam war. They realise that Europe may not support them were they to do more than issue 'grave warnings' and propose useless trade sanctions. Such is the weakness of the 'wall of untempered mortar' that, were the Americans to refuse to supply the Soviet Union with the goods she needs, America's 'allies' would not only willingly but eagerly fill the gap.

Present European policies seem designed to drive the United States into isolation once again, and such an attitude by the United States would be wholly understandable. The United States should realise, though, that there is now no fortress to which she can withdraw. Should she decide upon such a course it will be but a few years before Europe is subjugated by the Soviet Union and the mainland of America be directly threatened. You cannot talk isolation to an intercontinental ballistic missile!

Europeans should consider well, when engaging in what now seems to be the favourite European bloodsport of plucking the feathers of the great American eagle, that they have no hope of freedom except sheltered under the canopy of the American nuclear umbrella. America, on her part, must make it plain to Europeans that she will not hesitate to fight for the freedom and security of her allies.

## THE DIRE WARNINGS OF GENERAL SIR WALTER WALKER.

General Sir Walter Walker, KCB, CBE, DSO, was, until his retirement, NATO Commander-in-Chief, Allied Forces Northern Europe. Previously he was Deputy Chief of Staff in charge of Plans, Operations and Intelligence at Headquarters, Allied Forces Central Europe.

As the writer of the introduction to General Walker's book"Wake Up or Perish" says in the introduction:

".... there can be no one more able or better qualified than General Walker to spell out the grave dangers we are facing — with the exception of Mr. Brezhnev himself, and he is hardly likely to oblige."

(Brigadier G.H.N. Wilson)

The opening words of the General's book are as follows:

"This is the third time during my life that the security of this country — not to mention the West as a whole — is in peril as a result of, first, the neglect by political leaders in the face of an obvious military threat, and second, the listless and suicidal indifference to which the majority of our people have sunk. Never has the world situation been so grave and dangerous since World War II. Events are showing, and will continue to prove that my repeated warnings about the menace of Russia's massive military might and her aggressive and expansionist intentions have been a modest understatement.

Appeasement — now known as Détente — was the policy of the British and Allied Governments before the Second World War. A futile Appeasement which led to destruction on an unimaginable scale. Hundred of thousands of brave men and women fought heroically for a better world. They laid down their lives for justice and freedom. What is happening around us today is an insult to their memory. EVERY HEART OF THE POLITICAL LEADERS OF THE WEST IS FAINT AND EVERY HEAD IS SICK."

The General warns not only of the intention of the Soviet Union to subjugate Europe but also of their ability to subjugate Europe. In as hard-hitting a treatise as it has been my pleasure to read, General Walker warns of the total inadequacy of NATO to meet a Soviet attack and unequivocally states his view that Soviet policy is nothing less than the conquest of the world for Communism.

When I was in the Soviet Union I was surprised to see the complete and utter dedication, a dedication amounting to worship, which the Soviet regime bestow on Lenin. Queuing outside the Mausoleum in Red Square in those seemingly endless lines of people waiting to see the body, we were constantly under surveillance, our pockets were prodded and searched and when we reached the steps leading to where Lenin lay, even the sound of our footsteps drew a sharp rebuke from the guard. The face of Lenin gazes down from statues, walls, from book covers and stamps and indeed from every conceivable place. To the Russian citizen the word of Lenin is the word of God.

General Walker quotes Lenin as saying "We must communise the world, and encircle the United States, and, if they do not surrender, we shall destroy them." You can be quite sure that if Lenin said it, however long it takes to achieve, it will remain Soviet policy. So much for Soviet disclaimers when they are charged with constructing a vast machine for waging a war of aggression. Despite their constant assurances that this massive arsenal is for self-protection — against what antagonist one wonders — the policy laid down by the master, Lenin, is one of aggression not of self-protection.

N.A.T.O. — 'Wall of untempered mortar'! The military know it and the politicians know it, another great exercise in fooling most of the people most of the time. The latest chapter in the age-old doctrine of peace without sacrifice.

## PEACE, THEN SUDDEN DESTRUCTION.

The prophet and apostle Paul, in his first Book to the Thessalonians, predicts:

> *For yourselves know perfectly that the day of the Lord so cometh as a thief in the night. For when they shall say, Peace and safety, then sudden destruction cometh upon them, as travail upon a woman with child, AND THEY SHALL NOT ESCAPE.*
>
> 5: 2, 3

A thief arrives with stealth and when the householder is either absent, asleep or unguarded. 'Travail' arrives at a time which can be calculated within a certain approximation.

We know that we live in the time which will see the final 'run-in' to the Battle of Armageddon, we have the 'time indicators' provided by the ancient seers to guide us as to when to expect the travail. Let us not expect the Soviet Union to announce her intentions regarding Palestine with a loud knocking on the international door — that's not how the thief arrives. Just as the stock-in-trade of the thief is surprise, so, says the prophet, just when everyone is crying 'Peace and safety' will the armies of Gog and Magog strike when everyone is least expecting them to do so.

Ministers of religion who support the peace movements which today proliferate should stop consulting 'their own hearts' and 'following their own spirits'. If they are anything, they should be men of the book, men of the prophets, men of the ancient seers — if they are not that, then they are nothing. Stop! Think! Read what the ancient seers have to say. They call

236

themselves 'Christians', then they should study closely what the 'Christ' had to say and what His disciples had to say about the 'last days' — they will find that He held out little hope for 'peace'.

I am not unaware that, by now, some of my readers will be suspecting me of having broken my own precept. Did I not say that we should always apply the prognostications of the ancient seers to those to whom they were addressed? Why then am I writing of the 'walls of untempered mortar' prophecy in the context of the Jewish State of Israel and Britain and America when it was addressed to Israel alone? That I will explain in my chapter "The Mystery of the Missing Millions".

# 16.
# The Mystery
# of the Missing
# Millions

"In these last years of my life there is a message of which I conceive myself to be the bearer. It is a very simple message which can be well understood by the people of our countries. It is that we should stand together, in malice toward none, in greed for nothing, but in defence of those causes which we hold dear, not only for our own benefit but because we believe that they mean honour and happiness for long generations of men."

"We ought, as I said to the Congress of the United States in the dark hour of 1941, to walk together in majesty and peace. That, I am sure, is the wish of the overwhelming majority of the 200,000,000 Britons and Americans who are spread about the globe. THAT THIS IS OUR DESTINY, OR AS MOST OF US WOULD PUT IT, THE WILL OF GOD, SEEMS SURE AND CERTAIN. How it is to be expressed, and in what way and in what hour it is to be achieved I cannot tell.''

Winston Churchill speaking to the Virginia State Legislature on March 8th, 1946.

According to the ancient seers, the United States of America and Great Britain will shortly reunite into one nation.

This coming world federal empire will, in addition to Britain and America, include all those nations born of and populated by the British mother country.

Whatever political, military and economic liaisons exist between Britain and Europe, America and her allies, will soon be set aside in favour of a recognition of common destiny between all those who have sprung from the Anglo-Saxon, British and Celtic stocks. The Scandinavian countries, too, will belong to what we may, for the want of a better term, call "The Anglo-Saxon Federation".

The economic sufferings of both the United States of America and Great Britain will continue and intensify and their perplexity deepen until they recognise their true destiny — UNITY. The place of Britain is outside Europe and united with our kith and kin throughout the world.

Just as Britain will experience ever increasing economic distress while she is in Europe, so America will experience not only economic distress but other political and national perplexities until she accepts that Britain's throne is her throne and Britain accepts that America's 'United States' are the states to which she should belong. Unless, or rather until, this situation, foretold many thousands of years ago by the ancient seers, is realised in our countries, the United States will experience the peril of one Latin American country after another being conquered for the Communist cause.

Perhaps you find the prediction of the coming union of Britain, the United States of America, Commonwealth countries and Scandinavian countries surprising. Here is a more surprising prediction — The Jewish State of Israel will also be part of the worldwide kingdom.

Quite naturally, the reader will wish to know how the above conclusions have been reached, especially as the actual names of the countries concerned — apart from the Jewish State of Israel — are not mentioned by the ancient seers.

This chapter will be devoted to showing that, though not mentioned by their modern names, the great nations of the Western world WERE spoken of by the prophets, and their destinies in the 'end time' carefully predicted.

It behoves everyone in the Western world to examine carefully what the ancient seers had to say and, in view of their record of accuracy in other matters, to heed what they have to say about US in our day.

## THE COMING WORLD EMPIRE.

We have seen that the year 1917 ushered in the terminal period of earth's existence as we know it. We have seen, too, that, just as foretold by the prophet Ezekiel, the Soviet Union occupies the territories written of as the land of Gog and Magog. Thus we identify the Soviet Union as being the prime mover among those nations which will come against the land of Palestine at the Battle of Armageddon.

The prediction of the ancient seers regarding the gathering of the Jews in their own land has taken place, as have so many other of their prophecies. We are left with little other option than to believe their prophecies regarding the Battle of Armageddon will also be fulfilled, and be fought between the protagonists they predict.

All the utterances of the ancient seers we have studied lead us to believe we live in momentous days — I would go so far as to say THE most momentous days of earth's history to the present time.

Prophecy certainly tells us so, and who would deny that our own observation of the world around us tells us so with equal emphasis? Few thinking men would deny the possibility that we may be living in the final days of earth's existence — that we have the capability of universal destruction is beyond doubt.

Human reason leads us to a much more pessimistic view of the future of planet earth than does prophecy. Reason leaves us in no doubt, that the day will come when some evil or demented person somewhere, will use the awful destructive capability which now exists among the nations. There are a few innocents, it is true, who really believe the bomb can be 'banned' and how most of us wish that were so, but we know, don't we, that no-one can now 'un-invent' the bomb — it is with us until the end of human history.

## A NEW DIMENSION TO WORLD TERROR.

Humanity produces with monotonous regularity the evil and the insane who somehow gain power. The Lenins, Stalins, Hitlers and Mussolinis with their dreams of power push the world to the brink of the abyss despite the wishes of ordinary men and women just to live in peace. Horrifying as the wars of the past were, however, we have not seen a war of extermination such as would be waged were the world to go to war again. Our fear is compounded when we realise that not only Russia, America and Britain have the power to wipe out continents: Other less stable nations have the capacity, too.

Even in 'peacetime' terror stalks the earth, our towns and cities raked by bullet and blasted by bomb, not from some enemy without but from the terrorist within.

There is no way in which the terrorist can be placated for they have differing ends in view. Often they are fighting for opposites and for a nation to satisfy the one is for that nation to be blasted by the fury of the other. It is indeed a depressing thought that within five or ten years the street terrorist will have at his disposal nuclear weapons, ground to air missiles and the ability to wage germ warfare.

A spectre of whole cities held hostage looms before us: The spectre of communities the size of New York, London and Berlin being wiped out at the whim of some demented zealot. We have become all too familiar with the hijacking of aircraft, but such is as nothing compared with hijacking of a city, or even a nation, by a terrorist or perhaps by a mentally sick person. We should always be mindful that, nuclear weapons apart, germ warfare has now reached the point where a phial of germs, half the size of a fountain pen, would be enough to start an epidemic capable of depopulating Moscow, London or New York.

We live in the age of crazy senseless killing. Think of the insane reasoning behind the shots which hit President Reagan and the seemingly equally senseless reason a young Turk gave for shooting the Pope. We live in the age, not only of the mighty military machine, but of the idealistic terrorist and the crazy assassin.

That is the picture reason must bring before us — a picture of possible, even probable, destruction. I am pleased to say that the ancient seers paint a much more hopeful picture. True, they tell of terrible tribulation until the end of the age, with wars, famines, pestilence, insurrection, violence — in fact a concentration of all those things which have afflicted mankind throughout history as the terminal years draw to their close.

## PREDICTED – A WORLD AT PEACE.

They also foresee civilisation surviving, however. Having groped it's way through the valley of the shadow of death, mankind, they predict, will emerge into proud uplands of splendour, a world at peace where 'the lion will lie down with the lamb', a world where the nations will learn war no more.

Such a world is unforeseeable. But why — if, as we have seen, the seers have been correct in their other prognostications, should they not also be correct in this? If, as it would appear, a supernormal or supernatural power has seen fit to communicate earth's history to certain men, is it beyond the realms of possibility that that supernatural power will intervene in the history of planet earth at the critical moment? May it be that even now the mighty universal voice is preparing to boom "Mankind — thus far but no further — STOP!"

It is interesting to note that the word used to describe the tribulation through which the earth will pass during the terminal years is 'travail'. Most kinds of pain tell us there is something going wrong. 'Travail' is different, it's pain alright, but it is not an indication that there is something wrong, it is an indication that something 'new' is about to be 'born'.

The prophets tell us that there is a new day coming — I want them to be right for what they offer is a far brighter prospect than we may expect from an intellectual assessment of the current world situation.

## THE MISSING MILLIONS

You will remember that I have continually drawn a distinction in this book between The House of Judah, otherwise known as the Jews or The Jewish State of Israel, and the ten-tribed House of Israel.

We have seen Russia in prophecy and other named nations, the Egyptians, Persians, Libyans, Ethiopians, Syrians, the Turks and the Jewish State of Israel.

The prophet Ezekiel, however, foresees something happening in the last days which, on the face of it, is a mystery. He foretells of a nation, a nation numbering millions of people, who disappeared from the face of the earth — as far as any possibility of identification was concerned — reappearing before the Battle of Armageddon and being positively identified.

Ezekiel, you will remember, had a vision of a Valley of Dry Bones. His prophecy tells of how he saw the bones come together and live. This was the prediction of the resurrection of the nation of Israel.

The vision of the Two Sticks follows the vision of the Valley of Dry Bones and preceeds Ezekiel's vision of Armageddon.

What we are about to read, therefore, was destined to take place AFTER the resurrection of Israel and BEFORE Armageddon — in OUR DAY AND GENERATION.

## EZEKIEL'S VISION OF THE TWO STICKS.

*The word of the Lord came again unto me, saying, Moreover thou son of man, take thee one stick, and write upon it, For Judah, and for the children of Israel, his companions; then take another stick, and write upon it, For Joseph, the stick of Ephraim, and for all the House of Israel, his companions;*

*And join them one to another into one stick, and they shall become one in thine hand.*

*And when the children of thy people shall speak unto thee, saying, WILT THOU NOT SHOW US WHAT THOU MEANEST BY THESE?*

*Say unto them Thus saith the Lord God: Behold, I will take the stick of Joseph, which is in the hand of Ephraim, and the tribes of Israel, his fellows, and will put them with him, even with the stick of Judah, and make them one stick, and they shall be one in mine hand.*

*And the sticks upon which thou writest shall be one in thine hand before their eyes.*

*And say unto them Thus saith the Lord God: Behold I will take the children of Israel from among the nations, to which they are gone, and will gather them on every side, and bring them into their own land.*

*And I will make them one nation in the land upon the mountains of Israel, and one King shall be King to them all; AND THEY SHALL BE NO MORE TWO NATIONS, neither shall they be divided into two kingdoms any more at all.*

The Book of the Prophecy of Ezekiel 37: 15-22

It is essential to my theme that I spend some little time in describing some of the early history of Israel. What I have to say may be a little complicated and perhaps a little 'dry' to some, but the validity of the conclusions I wish to draw from the prognostications of the prophets depends strongly upon the REAL facts concerning the history of Israel.

I ask you therefore to read this chapter carefully for the conclusions we shall reach are startling, exciting and comforting for the British, American, Anglo-Saxon, Celtic peoples and the nations that have sprung from them.

Ezekiel, his prophetic eye looking down over two thousand five hundred years to our day, foretold the following:

1. The 'missing millions' of the 'lost' House of Israel would be found. A world shattering discovery would cause the Ten Tribes who had been separated from Judah (the Jews) for thousands of years to be recognised.

2. This would happen between the resurrection of the Jewish State of Israel (1917-1948) and the Battle of Armageddon.

3. Since one cannot join that which is not first 'separate', the prophecy of Ezekiel refutes the contention of those who believe that the ten tribes rejoined the House of Judah at some time in the past. The Jews do not believe this, by the way, they still pray for the uniting of their kinsmen of the other tribes.

4. Ezekiel's prophecy, too, refutes those who would have it that the ten-tribed House of Israel were irretrievably absorbed into the Gentile nations. According to Ezekiel there is no doubt that, though scattered among the nations, their individual national identity was preserved.

5. When, as the prophet predicts, the joining together of the House of

Judah and the House of Israel takes place in these, the terminal years of dispensation, the political implications will be such as to rend the political world assunder as an earthquake rends the earth. It will be one of the most politically significant events of all time.

6. Ezekiel predicts that the House of Israel, having been recognised and rejoined with the House of Judah, will be one Kingdom and have one King. From that time hence Israel will never again be divided.

7. Each of the prophets would seem to contradict himself about this coming King. We have seen how the prophecies of Daniel and other of the ancient seers regarding the coming Messiah/God/King of Israel were fulfilled in the coming of Jesus of Nazareth who was called 'the Christ'. Yet in many other prophecies we have the vision of a king who will come at the end of the age, take control of Israel, occupy the throne of Israel and rule with a rod of iron the nations of the world. The Jewish State has been resurrected as foretold by the prophets but — WHERE IS THE KING? We shall examine that mystery more fully in another chapter, but please accept for now that any contradiction is only apparent.

## THE CHOSEN PEOPLE.

Modern thought is very much against anything which smacks of racial preference but we should not ignore the fact that a great universal spirit which was at all times in accord with 'modern thought' would be forever changing it's character. The rapidity with which 'modern thought' changes can be seen in the Soviet Union, where people are confined to concentration camps today for expressing the same opinions which were obligatory a few years ago under Stalin.

The "god made in man's image" is, of course, forever changing — in his time he has been racist and anti-racist, pro-slavery and anti-slavery, capitalist and communist, Catholic and Protestant, pro-war and anti-war, pro-abortion and anti-abortion — he has even been an anti-semitic.

Our ancient seers knew of no such great universal spirit — they knew only of the great universal spirit who orders things 'after his own will'.

We may like it or we may not like it, the fact still remains that according to the teachings of the ancient seers, the great universal spirit DID choose men for no other reason that it was HIS WILL so to do. Similarly he chose one nation from the whole of the human race to be a servant nation — the nation of ISRAEL. THAT NATION WAS ULTIMATELY TO RULE THE WORLD.

Though a few Christian teachers have recognised the God who 'does according to His will', the majority find the doctrine strongly at variance with their "god made in the image of man".

Rather as the maker of a soap powder seeks to find a product acceptable to the buying public, so our churches seek a god acceptable to their 'buying public'. There are a few, of course, who are to be absolved from that criticism — the great Baptist preacher, the late Charles Haddon Spurgeon once remarked that men "will have God anywhere except on his throne".

John Whitfield was at variance with John Wesley on the matter, during the whole of their ministries, and of course John Calvin lent his name to a whole system of theology which propounded the doctrine of pre-destination and the absoluteness of the sovereign will of God.

This book is not, however, concerned with what the various branches of the Christian church believe nor what modern leaders of the Christian church, past or present, propagate. We are concerned solely with what the ancient seers taught and foresaw, and with that great universal spirit who, they believed, existed and exists, doing 'according to his own will' regardless of what the will of man may be.

## THE HISTORY OF ISRAEL.

Let it be said that whatever our social views, the prophets did teach of a universal spirit (God) who chose, and granted a special place in history, to a nation — the nation of Israel.

Let us now look briefly at how the nation of Israel came into being.

It is important to note that Abram — later renamed Abraham — was a Shemite NOT A JEW NOR AN ISRAELITE.

He dwelt in Ur of the Chaldees about 2000 B.C. and was the father of the Israelite, Arab and many of the Asiatic peoples, as we shall see.

The prophet Moses tells us how Ishmael, Abram's first son, came to be born:

*Now Sarai, Abram's wife, bore him no children: and she had an handmaid, an Egyptian, whose name was Hagar.*

*And Sarai said unto Abram, Behold now, the Lord hath restrained me from bearing: I pray thee, go in unto my maid; it may be that I may obtain children by her. And Abram harkened to the voice of Sarai.*

Genesis 16: 1-2

I read in a newspaper a few days ago of a surrogate mother — the young lady thought she was being very 'with it' — times don't change much, do they? No doubt the reporter who wrote the story was unaware that his 'exclusive' had been written many thousands of years ago.

Abraham's second son, Isaac, was born in somewhat different circumstances.

We turn again to the Book of the prophet Moses and read the record:

*And God said unto Abraham, As for Sarai, thy wife, thou shalt not call her name Sarai, but Sarah shall her name be. And I will bless her, and give thee a son also of her: yea, I will bless her, and she shall be a mother of nations; kings of people shall be of her. Then Abraham fell upon his face and laughed, and said in his heart, Shall a child be born to him that is an hundred years old? And shall Sarah that is ninety years old, bear?*
*And Abraham said unto God, Oh, that Ishmael might live before thee!*
*And God said, Sarah, Thy wife, shall bear thee a son indeed; and thou shalt call his name Isaac: and I WILL ESTABLISH MY COVENANT WITH HIM for an EVERLASTING COVENANT and with his seed after him.*

Genesis 17: 15-19

## ISAAC'S SONS.

Isaac was a Shemite and a Hebrew, NOT A JEW AND NOT AN ISRAELITE. The prophet Moses tells us how the first two sons of Isaac were born:

*And Isaac was forty years old when he took Rebekah as his wife, the daughter of Bethuel the Syrian of Paddan-aram, the sister to Laban the Syrian.*
*And Isaac entreated the Lord for his wife because she was barren; and the Lord was entreated by him, and Rebekah, his wife conceived.*
*And the children struggled together within her; and she said, If it be so, why am I thus? And she went to enquire of the Lord.*
*And the Lord said unto her, Two nations are in thy womb, and two manner of people shall be born of thee; and one people shall be stronger than the other people; and the elder shall serve the younger.*
*And when her days to be delivered were fulfilled, behold, there were twins in her womb.*
*And the first came out red, all over like a hairy garment; and they called his name Esau [meaning 'man of the earth']*
*And after that came his brother out, and his hand took hold on Esau's heel; and his name was called Jacob.*

Genesis 25: 20-26

As the firstborn, Esau should have inherited the line of promise from his father Isaac.

The boys grew and we are told that Esau became a hunter and Jacob a 'quiet man dwelling in tents'.

Esau came in from the fields one day feeling faint, though, it would seem, his faintness was of a serious nature for he said to his brother Jacob "Behold, I am at the point to die:". Jacob was at the time boiling pottage and the stricken hunter asked him for food.

Jacob made a cruel bargain with his brother "Sell me this day thy birthright ... swear to me this day; and he (Esau) swore unto him: and he sold his birthright unto Jacob. Then Jacob gave Esau bread and pottage of lentils;" (Genesis 25: parts of 31 and 33). That, of course, is the origin of the saying which is still much used "Selling one's birthright for a mess of pottage."

So the line of promise passed, not to the descendants of Esau, but to the descendants of Jacob.

Of course, the bargain struck between the two brothers was not necessarily binding upon the father for the birthright was in fact his to bestow and was not, at the time of the bargain, Esau's to trade. Further treachery was necessary to wrest the birthright from the careless, but generous and faithful, Esau.

Isaac was old and anticipating his death when he asked Esau to go and bring him venison that he may eat. The faithful Esau went forth at his father's request, to hunt and fulfil his father's wish. The love of Isaac for Esau is plainly shown in the narrative.

Meanwhile Rebekah, Jacob was always her favourite son, told Jacob of the discussion between Esau and Isaac and an elaborate plot was brought about to cause the blind Isaac to bestow the birthright on Jacob.

Jacob, dressed in Esau's clothes, clothes which bore all the odorous characteristics of the hunter of his day, simulated the hairiness of Esau's hands by covering them with the skins of goat kids. Let Moses complete the story:

> *And Jacob went near unto Isaac, his father; and he felt him, and said, The voice is Jacobs voice, but the hands are the hands of Esau. And he recognised him not, because his hands were hairy, as his brother Esau's hands: so he blessed him.*
> *And he said, Art thou my very son Esau? And he [Jacob] said, I am.* Genesis 27: 23-24

Thus did the birthright and the blessings pass from Isaac to Jacob.

## JACOB'S SONS.

Jacob was NOT A JEW but he did become the first ISRAELITE.

The name of Jacob was changed to 'Israel' at Peniel and his sons became the 'children of Israel'.

The nation of Israel did not commence with either Abraham or Isaac, though they were patriarchs of Israel, but with Jacob whose name was changed to Israel. All the covenants and blessings promised to Abraham and Isaac were now vested in Jacob.

Jacob had twelve sons:

Reuben (the firstborn)
Simeon
Levi
Judah (Father of the House of Judah and the Jewish
    State of Israel)
Issachar
Zebulun
Joseph ———————————————————⌈— Ephraim
                                                                 (sons)
Benjamin                                            ⌊— Manassah
Dan
Naphtali
Gad
Asher

The line of promise should have gone through Reuben being the firstborn, but Jacob (Israel) decided otherwise: His son Joseph was his favourite son.

I cannot emphasise too strongly the fact that it is not possible to understand the prognostications of the ancient seers if we do not first understand the line of promise from Abraham to the children of Israel. Because students of prophecy have persistently misread this 'line of promise', they have consistently arrived at erroneous conclusions about what the prophets predict will happen during the 'end time' of earth's history.

It has been commonly believed and taught that the Jews were the 'chosen people' and the sole inheritors of the promises made by 'God' to Abraham, Isaac and Jacob — THEY WERE NOT. To prove the point I now quote, at length, the prophet Moses' account of how the birthright was passed down from Israel (Jacob) to his descendants:

*And Israel [Jacob] beheld Joseph's sons, and said, Who are these? And Joseph said unto his father, They are my sons, whom God hath given me in this place. And he said, Bring them I pray thee, unto me, and I will bless them.*

*Now the eyes of Israel [Jacob] were dim for age, so that he could not see. And he brought them near unto him; and he kissed them, and embraced them.*

*And Israel said unto Joseph, I had not thought to see thy face; and, lo, God hath shown me also thy seed.*

*And Joseph brought them out from between his knees, and he*

*bowed himself with his face to the earth.*
*And Joseph took them both, Ephraim in his right hand toward*
*Israel's left hand, and Manasseh in his left hand towards Israel's*
*right hand, and brought them near unto him.*
*And Israel stretched out his right hand, and laid it on Ephraims*
*head, who was the younger, and his left hand upon Manasseh's*
*head, guiding his hands knowingly; for Manasseh was the first*
*born.*
*And he blessed Joseph, and said, GOD, BEFORE WHOM MY*
*FATHERS, ABRAHAM AND ISAAC DID WALK, THE GOD*
*WHO FED ME ALL MY LIFE LONG UNTO THIS DAY, THE*
*ANGEL WHO REDEEMED ME FROM ALL EVIL, BLESS*
*THE LADS; AND LET MY NAME BE NAMED UPON THEM,*
*AND THE NAME OF MY FATHERS ABRAHAM AND*
*ISAAC; AND LET THEM GROW INTO A MULTITUDE IN*
*THE MIDST OF THE EARTH ... AND HE BLESSED THEM*
*THAT DAY, SAYING, GOD MAKE THEE AS EPHRAIM*
*AND MANASSEH.*

Genesis 48: Parts of 8 — 20

The line of promise and of blessing did not pass to ANY of the twelve sons of Israel but to the two GRANDCHILDREN of Israel, the sons of Joseph, Ephraim and Manasseh.

*Now the sons of Reuben, the firstborn of Israel for he was the*
*firstborn; but forasmuch as he defiled his fathers bed, HIS*
*BIRTHRIGHT WAS GIVEN UNTO THE SONS OF JOSEPH*
*[EPHRAIM AND MANASSEH], the son of Israel, AND THE*
*GENEALOGY IS NOT TO BE RECKONED AFTER THE*
*BIRTHRIGHT. For Judah prevailed above his brethren, and of*
*him came the prince; BUT THE BIRTHRIGHT WAS JOSEPHS.*

1. Chronicles 5: 1, 2

Nothing could be more plain than that and it is difficult to see how so many generations of theologians (so-called) have persisted in the view that the descendants of Judah are the inheritors of the promises to Israel. It seems that only the Jewish theologians have recognised the facts regarding the line of promise.


## THE SPECIAL PROMISE TO THE HOUSE OF JUDAH.

After he had passed the line of promise to the sons of Joseph, Israel gathered all his sons to him and gave each his own special blessing and a prediction of what would happen to them in the 'last days'.

For our present purpose we need only consider the special prediction of Israel regarding the Jews (Judah).

# LINE OF INHERITANCE.

ABRAHAM

ISAAC

JACOB

(Whose name was changed to 'Israel' — he was therefore the first Israelite).

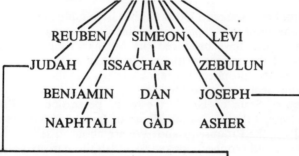

REUBEN  SIMEON  LEVI

JUDAH  ISSACHAR  ZEBULUN

BENJAMIN  DAN  JOSEPH

NAPHTALI  GAD  ASHER

Judah went captive into Babylon and later returned to Jerusalem and is today known as the Jewish State of Israel. The 'seven times' punishment period commenced 604-586 B.C. and was to expire 2520 years later in 1917.

MANASSEH

Manasseh went captive in 730-732 B.C. and their seven times punishment period was to come to an end 2520 years later in 1787-1789.

EPHRAIM

Ephraim went captive into Assyria in 723-721 B.C. and their seven times punishment period was to come to an end 2520 years later in 1798-1800.

*Judah, thou art he whom thy brethren shall praise: Thy hand shall
be in the neck of thine enemies; thy father's children shall bow
down before thee.
Judah is a lion's whelp: from the prey, my son, thou art gone up:
he stooped down, he crouched as a lion, and as an old lion. Who
shall rouse him up?*
*THE SCEPTRE SHALL NOT DEPART FROM JUDAH, NOR
A LAWGIVER FROM BETWEEN HIS FEET, UNTIL
SHILOH [THE MESSIAH/GOD] SHALL COME; and unto him
shall the gathering of the people be.*

Genesis 49: 8-10

That prophecy, spoken 1430 B.C., has been quite literally fulfilled for,
though Israel went into captivity and lost her language, her identity, and
her religion, the Jews produced the Messiah/King and remained the
custodians of the ancient writings. We owe it to the Jews that the vast
library of ancient prophecy is available to us, and the world cannot begin
to assess the debt it owes to the greatest Jew of all.

The Jewish State of Israel is now in possession of Palestine, the
prophets foretell that the whole House of Israel will have representation
territorially in the Promised Land. We are about to see the fulfilment of
the 3,400 year old prophecy spoken to Judah those many years ago "unto
him (the Messiah/God who came out of Judah) will the gathering of the
people be."

Unless the ancient seers were wrong and their great predictor — the ever
existing one — has failed them, there must be on earth today a nation or
company of nations descendant from the ancient House of Israel.

If that is not so then the Jewish scriptures stand discredited as does the
Christian Bible, for it, too, is based upon the writings of the ancient seers,
prophets and law-givers. This is as serious a matter as that!

Where, then, is the nation or group of nations who are the descendants
of the ancient House of Israel? Of the nations on earth today, who is
destined to fulfill the prognostications of the ancient seers? If we find the
answer to those questions we find the key to the future political
development of the planet earth.

## THE DIVISION OF THE KINGDOM OF ISRAEL.

From the time of Israel's (Jacob's) handing on of the birthright to
Ephraim and Manasseh, Joseph's children, to the final division of the
House of Israel from the House of Judah (the Jews) is a period of time
which may be ignored for our present purpose, for it is the division of
Israel which concerns us here.

*So when all Israel saw that the king harkened not unto them, the people answered the king, saying, What portion have we in David? Neither have we inheritance in the son of Jesse. To your tents, O Israel, Now see to thine own house, David. So Israel departed to their tents.*

*But as for the children of Israel who dwelt in the cities of Judah, Rehoboam reigned over them.*

*Then King Rehoboam sent Adoram, who was over the forced labour; and all Israel stoned him with stones, that he died. Therefore King Rehoboam made speed to get him up to his chariot, to flee to Jerusalem.*

*SO ISRAEL REBELLED AGAINST THE HOUSE OF DAVID UNTO THIS DAY.*

*And it came to pass, when all Israel heard that Jeroboam was come again, that they sent and called him unto the congregation, and made him king over all Israel; THERE WAS NONE THAT FOLLOWED THE HOUSE OF DAVID, BUT THE TRIBE OF JUDAH ONLY.*

*And when Rehoboam was come to Jerusalem, he assembled all the house of Judah, with the tribe of Benjamin, an hundred and four-score thousand chosen men, who were warriors, to fight against the house of Israel .... but the word of God came unto Shemaiah, the man of God, saying, Speak unto Rehoboam, the son of Solomon, king of Judah and Benjamin, and to the remnant of the people saying, Thus saith the Lord, Ye shall not go up, nor fight against your brethren, the children of Israel. Return every man to his house; for this thing is from me.*

1. Kings 12: 16-24

Note carefully that the Kingdom of Israel was permanently divided "So Israel rebelled against the house of David unto this day." That Judah was joined only with the tribe of Benjamin "And when Rehoboam was come to Jerusalem, he assembled all the house of Judah, with the tribe of Benjamin, an hundred and fourscore thousand men, who were warriors to fight against the house of Israel."

## THE HOUSE OF ISRAEL GO CAPTIVE INTO ASSYRIA.

The Jews dwelt in the land of Palestine as a national entity 136 years after the House of Israel went captive into Assyria. It is quite incorrect to speak simply of "The Captivity", as some theologians are prone to do, there were two distinct captivities. The House of Israel were taken captive into Assyria in the year 722 B.C. and the House of Judah taken captive into Babylon in the year 586 B.C.

Though the Jews returned from their captivity in Babylon and never lost their national identity, the House of Israel suffered quite a different fate for they never returned to Palestine from their captivity in Assyria.

In his very capable book "Documents of Destiny", F. Wallace Connon makes this very pertinent comment.

"There is one peculiar difference between the two captivities which is very important: in the case of Judah their land was left desolate, as if in readiness for their return, which was also prophesied, but in the case of Israel the Assyrians put other peoples in their land; they were not to return to settle as Judah did."

So the Kingdom of Israel (The House of Israel) came to it's end in the year 722 B.C., taken captive by Tiglath-Pileser, the king of Assyria. From that time forth, even unto our day, the millions of people forming the ten-tribed House of Israel have been 'lost'. They do not appear in the pages of history but they do remain in the pages of prophecy.

## THE PROPHETS FORETELL THE CAPTIVITY OF THE HOUSE OF ISRAEL.

The removal of the House of Israel from the land of their fathers came as no surprise to the prophets of Israel, for it had been predicted by the prophets many years before. Israel was to be divided, destroyed and expelled from the promised land.

Seven hundred years before the event, the prophet Moses had written:

*I call heaven and earth to witness against you this day, that ye shall soon UTTERLY PERISH from off the land whereunto ye go over Jordan to possess it, but shall utterly be destroyed. And the Lord shall scatter you among the nations, and ye shall be left few in number among the heathen, whither the Lord shall lead you.* Deuteronomy 4: 26-27

Yet again in the year 1451 B.C. the prophet Moses prophesied:

*The Lord shall bring thee, and thy king which he shall set over thee, unto a nation which neither you nor your fathers have known; and there shalt thou serve other gods, wood and stone. And thou shalt become an astonishment, a proverb, and a byword, among all nations whither the Lord shall lead thee.* Deuteronomy 28: 36,37

That, of course, was written before the division of the House of Judah from the House of Israel and therefore refers to both.

Is it not fascinating that the prophet foretells the setting up of the kingdom over 400 years before the first king of Israel and also foretells the captivity?

"Thou shalt become a proverb" and indeed Judah went on to become a proverb — "The Wandering Jew" — and the House of Israel did turn to the worship of gods of wood and stone.

We see from the above that the House of Israel was to change it's religion, we should note that well for we will fail to identify the House of Israel if we expect to find it adhering to the Hebrew faith.

The last historic record of the existence of the ten-tribed House of Israel comes from the Jewish historian Josephus, writing in the first century A.D

*The entire body of the people of Israel remained in that country; wherefore there are but two tribes in Asia and Europe subject to the Romans, while the ten tribes are beyond the Euphrates till now, and are an immense multitude not to be estimated by numbers.*                                                         Book XI

## FURTHER EVIDENCE OF THE CONTINUED EXISTENCE OF THE HOUSE OF ISRAEL AS A NATIONAL ENTITY AFTER THE CAPTIVITY.

The prophet Amos foretold that though the House of Israel would be sifted among the nations, not a grain would be lost:

*Behold, the eyes of the Lord God are upon the sinful kingdom, and I will destroy it off the face of the earth, except that I will not utterly destroy the House of Jacob, saith the Lord. For, lo, I will command, and I will sift the House of Israel among all nations, as grain is sifted in a sieve; yet shall not the least kernel fall upon the earth.*

The Book of the Prophet Amos 9: 8-9

In the last great prophecy of the last of the prophets of Israel in the Apocalypse, John sees Israel still existing at the end of time:

*And he carried me away in the Spirit to a great and high mountain, and showed me that great city, the holy Jerusalem, descending out of heaven from God .... And [it] had a wall great and high, and had twelve gates, and at the gates twelve angels, and names of the TWELVE TRIBES of the children of Israel.*

Apocalypse 21: 10, 11

Quite obviously it was his understanding that the ultimate world order would be an order in which the TWELVE tribes of Israel would play their full part.

Jesus of Nazareth, too, spoke of the continued existence of the House of Israel when He said: *"I come not save to the LOST SHEEP of the house of Israel."* He was not speaking *of* the Jews, for he was speaking *to* the Jews. They were not lost — everyone knew where they were — they were in Palestine.

I cannot emphasise too strongly that the promises given to Israel via Abraham, Isaac and Jacob were irrevocable.

According to the ancient seers there was a 'contract' or 'covenant' between the patriarchs and the great universal spirit, the spirit for which they had a number of names which we have consolidated into the word 'God' but of whom they often spoke as 'The Lord'.

There hangs, therefore, upon the ultimate and literal fulfilment of the covenant promises to the children of Israel, not only the reputations of the prophets but also the veracity of 'God' Himself.

The seriousness and solemnity which the ancient seers attached to the promises of God to Israel, is well expressed by the prophet Paul who, when referring to the promises made by 'God' to Abraham, said:

*For when God made promise to Abraham, because he could swear by no greater, he sware by HIMSELF.*

Hebrews 6:13

Oaths are sworn lightly today, and many people do not care much if they break their word, but in the days in which the ancient seers lived an oath was a very serious matter. That God should swear an oath to carry out His promise was solemn indeed.

## THE PROMISES MADE TO JUDAH (THE JEWS).

We have seen that the promises made to Judah were twofold:

1. That they would remain the kingly tribe until the Messiah came.
2. That they would remain the possessors of the Law.

Both those promises were literally fulfilled.

## THE PUNISHMENT OF THE HOUSE OF ISRAEL.

After the division of the Kingdoms in 970 B.C. the House of Judah and the House of Israel went their separate ways. They sinned their separate sins and they incurred each their own punishments.

I want for a few moments to examine the punishments which were to befall the House of Israel.

## 1. THE HOUSE OF ISRAEL WAS TO BE BANISHED FROM PALESTINE.

*But if ye shall at all turn from following me, ye or your children, and will not keep my commandments and my statutes which I have set before you, but go and serve other gods, and worship them.*
*Then will I cut off Israel out of the land which I have given them, and this house which I have hallowed for my name, will I cast out of my sight;*

1. Kings 9: 6, 7

The House of Israel DID worship other gods and WAS banished from the land of Palestine. The one place, therefore, we SHALL NOT find the ten lost tribes is in Palestine.

## 2. THE HOUSE OF ISRAEL WAS TO LOSE IT'S IDENTITY.

The prophet and apostle Paul prophesying to the Romans, discourses at length on the 'grafting into the Olive Tree' of Gentiles. It is a theological discourse which does not concern us here, so I will not quote it at length.

You will remember that just as the Jew was the 'fig tree', so the House of Israel is signified by the 'olive tree'. Paul is therefore speaking to the Romans about the House of Israel, not the Jews.

*For I would not, brethren, that ye should be ignorant of this mystery, lest ye should be wise in your own conceits: that BLINDNESS IN PART HAS HAPPENED TO ISRAEL, UNTIL THE FULNESS OF THE GENTILES COME IN.*

Romans 11:25

The phrase 'until the fulness of the Gentiles come in' of course means 'until the times of the Gentiles come to an end'. Therefore Israel was to be 'BLIND' until the end of the times of the Gentiles.

It is true to say that the House of Israel has become blind to her own identity but since the 'times of the Gentiles' were fulfilled in 1917, Israel ought to be now regaining her sight.

Here is another prophecy foretelling the loss of identity of the House of Israel, written in the 8th century B.C.:

*I will no more have mercy upon the House of Israel, but I will utterly take them away. But I will have mercy upon the house of Judah, and will save them by the Lord their God .... Yet the number of the children of Israel shall be like the sand of the sea, which cannot be measured nor numbered; and it shall come to pass that, in the place where it was said to them, Ye are not my people, there shall it be said unto them, Ye are the sons of the living God.*

Prophecy of Hosea 1: Parts of 6-10

The House of Israel, unlike the House of Judah, was to lose it's identity. Where ever they are, therefore — they will not be called ISRAEL.

## 3. THE HOUSE OF ISRAEL WAS TO LOSE IT'S RELIGION.

Note again in the following quotation the distinction drawn by the prophet Hosea between the House of Israel and the House of Judah:

*My people ask counsel of their idols, and their staff declareth unto them; for the spirit of harlotry hath caused them to err, and they have played the harlot, departing from under their God. They sacrifice upon the tops of the mountains, and burn incense upon the hills, under oaks and poplars, and elms, because the shadow of them is good; therefore your daughters shall commit harlotry, and your spouses shall commit adultery ..... Though thou, Israel, play the harlot, yet let not Judah offend EPHRAIM IS JOINED TO IDOLS; LEAVE HIM ALONE.*
The Book of the Prophet Hosea 4: Parts of 12-18

Just as we should not look for the House of Israel existing under the name of Israel, nor look for it in the land of Palestine, neither should we expect to find the House of Israel worshipping in the way their fathers did.

The religion the House of Israel carried with them from Palestine is described in the prophecy quoted above, it was certainly not the religion of their fathers.

## 4. THE HOUSE OF ISRAEL WAS TO LOSE IT'S LANGUAGE.

The prophet Isaiah makes it quite plain that he is speaking of and to the House of Israel (Ephraim) not Judah in his 28th chapter. He commences the chapter "Woe to the crown of pride, to the drunkards of Ephraim".

In verse eleven of the same chapter, still prophesying of the House of Israel, he says:

*For with stammering lips and another tongue will he speak to this people.*

We must not expect, therefore, that the ten 'lost' tribes of Israel will speak the Hebrew language.

## 5. THE SEVEN TIMES PUNISHMENT PERIOD PRONOUNCED ON THE HOUSE OF ISRAEL.

Here we have, perhaps, the only similarity in the destinies of the two parts of Israel from the time of the division. The length of both their punishment periods was to be the same 'seven times', or 2520 years.

We shall return to that later, but meanwhile do not forget that since their punishment era's commenced on different dates they would also terminate on different dates.

## WHY HAVE THE JEWS NOT REALISED THE TEN TRIBES WERE MISSING BEFORE NOW?

It is quite a reasonable question!

The Jewish State of Israel called itself "The Jewish State of Israel" and not just 'The State of Israel' because of their official recognition of the existence somewhere in the world of the other part of Israel — the House of Israel.

Why, it may be asked, have the Jews not been more aware of the existence of the 'lost tribes' before now? The answer is that they have always been concerned for the fate of their lost brethren.

We have seen that Jesus, in His day, spoke of "the lost sheep of the House of Israel".

The prophet and apostle James, writing in the first century A.D., commenced his Epistle by addressing it to the "Twelve tribes which are scattered abroad."

Josephus the Jewish historian tells, as we have seen, that the ten tribes of the House of Israel were existing in vast numbers "the other side of the Euphrates" in his day.

In later years, but still many years ago, the Jewish Encyclopaedia wrote:

"If the Ten Tribes have disappeared, the literal fulfilment of the prophecies would be impossible. If they have not disappeared obviously they must exist UNDER A DIFFERENT NAME."

As far back as 1879 the Jewish Chronicle stated:

"The Scriptures speak of a future restoration of Israel, which is clearly to include both Judah and Ephraim. The problem then is reduced to it's simplest form. THE TEN TRIBES ARE CERTAINLY IN EXISTENCE. All that has to be done is to discover which people represent them."

In 1918 a Rev. Merton Smith wrote to Dr. Herts, Chief Rabbi of the British Empire, asking his views on the composition of the Jewish people. Here is Dr. Hertz' reply:

"The people known at present as Jews are the descendants of the tribes of Judah and Benjamin, with a certain number of the descendants of the tribe of Levi. So far as is known there is not any further admixture of the tribes."

The theory I propound, that the Jewish State of Israel and those nations which have sprung from the House of Israel will again become one nation in the last days, is no new concept to the Jewish Hierarchy — they have known about it for thousands of years. As the Jewish Chronicle remarked "All that has to be done is to discover which people represent them."

That the identity of the ten lost tribes of the House of Israel has never been revealed is the fault of no-one. In years past, the time had not come for the revelation of this people — the time has now arrived.

## THE PROMISES TO THE HOUSE OF ISRAEL
## (EPHRAIM AND MANASSEH)

We have seen in our past deliberations on the prognostications of the prophets, how very easy it is for people, living at times of prophetic fulfilment, not to recognise the significance of the events which are taking place around them.

I am putting the proposition that the British, American, Celtic, Anglo-Saxon and Scandinavian people are in fact the House of Israel, and are therefore the subject of the ancient seers predictions regarding the fortunes and misfortunes of the House of Israel in the 'last days'. If this proposition is true then the British Commonwealth of Nations and the United States of America are destined to be the vehicle through which the great universal spirit will rule the world.

Before proceeding to the evidence for my proposal, I would make the point that we have established that we are living in the 'last days' and therefore in the days in which it was predicted the lost House of Israel would be identified and reunited with the House of Judah.

Because the name 'lost tribes' gives a picture of a band, or several bands of wilderness wanderers, we must dispel from our minds the thought that the people we are looking for will be people living in some wilderness in rather primitive conditions. The ancient seers make it quite plain that, when they are found, the ten tribed House of Israel will be among the most civilised and powerful nations on earth.

There are very definite prophetic statements as to:

1. The 'size' of the House of Israel when it will be found.
2. The place from which the large group of nations comprising the House of Israel would spread.
3. The period in history when they would emerge from obscurity into the greatness foretold for them.

One stumbling block to the discovery of the House of Israel, and stumbling blocks there had to be, for Israel could not be 'found' before the appointed time, has been the attitude of many Christian churches who have somehow seen the belief that ten tribed Israel still exists as a real nation as a threat to their gospel.

This view is one with which I have to disagree most strongly. Though not the member of any church myself, I must say that anything which establishes the veracity of the ancient prophets must also establish the authority of the teachings of Jesus and anything that adds weight to the claims of Jesus must be good for the Christian church. Conversely, if it can be shown that the teachings of the ancient prophets have failed the whole edifice of mystical Christianity, or should I say 'miracle based' Christianity, comes crashing down. Of course, there is then left the residual Christian social philosophy but that is no better than any other 'do-good' philosophy.

The Messiah/God/King depends upon the ancient seers for confirmation of His identity and the 'supernatural based' Christian faith depends upon the literal existence of the Messiah/God/King, the veracity of the prophets and therefore upon the latter day fulfilment of the predictions regarding the ten tribed House of Israel. If the promises of the 'Ancient of Days' can be abrogated or changed in one instance, then there is no certainty such as the evangelical Christian teaches he has.

## THE HOUSE OF ISRAEL WAS TO BE A 'GREAT AND MIGHTY NATION'.

It was the prophesied destiny of the House of Israel to become a great and mighty nation. There is evidence to suggest, though not clear enough evidence for me to be dogmatic about it, that the word 'Great' was to appear in the name of the resurrected and restored Israel.

Here are the prophecies which foretell this, written 1450 years before Christ was born: In reading these prophecies, keep in mind the 'line of promise' as we have previously traced it.

*And I will make thee a great nation, and I will bless thee, and make thy NAME GREAT; and thou shalt be a blessing. And I will bless them that bless thee and curse them that curse thee.*
Genesis 12:2

"I will make thy name GREAT". I do not put it forth as a proof of Britain's identity as Israel, but is there not some significance in the fact that these islands have become known as GREAT Britain?

Certainly, the British nation and the American peoples fulfil that prophecy spoken 3400 years ago.

## THE LATTER DAY HOUSE OF ISRAEL WAS TO BE 'A NATION AND COMPANY OF NATIONS'.

There has never been an organisation of nations on earth such as those nations known as the United States of America and the British Commonwealth of Nations. Truly there is the so-called Union of Soviet Socialist Republics, but that is held together by the tyranny of oppression not the freewill of it's peoples.

Not only those of a particularly religious turn of mind have noted the human miracle we call the British Commonwealth of Nations. A former Prime Minister of Canada said:

"The colonisation and development of the British Empire is in furtherance of the Divine purpose. I still think that this was no accident, but part of the great purpose of the Infinite, that we should have carried these responsibilities as we have."

Lord Bennett

ALL the Commonwealth countries of the British Commonwealth of Nations are members of FREE CHOICE, as are the member states of the United States of America.

The prophet, speaking about 3,400 years ago, peering down through time to the 'last days' foretold:

*And God said unto him [Jacob], Thy name is Jacob: thy name shall not be called any more Jacob, but Israel shall be thy name: and he called his name Israel. And God said unto him, I am God Almighty: be fruitful and multiply; A NATION AND COMPANY OF NATIONS shall be of thee, and kings shall come out of thy loins.*

Genesis 35: 10,11,12

"A Nation and Company of Nations" — could one describe the British and American people in more accurate terms?

"Of course", someone may say, "there are the Arabs and other nations which have descended from Abraham. No, the promise went not to any other nation than the nations founded by the grandsons of Israel, Ephraim and Manasseh, for have we not seen that they were the inheritors of ALL the promises given to the ancient fathers?

The Jews have certainly not fulfilled that prophecy nor were they supposed to. Perhaps now, my reader will recognise why I have been fastidious in defining the 'line of promise' and now see how, unless one does differentiate between things that really differ, it is impossible to understand the message of the prophets as it is applicable to the destiny of our world.

## BANISHED FROM THE PROMISED LAND – IN WHAT KIND OF PLACE WERE THE TEN TRIBES OF THE HOUSE OF ISRAEL TO GATHER?

The House of Israel was not to be found in Palestine. The ancient seers, however, gave clues to where Israel would be found.

In the Second Book of Samuel, the author of which is unknown, there is a prophecy of Israel having an 'appointed place' waiting for them.

It is a place other than Palestine, because Palestine had been given to the twelve tribes many hundreds of years before. This 'appointed place' was also to be the permanent home of the children of Israel because once they were there they would never again be moved. As we have seen, this simply is not true of Palestine. Both the House of Judah and the House of Israel were deported from Palestine, the House of Israel never to return and the House of Judah were to be ousted from possession of the land for many thousands of years.

In this knowledge, that it is not Palestine being spoken of, let us read the prediction of the prophet, made over 1,000 years before the time of Christ.

> *Moreover I [God Almighty] will appoint a place for my people Israel, and will plant them, that they may dwell in a place of their own, AND MOVE NO MORE,*
>
> 2. Samuel 7:10

This appointed place was to be a place of safety and having settled in the new land, the House of Israel would MOVE NO MORE.

Over a thousand years later, the prophet John in the Apocalypse, had the vision of the 'woman clothed with the sun, and the moon under her feet, and upon her head a crown of twelve stars''. The reference is, of course, to the nation of Israel. John saw 'a great red dragon' persecute the woman and says:

> *The woman fled into the wilderness, where she hath a place prepared of God, that they should feed her there a thousand two hundred and three score days.*
>
> Apocalypse 12:6

The 'place prepared of God' and the 'appointed place' are obviously one and the same place. So we have two prophets separated in time by over a thousand years, foretelling that Israel would have a place prepared for her to escape those who would destroy her. In this 'appointed place' they would grow into a great and mighty nation, and a nation and company of nations would come of them.

John knew well that Palestine was the appointed place for Judah, but he also foretold that Israel of the ten tribes would have another home and another 'appointed place'.

The word 'wilderness' is interesting. It does not mean a desolate place as we imagine but rather a desirable, virgin and fertile land.

Hosea the prophet, writing 740 B.C., tells of how Israel will be 'lured' into the wilderness. His prophecies referred to the ten tribed House of Israel.

*Therefore, behold, I will allure her, and bring her into the wilderness, and speak comfortably unto her.*

Hosea 2:14

Here again, the prophet is speaking of a place other than Palestine for the people of Israel had previously been promised possession of Palestine.

Jeremiah, the weeping prophet, writing after Israel had been taken captive into Assyria, makes a quite remarkable prophecy:

*At the same time, saith the Lord, will I be God of all the families of Israel, and they shall be MY people. Thus saith the Lord, THE PEOPLE WHICH WERE LEFT OF THE SWORD FOUND GRACE IN THE WILDERNESS;*

Jeremiah 31:1, 2

## THE WILDERNESS IN THE ISLANDS.

It is the prophet Isaiah who gives us a vital clue as to where 'the wilderness' may be:

*Sing unto the Lord a new song, and His praise from the END OF THE EARTH, ye that go down to the sea, and all that is therein: THE ISLES, and the inhabitants thereof. Let the wilderness and the cities thereof lift up their voice, the villages that Kedar doth inhabit: let the inhabitants of the rock sing, let them shout from the top of the mountains. Let them give glory unto the Lord, and declare his praise IN THE ISLANDS.*

There are several very important points to note in this prophecy of Isaiah:

1. The 'wilderness' was not a place of bareness and sadness but a place of plenty and gladness.
2. The 'wilderness' was to be situated in the Isles.
3. The 'Isles' were to be situated 'at the end of the earth'.

The limit of the earth as it was known in the days of Isaiah was the North Sea coast of Europe and the Islands that were in the uttermost part of the earth were none other than the British Islands.

# A SHORT RESUMÉ.

We have now seen the following:

1. The House of Israel was banished from Palestine.
2. The banished House of Israel would lose the name 'Israel' and be called by a new name.
3. The House of Israel was to leave it's old religion and find a new religion.
4. The House of Israel would lose it's language and speak a new language.
5. The House of Israel would start to come to greatness 'seven times' or 2520 years after her punishment era had commenced.
6. The House of Israel would not, during that time, rejoin with the Jews.
7. At the end of the punishment period the House of Israel would become 'A great and mighty nation', her name would be 'Great' and she would be the centre of 'a nation and company of nations'.
8. The House of Israel was to occupy a country in which they would prosper and 'be moved no more'. That country was to be in the 'isles' at the 'uttermost part of the earth'.

## CAN WE IDENTIFY 'THE ISLANDS'?

We have already seen that the Islands were at the uttermost part of the earth. The prophet Jeremiah also speaks of Israel as being in the islands.

*Hear the word of the Lord, O ye nations, and declare it in THE ISLES AFAR OFF, and say, He that scattered Israel will gather him, and keep him, as a shepherd doth his flock.*
                                                                Jeremiah 31: 10, 11

The prophet makes it quite plain that the isles are 'afar off'. That, of course, precludes the islands which dot the Mediterranean. Quite apart from which, none of those islands can be said to have produced a nation whose numbers are as multitudinous as the sand of the sea, nor could any of them be described as a great and mighty nation, or be said to have founded a nation and company of nations.

We should note the precise expressions used, well. The Islands were to be at 'the END of the earth' not the 'ENDS of the earth'. The word 'end' is in the singular, making it certain that the prophet was speaking of the 'end' of the known world in one particular direction, not all directions in general. Then again, note that the singular is again used in the term 'the uttermost PART of the earth'.

How do we know that the 'uttermost part of the earth' and 'the end of the earth' means the part in the direction of Britain from Palestine?

Because the prophet tells us so!
Isaiah, in that great passage referring to the end time, says of the House of Israel:

*Behold, these shall come from afar: and, lo, these from the north and from the west: and these from the land of Sinim.*
Isaiah 49:12

"The north and west" is the Hebrew way of saying the north-west. The House of Israel is to come from the Islands at the uttermost part of the earth to the north-west of Palestine. It is a fact not open to doubt that the 'end of the earth' to the north-west of Palestine was, in the days of the ancient seers — the British Isles.

No other islands north-west of Palestine have ever grown into a 'great and mighty nation' or 'a nation and company of nations'. No islands of the Mediterranean have produced a people whose numbers are 'as the sand of the sea'. There can be no doubt that the islands referred to by the ancient seers are the British Islands.

Jesus of Nazareth, we have read, said that He had come to 'the lost sheep of the House of Israel'. His reply then, to His disciples when they asked Him "Lord, wilt thou at this time restore again the Kingdom to Israel?" is far more meaningful than has ever been realised:

*It is not for you to know the times or the seasons, which the Father hath put in His own power. But ye shall receive power, after that the Holy Ghost is come upon you; and ye shall be witnesses unto me both in Jerusalem, and in all Judea, and in Samaria, and unto the uttermost PART of the earth.*
Acts 1:6

Had He so desired, this was the opportunity for Jesus to have exploded forever the idea of a future EARTHLY kingdom of Israel. Jesus did no such thing, on the contrary He made it plain that the kingdom WOULD be restored, but reminded His disciples that it was not for them to know when. In His reply He uses the same word formula as the ancient seers before Him, the singular 'uttermost PART' of the earth.

It is interesting to note that in 1931 Pope Pius XI proclaimed in an address that St. Paul not Pope Gregory first introduced Christianity into Britain. Theodore Martin of Lovan writes:

"Three times the antiquity of the British Church was affirmed in Ecclesiastical Councils. 1) The Council of Pisa, A.D.1417; 2) Council of Constance A.D.1419; 3) Council of Siena, A.D.1423. It was stated that the British Church took precedence of all other Churches, being founded by Joseph of Arimathea, immediately after the Passion of Christ."

# THE HOUSE OF ISRAEL TO INHERIT A GENTILE EMPIRE.

Using the imagery of the House of Israel as the restored 'wife' of the 'Lord' the prophet Isaiah foretold 2682 years ago that the restored House of Israel would inherit Gentile nations. Read what Isaiah said those many years ago and see if you cannot see the colonial period of British history in his words:

*Sing, O barren, thou who didst not bear; break forth into singing, and cry aloud, thou who didst not travail with child; for more are the children of the desolate than of the married wife, saith the Lord.*
*ENLARGE THE PLACE OF THY TENT, and let them stretch forth the curtains of thine habitations; spare not, lengthen thy cords, and strengthen thy stakes;*
*For thou shalt break forth on the right hand and on the left, AND THY SEED SHALL INHERIT THE GENTILES, and make the desolate cities to be inhabited.*
The Book of the Prophet Isaiah 54: 1-3

The inhabitants of the British Isles did just that. Suddenly, at a certain time in history they began to 'enlarge the place of their tent'. The British Empire did inherit may Gentile countries and populate many desolate areas. Canada, Australia, New Zealand, Newfoundland and, through the Pilgrim Fathers, the United States of America, to name but a few.

From this tiny island home of ours, this island shrouded in the cold mists of the sea, sprang a worldwide population. Nations were developed where nationhood had been unknown before, and despite the snide remarks of some of our Marxist acquaintants, ultimately freedom was given, by Great Britain, to more people than have received freedom from any other nation on earth. Yes, my Marxist friend, I say again, when your Soviet Union has given freedom to one quarter as many people as this Great Britain of ours has, then I will listen to your prattle about 'imperialism'.

The world received a language, too — English. Now spoken by more people than any other language on earth, a great international language.

## THE ERA OF HISTORY WHEN THE HOUSE OF ISRAEL'S PUNISHMENT WAS TO CEASE.

We have seen that the history of the British people, and the place from which they sprang into world leadership, conform completely with the predictions made by the prophets.

I would remind you at this point that there were, in fact, to be two separate peoples in the House of Israel, Ephraim and Manasseh. You will remember, if you think back to the 'blessing' given by Israel the Patriarch, he foretold that one would be 'A nation and a company of nations' and the other would be 'A great people'. He also foretold that the 'elder would serve the younger.'

Is it mere chance that this British nation, which conforms so closely to the predictions of the prophets, divided into two major parts — the British Commonwealth of Nations and the United States of America?

You will remember I said there was one thing common to the House of Judah (the Jews) and the two parts of the House of Israel (Ephraim and Manasseh). Each was to have the same 'seven times punishment' period.

Judah's punishment began when she was taken captive into Babylon and the first 'Beast' Nebuchadnezzar was made associate king of Babylon in 603 B.C. we have seen how exactly 'seven times' or 2520 years later, in 1917, Jerusalem was delivered and a national home for the Jews proclaimed.

Manasseh's punishment period commenced at an earlier date, however, in 734—732 B.C. the tribes of Gad, Reuben and part of Manasseh were taken captive into Assyria — Manasseh's punishment period of 2520 had commenced.

The termination dates of the 2520 years of punishment for Manasseh should therefore have terminated in the years 1787-1789. Is it pure coincidence that in 1787 the first Constitution of the United States of America was drawn? It then had to be ratified by each of the individual states, this was done by 1789 when the first Government of the United States of America was formed with George Washington as President.

Ephraim's punishment period began in 723-721 B.C., later than that of Manasseh. Shalmaneser, king of Assyria, besieged Samaria and the Ephraimites were taken into captivity.

Simple arithmetic shows us that the expiration of the 2520 year punishment period should have been in 1798-1800 A.D.

Most people today, I think, assume that the United Kingdom was established before the United States of America came into being but that is not so the United States of America came into being before the United Kingdom — JUST AS THE ANCIENT PROPHET SAID IT WOULD!

Towards the end of the eighteenth century the Catholics in Ireland were in rebellion against Protestant rule. Aid was sought by them from France. Now note the dates carefully, and see, if you can detect the moving of the invisible hand in them. In 1798 it was decided to unite Ireland with Britain and the union became official in 1800. Thus, in 1800, the exact year foretold by the ancient seer, the United Kingdom was formed and the Union Jack became the national flag of the United Kingdom.

When the year 1700 dawned, England had a population of a little over five million dwelling in a small group of islands and torn asunder by strife. Compare that with the number of people of British stock in the world today, quite apart from the vast numbers of non-British stock living in the British Commonwealth of Nations, and I will leave it to my reader to decide whether a national 'resurrection' took place.

Britain and America arose and prospered at exactly the time in history the ancient seers had said the lost ten tribes of the House of Israel would complete their punishment period and become 'a nation and company of nations' and a 'great people'.

The prophets said two nations would appear and become great at that time in history and two nations did — chance or providence?

## THE WAY IN WHICH THE PEOPLE OF THE 'ISLANDS' WOULD SPREAD, FORETOLD.

Not only did the prophets foretell the expansion of the House of Israel from their 'Islands of the sea' but in exactly what directions and in what directional order they would spread.

*And thy seed shall be as the dust of the earth, and thou shalt spread abroad to the west, and to the east, and to the north, and to the south: and in thee and in thy seed shall all the families of the earth be blessed.*

Genesis 28:14

There is a considerable amount of crooked thinking in the world today. We in Britain and America are berated, and unfortunately we sometimes listen and allow ourselves to be given national moral inferiority complexes, for not feeding and industrialising the underdeveloped countries. The fact is that no two countries have done more to feed the hungry and lend money to develop the underdeveloped countries than Britain and America. With all our faults, and there are plenty of people who will gleefully point those out without me doing so, wherever freedom reigns supreme today, it is because of either the effort or blood or both of either the British or American people.

Asia is free because the United States of America's reaction to the Japanese attack on Pearl Harbour, and those parts of Europe and Africa which are free, enjoy that status because of the Allied defeat of Italy and Germany during the last war.

"Bring the poor nations of the earth up to our standard of living" cry the do-gooders, but at the same time condemn our standard of living as using too much of the earth's resources. "Establish new industries in the poor and backward countries" cries the Marxist blithely — all very fine but the Marxist must surely stop using his influence in the trade unions to establish import controls, otherwise to whom will the new industries we have so established sell their products?

The ancient seer foretold that in the resurrected Israel of the latter days would 'all the families of the earth be blessed'. The Christian will argue that the promise was fulfilled in the Gospel of Jesus Christ. Surely even the most evangelical Christian will have to admit that the Gospel of Jesus Christ is valueless to those who have not heard it. Is it not the teaching of almost all churches that to be a beneficiary of the Gospel one has to 'believe' it? How can one believe something one has not heard? So the very corollary of the Christian position is that it is the hearing of the Gospel which brings blessing to the individual and nation, not it's unknown existence.

Who have been the most ardent spreaders of the Gospel? Britain, America, the Anglo-Saxon peoples and the Scandinavians! Even by the criteria that the 'blessing' spoken of in Genesis is not temporal but spiritual, the fact remains it is the British and American people who have fulfilled the prophecy. Though the Jews were the tribe into which the Messiah was born, it was not through them, quite the contrary, that the 'blessing' of the Gospel sped around the world.

The 'blessing' spoken of was tied in with the prophecy of the spreading of Israel to the west, the east, the north and the south. One ignores the context of a prophecy at one's peril — that is the context, that the blessing was to be associated with the 'spreading abroad'.

Is it pure chance that the first colonisation from the British Isles was Newfoundland to the WEST. The second direction in which Britain colonised to India in the EAST. Then, in the 18th century, Britain gained Canada in the NORTH and then Australia, New Zealand and South Africa in the SOUTH. The prophet did not say north, south, east and west as most would say but "West, East, North and South" — a most unusual order— but the precise order in which Britain did spread abroad.

## THE PROMISED ISLES.

There was a very special, important and yet little noticed prophecy spoken to the House of Israel 2700 years ago. It's a very short prophecy, written by the prophet Isaiah under the inspiration of the 'Lord'. Once the House of Israel had been restored and resurrected he promised:

*NO WEAPON THAT IS FORMED AGAINST THEE SHALL PROSPER.*

Isaiah 54:17

In 1066 A.D. the last people of Israelite stock arrived in the British Isles — since then no successful invasion of these islands has taken place.

In 1588 the mighty Spanish Armada assembled for the invasion of England. Britons are, of course, very proud of the part their navy played in the destruction of the Armada and the story of the heroic Sir Francis Drake used to be recounted with pride in our schools until it came to be considered more politically expedient, for some, to denigrate Britain's role in world history. Queen Elizabeth I, however, had other views as to how the Armada met it's doom. Sir Francis Drake must have his share of the credit, as must the fighting men of our navy, but so must the powerful wind which blew at the time of the Armada, destroying numerous ships on the rocks around our coasts.

Queen Elizabeth I seems to have had no doubt from whence the decisive help came. On the medal struck to commemorate the defeat of the Armada she had inscribed the words "He (God) blew and they were scattered."

An army from France, Spain and Holland joined forces with revolutionary forces in Ireland from whence they proposed to invade England. The force was strong and the peril to England great. The invasion fleet was delayed by contrary winds for eighteen days, the invading armies' supplies ran out and the proposed invasion abandoned.

In 1815 the defeat of the British by Napoleon at Waterloo seemed inevitable. The British commanders knew well they had little chance faced with the might of Napoleon's artillery. Battle lines were drawn but the night before Napoleon was to have brought his artillery into position there was a period of torrential rain which delayed the bringing into position of the artillery because of the muddy conditions. By the time Napoleon was ready for the fray, Blucher had arrived with his army and Britain, instead of going down into the valley of defeat, gained a victory which is celebrated to this day. "No weapon which is formed against thee shall prosper."

1915 at Ypres and the Germans had a new secret weapon — GAS! The success of this new weapon depended, of course, on the direction of the wind. With typical German thoroughness Dr. Schmaus, the head of the German Meteorological Department, was consulted and he picked a time when the wind was certain to remain in the same direction for more than a day. He, in fact, gave the German Command an assurance that the wind would remain in the same direction for at least 36 hours.

The gas was released and THE WIND CHANGED almost immediately, the swirling clouds of deadly vapour swept down upon the German army. Had the wind not changed the British army, completely unequipped to meet this kind of warfare, would have been decisively defeated.

A baffled Dr. Schmaus wrote later, in his official report: "In forty years of meteorological records of the German Government THE WIND NEVER ACTED SO PECULIARLY BEFORE."

We who lived through the last war and beheld the spectacular "few" winning the Battle of Britain and know of the strange calm which affected the waters of the North Sea at the time of Dunkirk, need no reminding of seeming acts of providence that took place in those days.

The whole might of the Third Reich was halted at the channel ports — how and why? There is still no satisfactory explanation as to why Hitler and his henchmen, determined men as they had proved themselves to be, ingenious in warfare and ruthless in the execution of their plans, allowed Britain the 'breathing space' which we so urgently required. Why the mad plunge into Russia at that moment? Why the turning of the bombers from strategic targets to civilian targets just as the Germans were on the brink of destroying the R.A.F.? Certainly the Germans had no lack of information about the condition of aircraft, crews and runways. The theory that a few bombs dropped on German cities caused the German High Command to retaliate against British cities and abandon military targets does not suffice or convince: The German airforce was able to hit both civilian and military targets. If there is a better answer to the conundrum than "No weapon that is formed against thee shall prosper", historians do not seem to know of it.

Britain has a reputation, equalled only in these latter days by that of the armed forces of the Jewish State of Israel, of defeating enemies which seem certain to defeat her. Our history is peppered with inexplicable events, miracles of good fortune some would say. Is that what they really are or are they 'Providential Acts' or 'Divine Intervention'? Or are they fulfilments of the prophecy "No weapon which is formed against thee shall prosper"?

There is so very much more to say in this chapter, but then, to pursue each prophecy fully to it's conclusion would turn this chapter alone into a volume.

I would exhort you at this point to turn back to the commencement of this chapter and read again my view that there is to be, in the near future, one united and mighty kingdom composed of the British Commonwealth of Nations, the United States of America and the Scandinavian countries.

The hope that Winston Churchill spoke to the Virginia State Legislature on March 8th, 1946, was in accord with the 3400 year old predictions of the prophets. I wonder if he knew? Or was it that, for a fleeting moment, the 'voice' that spoke of old through the ancient seers spoke again through that man of destiny?

# 17. The Greatest Hoax of All Time

Undoubtedly the question will be asked: If the House of Israel was a civilised people, as we know it was, and if we contend that the first inhabitants of the British Isles were the descendants of the House of Israel, how can it be explained that the early inhabitants of the British Isles were uncivilised?

A very good question. Obviously the answer must lie in one of the following:

1. We are mistaken in our assertion that the earliest inhabitants of the British Isles were of Israelitish origin and they are therefore not

ancestors of the nation which is to fulfil the predictions of the ancient seers and inherit the promises of the patriarchs.
2. The House of Israel lost it's civilisation during it's long journey from Palestine to these islands.
3. The early British were not the 'painted savages' historians would have us believe but rather a highly civilised people long before the arrival of the Romans on these shores.

Were we to accept the first view then we would be left with the unaccountable facts of our previous chapter. How did it come about that a nation and company of nations (The British Commonwealth) and a great people (The United States of America) came to power exactly when the ancient seers predicted the House of Israel would come to Power? Then again, how has it come about, if these nations are not the House of Israel, that they have fulfilled precisely the predictions of the ancient seers as to the area of the earth's surface where ancient Israel were to make their home? How can we explain the fact that the British and American people have fulfilled all the 'marks' of the House of Israel if some other nation exists which IS the House of Israel? Where is that nation?

Our second alternative is unacceptable also, because we must consider it unlikely that an uncivilised band of savages would survive the migratory travels and the attendant conflicts which brought them from Palestine to this land.

So we are left with the third alternative, that the early settlers in these islands were not the 'savages' history has portrayed them to be, but a highly civilised society long before the Romans reached these shores.

It will be the contention of this chapter that history has been subjected to a hoax — a hoax which was carefully planned, brilliantly executed and which has succeeded for almost two thousand years.

I will seek to show that while Rome was yet pagan, the ancestors of the British and American peoples were living in a highly civilised society in the British Isles.

## IT IS A FACT OF HISTORY THAT THE TYRANT INVARIABLY MALIGNS HIS VICTIM.

Have you read Adolf Hitler's "History of the Jewish People"? Fortunately not! Adolf Hitler did not live to write it and he did not conquer widely enough, or for long enough, for his views to become accepted as fact.

Can you imagine, though, had Adolf Hitler prevailed, how different the history books in our schools would be today? Can you imagine what today's generations of school-children would be learning about the Jews?

It is an unfortunate but unavoidable fact that the writing of history is highly derivative. Few people, fifty years after an event, can remember much of what happened seventy-five years ago and, of course, further back than that none of us know anything other than that which we derive from another source.

Today, of course, we have films, photographs, recordings and a wide dissemination of the written word, and there is more latitude for a historian to find new facts and a different view. It is still, however, true that author copies author and, by constant repetition, a 'view' of history becomes a 'fact' of history.

In totalitarian societies such as the Soviet Union, photographs are altered to accord with the Communist Party's current view of history and I think we are all aware of how, even in our own country, film can be manipulated to convey whatever message the film-maker wishes to convey.

Do you remember that ridiculous little dance Adolf Hitler did outside the train at Versailles just before the French signed the surrender? We 'KNOW' it happened because we've all seen it on film. It may surprise you to know that Hitler never did that silly little dance at all — by the simple trick of moving a few 'frames' of the film around, a wartime propagandist manipulated the film just to make Hitler look ridiculous — and succeeded.

History books are altered today in the Soviet Union to support current political opinion, and films are so 'doctored' or 'selected' that they give altogether a different impression from what really happened.

Yes, Adolf Hitler's "History of the Jewish People" would have been some book!

On 5th August 55 B.C., Julius Caesar sailed with two divisions from Witsand, near Calais, with the intent of invading Britain. The Romans landed on the Kentish coast.

THE HOAX which has lasted for almost two thousand years was about to be perpetrated.

Fifty-five days later, bloodied and bowed, having been beaten in battle and having failed to penetrate more than SEVEN MILES inland, Julius Caesar's army beat a hasty retreat. Whilst ashore, Caesar's army had suffered as humiliating and ignominious a defeat as any army has ever suffered. Under cover of darkness the Romans retreated to the comparative safety of the French coast.

A second invasion was mounted from Witsand on May 10th of the following year, 54 B.C. Though above a thousand ships were used and five legions — Gibbons puts the number of men at 60,000 — disembarked, the Roman army were again unable to penetrate inland for more than seventy miles. The campaign lasted until September 10th when peace was concluded at St. Albans.

Though the Roman army had successfully landed on British soil, a storm damaged the fleet, and, while his soldiers repaired their landing craft, Caesar whiled away the weary hours writing a description of the British people:

"Most of the inland inhabitants do not sow corn, but live on milk and flesh, and are clad with skins. ALL the Britains, indeed, dye themselves with wood (a misprint for 'woad') which occasions a bluish colour, and thereby have a more terrible appearance in fight."

Caesar. Gallic War. Volume 2.

It's surprising what some people can learn about "All" the British people in a few weeks — and without getting any further inland than seventy miles!

In view of the fact that it is traditional for conquerors not to say nice things about the people they wish to conquer, is it not surprising that it is with Caesar's ill-informed view of the British of his day, that most modern books on the history of Britain commence?

Thus the HOAX began, and, by sheer negligence, has been repeated by one historian after another. By constant repetition Caesar's flight of historic fantasy has come to be accepted as fact, and it is now widely believed that civilization in the British Isles commenced with the Roman occupation.

The basis upon which historians over the years have made their assumptions about the degree of British civilization existent prior to the arrival of Caesar is as nefarious as that: The writings of a tyrant, about a people he had hardly seen and in whose country he had only been for a few weeks, during which time he had been confined within a very tight perimeter, have become the foundation statements upon which a false edifice of British 'history' has been erected.

Caesar was fortunate — his HOAX worked. He was able to cause the world to believe, as it still believes, that the British were 'painted savages' until the coming of the Romans. How badly Caesar needed to hoax posterity, for, far from being the cultured, law giving, road building, civilising and elevating force we think of today, the Roman Empire was as cruel, corrupt and oppressive an imperialistic force as the world has ever seen. They built roads it is true — the Nazis built magnificent roads, the forerunners of our 'motorways'. The Romans were fine soldiers — so were the Waffen S.S. Despite such qualities, Rome was corrupt as the Third Reich was corrupt and cruel and oppressive to an even greater degree than Hitler's Germany or Communist Russia.

One day, perhaps, Belsen and Auschwitz will become as respectable as tourist attractions as the Colosseum in Rome, time heals and balms the hurt. Certainly no more degrading or agonising human suffering took place in Belsen than in the Colosseum.

Clever, cultured and brave the Romans might have been, but civilised they certainly were not. When it was proposed that the brutal Roman Gladiatorial sports be introduced into Athens a cynic philosopher exclaimed "We must first pull down the statue to Mercy which our forefathers erected fifteen hundred years ago.''

Today, as tourists wander around the place where men, women and children died in the name of sport, exclamations of wonder are expressed at this edifice of Roman ingenuity. At least Hitler and Stalin perpetrated their crimes in the name of vengeance not 'sport'.

The truth about the Roman Empire is that it rampaged across the face of the earth putting to death by fire and the sword millions of innocent people for no other reason than that they withstood the Roman insatiable imperialistic appetite. They also put to the sword, and even worse forms of death, many who did not withstand them but whose sole crime was that they happened to be 'there at the time'.

Rape and pillage followed the armies of Rome, and the best prisoners could expect was public exhibition in the streets of Rome followed by death, but, for many, no swift mercy came. Crucifixion, hanging by nailed hands, writhing in agony, both men and women, often naked, was a much favoured and 'enjoyable' spectacle. Men, women and children herded into the arena with wild beasts, while frenzied crowds watched them being torn limb from limb, eyes burnt from sockets, tongues cut out at the roots, and old and young disembowelled — all 'sport'.

Nothing was too vile to appeal to the Roman taste for excitement and nothing too depraved to be regarded as a sporting spectacle for the depraved citizens of those people who, it is alleged, civilised US — for under the stands of the Colosseum there were private 'viewings' of naked women being raped to death by animals.

Yes, Caesar certainly needed to 'cover his tracks' as did his dictatorial successors in later years. His need to denigrate the civilisations of his victims is understandable, but what is not quite so understandable is why historians have been so willing to accept, without too much protest, the myth of Britain's primitive condition when Caesar arrived. If it be true, and in my view it most certainly is, that the bad invariably drives out the good, the very characteristics of the Roman Empire would disqualify it from being a civilising influence in our country.

## WHO SAID THIS?

I have deleted a number of words from the following speech because they will surely identify the speaker, and the circumstances in which the speech was made. I do not want to give you any clues because I want you to guess when and where the speech was made and by whom.

You will see that it is a speech that stands majestically besides the inspiring words of President Abraham Lincoln in his Gettisburgh Address, the words of the bard William Shakespeare and the stirring war speeches of Winston Churchill, for it's magnificent command of the English language.

Who spoke these words? Where was he when he spoke them? When did he speak them?

"Had my government in Britain been directed solely with the preservation of my hereditary domains, or the aggrandizement of my own family, I might long since have entered this city an ally, not a prisoner: nor would you have disdained for a friend a king descendant from illustrious ancestors, and the dictator of many nations. My present condition, stripped of it's former majesty, is as adverse to myself as it is a cause of triumph to you. What then? I was lord of men, horses, arms, wealth; what wonder if at your dictation I refused to resign them? Does it follow, that because the (1) ........ aspire to universal domination, every nation is to accept the vassalage they would impose? I am now in your power betrayed, not conquered. Had I, like others, yielded without resistance, where would have been the name of (2) .....Where your glory? Oblivion would have buried both in the same tomb. Bid me live. I shall survive for ever in history one example at least of (3) .....clemency."

The words are the words of a proud man and the language the language of an educated man. Who spoke them?

No, they are not the words of Shakespeare but the British leader, Caractacus, who led the fight against the Romans in Britain until A.D.52. Such was his fame that when he was taken to Rome captive, over three million people crowded the streets of Rome to see the mighty Briton.

So well had the men of Caractacus fought that the Roman Emperor Claudius had to hasten to Britain with reinforcements, to personally take charge of the battle at Clune despite there being already three of Rome's most famous generals in the field — Aulus Plautius, Vespasian, who was later to become Emperor, and Titus, the general who was later to destroy Jerusalem.

After the battle, Caractacus sought shelter with the Queen of the Brigantes who betrayed him. He was taken prisoner while he slept.

Caractacus was accorded the privilege of addressing the Senate in Rome where he made the aforementioned speech. You can now, by the way, fill in the blanks: (1) "Romans" (2) "Caradoc" and (3) "Roman".

The lot of any foreign king captured by the Romans was not a happy one. Death was certain but never merciful, the ex-enemies of Rome would expect to be pulled behind chariots, disembowelled or to suffer any of a number of ghastly deaths the Romans reserved for their conquered foes.

Historians have failed to agree on a reason why Caractacus was pardoned and he and his family set free to return to Britain.

Let me ask you — is that speech the speech of a 'Barbarian'? Can we say of a man that has a command of thought and language such as that speech shows, that he was a 'savage'? I contend that Caractacus was a highly civilised person.

Remember, he was speaking to people who knew him and they knew his nation. He could not fool them nor could they fool him. Had he said anything in that speech which was not fact, the Romans would have laughed him to scorn, yet he speaks of:

> Hereditary domains.
> Being descendant from 'Illustrious ancestors'.
> Being 'Dictator of many nations'.
> 'Former majesty'.
> Having 'men, horses, arms, wealth'.

All these things, put together with the long hard struggle fought against the best commanders Rome could put in the field, and the majestic language of Caractacus' speech lead us to believe that there was a highly developed civilisation in Britain before the Romans came. Who were Caractacus' 'Illustrious ancestors' — the Kings of Israel perhaps?

Caractacus remained in Rome for seven years, where he and his family lived in the 'Palace of the British'. Do you think for one moment that the Romans would have provided a palace for the use of a 'savage' king?

## THE ROMAN G.I. BRIDES.

It is here that we can explode once and for all the myth that Rome brought Christianity to Britain. Britain was a Christian country while Rome was yet Pagan.

Gladys — it sounds an unusually modern name for an ancient Briton — the sister of Caractacus, was married to the Roman Commander-in-Chief, Aulus Plautius!

Tacitus, the historian, in his Annals, tells us how Gladys was brought to trial in pagan Rome, accused of being a Christian! When she was married Gladys took the name of Pomponia Graecina Plautius. We are told she had a considerable command of the Greek language — an odd proficiency for a 'painted savage'.

We are told by Tacitus that:

"Pomponia Graecina, a woman of illustrious birth, and the wife of Plautius, who, on his return from Britain, entered the city with the pomp of an ovation, was accused of embracing the rights of a foreign superstition."

That 'foreign superstition' was Christianity. Gladys was set free and several years later her husband Plautius, the Roman Commander-in-Chief, became — a Christian!

A 'painted savage' proficient in Greek — why most people in Britain are not proficient in Greek now! The Commander-in-Chief of the Roman army marrying a 'savage' and taking her back to Rome — does it pass the test of commonsense?

In A.D.45 the Roman Emperor Claudius offered the hand of his daughter, Venus Julia, in marriage to the British King Arviragus and they were married in Rome. Can you imagine a Roman Emperor allowing his daughter to marry a king from a land of 'savages'?

No, there are far too many holes in the 'painted savage' story for it to be seriously maintained.

## THE ANCIENT BRITONS.

In her excellent work "Celt, Druid and Culdee", Isabel Hill Elder writes "Wilford states that the old Indians were acquainted with the British Islands, which their books described as the sacred isles of the west, and called one of them Britashtan, or the seat or place of religious duty."

The popular idea that the ancestors of the British were painted savages has no foundation in fact. It was a custom and practice of the Picts and other branches of the Celtic and Gothic nations to make themselves look terrible in war, from whence came the Roman term 'savage'. The 'painting' was in reality tattooing, a practice still cherished in all it's primitive crudities by the British sailor and soldier.

Far from these ancestral Britons having been mere painted savages, roaming wild in the woods as we are imaginatively told in most of the modern histories, they are now, on the contrary, as disclosed by newly-found historical facts given by Professor Waddell, known to have been from the very first grounding of their galley keels upon these shores, over a millenium and a half (1500 years) before the Christian era, a highly civilised and literate race, pioneers of civilisation.

The universally held belief that the British are a mixed race has prevailed during many centuries; this belief, however, is now fading out of the scientific mind and giving place to the exact opposite. Britons, Celts, Gauls, Anglo-Saxons, Danes and Normans, when warring with each other, were kinsmen shedding kindred blood.

Professor Sayce, at a later date, in one of his lectures, observes that he "misses no opportunity of uprooting the notion that the people who form the British nation are descendant from various races, all the branches that flowed into Britain being branches of the self-same stock" Pages 16-17.

Having read Mrs. Elder's book as one of the many works of reference which it has been necessary to read during the writing of this book, I have it on my list of books for regular periodic reading, for, in these days when there are so many voices in Britain and America who would seek to denigrate our great nations, such a work is a source of encouragement in the battle not to let the greatness of our nations be lost by default.

It is to Mrs.Elder, too, that I am indebted for drawing my attention to the following quotation: It is a description by Strabo, of the visit to

Athens of a Druid astronomer of his day:

"He came not clad in skins like a Scythian, but with a bow in his hand, a quiver hanging on his shoulders, a plaid wrapped around his body, a gilded belt encircling his loins, and trousers reaching down from the waist to the soles of his feet. He was easy in his address; agreeable in his conversation; active in his dispatch and secret in his management of great affairs; quick in judging of present accuracies, and ready to take his part in any sudden emergency; provident withal in guarding against futurity; diligent in the quest of wisdom; fond of friendship; trusting very little to fortune, yet having the entire confidence of others, and trusting with everything for his prudence. He spoke Greek with a fluency that you would have thought that he had been brought up in the Lyceum; and conversed all his life with the academy of Athens."

Today there are still 'Druids' in Wales, though, I think, their order owes little, apart from it's name, to the Druids of ancient Britain.

In the Britain of the pre-Christian era, Druidism was, in fact, the organising force and civilising force both in Britain and, to a lesser extent, on the continent of Europe. In it's Order were the doctors of medicine, clergy, legal profession and politicians. The whole of national life centred around the Druid presence in the community.

Far from being the 'savages' the Roman's wrote us into history as being, before the Romans arrived in Britain there were over forty major universities here. According to Caesar, the youth of Gaul were sent to Britain for education and sixty thousand British youths were in British colleges.

## THE MYSTERY OF THE DRUID JESUS.

When Christianity came to these islands, it came while Rome was still worshipping it's Pagan gods and would do so for another two hundred or so years. We are always told how the Romans sent missionaries to Britain, the FACT is that BRITAIN SENT MISSIONARIES TO ROME. Past Popes have been the first to admit that the British Church was the first church, outside Palestine, in the world.

There seems to have been little antagonism between the ancient Druid faith and the newly arrived Christian faith. Seeing that the Druids were such a highly civilised society, is it not strange that whereas they were at no time willing to accept Roman gods, the Druids became so easily at one with the 'new faith' from Palestine? It can be truly said that, in no part of the world was Christianity so easily assimilated than in Druid Britain.

We have seen that as little as ten years after the crucifixion, British royalty was professing the Christian Faith.

The reason Druidism so easily accepted the Christian faith was because the Christian faith did not call upon them to change their own faith — Christianity came as an extension to their faith, not a change.

Today in Wales you can walk on Sunday evenings into the many chapels which conduct their services in Welsh, the language spoken by the ancient Druids. The minister will preach about the God called "Yesu" and the congregation will stand and sing to the God called "Yesu". The chapel will look like a Christian chapel, the minister will be dressed like a Christian minister and the congregation will be singing Christian hymn tunes, but all to the God "Yesu".

The Welsh chapels in Wales, in 1984, still worship "Yesu" and "Yesu" was the Druid God several hundred years before Jesus was born in Bethlehem of Judea.

This is one of the greatest mysteries you will find in this book, or in any other book for that matter, the fact that the chapels in Wales still, in 1984, sing praises to an ancient Druid God.

The reason? Because hundreds of years before Jesus was born in Palestine, the Druids of Britain were already worshipping — Jesus! The word "Yesu" in the ancient Welsh language means 'Jesus' and their God has been called Jesus from the earliest times.

No wonder the Druids had no problem in identifying themselves with Christianity — the name of Jesus was one with which they were already very familiar.

How did that come about? If they were, as we believe, the House of Israel, they would know of the writings of the ancient seers and would be expecting the Messiah-God. The name 'Jesus' means 'Saviour' — Israel in the Isles knew of the promise of the ancient seers that in Bethlehem there would be born a 'Saviour' a 'Jesus' or, in their language, a 'Yesu'.

# 18.
# The Ancient Seers Foretell an Event Which Will 'Out Science Fiction' Science Fiction

The ancient seers must have been as confused as anyone about the subject matter of some of their prophecies — they cannot have been unaware that many of their predictions regarding the Messiah-God were seemingly contradictory.

On the one hand we have portrayed a Messiah-God who would come in a meek and lowly form, who would be 'despised and rejected of men, a man of sorrows and acquainted with grief', who even the House of Judah would reject and who would die by crucifixion.

Other predictions regarding the coming Messiah-God were quite different. The Messiah-God was to come in majesty, he was to reign forever, 'King of Kings and Lord of Lords'. Messiah-God was to bring peace to the earth after conquering nations which had gathered at the battle of Armageddon. The Messiah's kingdom was to be the whole earth, all nations would bow the knee to him and he would thereafter rule them forever, in peace, but with a rod of iron.

· It is to the credit of the ancient seers that they made no attempt to reconcile that which would seem to have in it the seeds of discrepancy. It is the yardstick of their integrity and their faith, that they wrote exactly what was revealed to them and made no attempt to 'make sense' of those things in their prognostications which seemed to be contradictory.

We have seen how the prophecies of the ancient seers regarding the birth, life, death and resurrection of the Messiah-God were fulfilled in Jesus the prophet of Nazareth. It is obvious, though, that the prognostications of his sitting on the throne of his father David and ruling Israel were NOT fulfilled. Neither were the predictions that he would rule the nations of the world as 'King of Kings and Lord of Lords' fulfilled. Far from every knee bowing to him, he was rejected.

Attempts to 'spiritualise' these unfulfilled prophecies simply will not do — I once heard a minister, more ingenious than theologically informed, discourse at length on how the church is the 'Lord's Kingdom' and had conquered the hearts of people in every nation under heaven. Such, the minister proclaimed, was the meaning of Christ's Universal Kingship. One, of course, has to doubt whether a heart conquered by 'the church', of whatever denomination that church may be, is the same as a heart conquered by Christ as King. Even if we admit that it is, we must still doubt whether sufficient people are really convinced of the Christian faith, to enable us to say that they fulfil the prophecy that Jesus would conquer and rule the nations with a rod of iron.

There can be no doubt that the prophets contemplated a physical battle between the nations of the world and a physical response by a physical Messiah.

Just as both the prophets, Ezekiel, and John in Apocalypse, made it quite clear that the Battle of Armageddon is to be a real battle fought between real armies, so they also made it clear that the Messiah who will 'utter his voice before his army' will be a physical Messiah engaged in physical battle.

We therefore come face-to-face with a concept which 'out-science fictions' science fiction — that much discredited subject the 'Second Coming' of Jesus Christ.

## THE COMING KING.

There was a time, just a couple of hundred years ago, when people turned out in considerable numbers to watch the 'crackpots' who attempted — with the aid of various contraptions — to fly. Of course, the 'wise' knew they never would be able to fly. The world continued to smile at the 'crackpots', but the 'crackpots' continued trying and of course all the time the 'wise' knew they never would succeed — one day the 'crackpots' did fly .... and they're still doing it!

One cannot blame people for smiling at the mention of the 'second coming' of Christ for it had been used by ranters of all ages to strike fear into the hearts of their congregations, and often to pour money into the coffers of their churches.

In the mid 18th century 'second coming' fever reached such a pitch that people throughout the world were being warned to prepare for the sudden appearance of Jesus Christ. Even so well known a person as Lady Hester Stanhope, niece of William Pitt, took up residence in Lebanon so that she would be present at the 'second coming'.

It is reported that many sold their homes, withdrew their savings from the banks and gave their money to the poor unbelieving, who, they conceived, would be 'left behind' and therefore able to spend it.

The history of the doctrine of the 'second coming' has, as I have said, been discredited. Often it has been discredited through zeal but more often because it has been used as a rough-edged tool by preachers for their own ends.

Putting behind us our amusement at the antics of the past, we must ask ourselves one question: Did Jesus Christ and the prophets really foretell the Second Coming of the Messiah to Earth?

The past sixty years or so have seen some of the most horrific events ever to have happened upon the planet earth. Even now the whole world lives daily beneath the threat of blistering extinction by nuclear weaponry.

As we have seen, the prophets of old made it plain that our world would not be destroyed, but, with equal clarity, they foretold that, in our generation, the world would pass through a time of indescribable trouble and confusion politically, economically and militarily.

Jesus of Nazareth describes it thus:

> *And there shall be signs in the sun, the moon and the stars; and upon earth distress of nations with perplexity; the sea and the waves roaring; Men's hearts failing them for fear, and for looking after those things which are coming on the earth; for the powers of the heavens shall be shaken.*

> Luke 21: 25, 26

I would submit to you that that is a precise description of the attitude of world statesmen and thinking people today. Nations have always been distressed, but never quite so perplexed. Even at the zenith of the Great War it was possible to believe in 'the war to end wars' but who would believe such a thing today?

At the turn of the century mankind held the view that science would create a world of plenty and socialism would create a great 'international' of workers which would prevent war. Education would bring about the circumstances in which crime, poverty, disease, and indeed all the ills that had afflicted mankind from the days of his emergence from the cave, would gradually disappear. In hindsight there is little we can congratulate ourselves upon and perhaps less we can look forward to. "Distress of nations with perplexity" and "men's hearts failing them for fear and for looking after those things which are coming on the earth." Apt words indeed!

It was the prophet Jesus of Nazareth who said all this, you will remember. He said it during the discourse in which he foretold the destruction of the Temple and of Jerusalem. The discourse in which he foretold Jerusalem would be trodden down until 1917.

Is it not strange that the very conditions he forecast have taken place in the very generation in which he predicted they would take place?

But let us go back to the Mount of Olives for a moment for it is there, you will remember, that he made his prognostication. It was there, too, that the disciples had asked him the question to which all these predictions were the answer.

## THE MOUNT OF OLIVES DISCOURSE.

You will forgive me repeating once again the quotation, it IS important and I know that many of my readers will not go back to the page on which I originally quoted it:

*And Jesus went out and departed from the temple; and his disciples came to him to show him the buildings of the temple.*
*And Jesus said unto them, See ye not all these things? Verily I say unto you, There shall not be left here one stone upon another, that shall not be thrown down.*
*And as he sat upon the Mount of Olives, the disciples came unto him privately, saying, Tell us, when shall these things be? And WHAT SHALL BE THE SIGN OF THY COMING, and of the end of the age?*

Matthew 24: 1-3

We have previously dealt with the question "What shall be the sign of ... the end of the age." but the first part of this question is a puzzle. "What shall be the sign of thy coming?"

He was sitting before them and they ask him "What shall be the sign of thy coming?" Don't you think that to be a very mysterious question to ask? Why did they ask it?

They asked Jesus Christ of Nazareth what would be the sign of his coming, despite the fact he was sitting there in front of them, because he had made the claim that he would come to earth a second time in the 'last days'.

## THE COMING WORLD RULER.

We have seen that there have been people predicting the 'second coming' of Jesus Christ since the year 'dot'. There have, too, been many who have foretold the year in which he would come and the place to which he would come. People sold property, gave up jobs and sat on the mountains in white robes, at midnight, expecting the predictions of the preachers to come to pass. Nothing happened and most of us now have a rather amused love for the good old 'second comers' as they are affectionately known.

I have to admit that the concept of someone who died almost two thousand years ago in Palestine coming back to earth in this twentieth century offends my intellect. My mind finds it impossible to accept or grasp. There is no doubt that Jesus of Nazareth was taken and nailed to a cross — almost two thousand years ago! Yet there is absolutely no doubt either that he taught he was going to come back to earth to save this world of ours from destruction at the end of the age.

Yet, there is, too, another aspect of this which could offend my intellect. It is that, as we have seen, all the things Jesus foretold would happen in the world have happened. The things foretold by the ancient seers who lived centuries before Jesus, came to pass in the minutest detail: The date of the birth of Jesus, the town in which he would be born, the family into which he would be born, the fact his family would come from Nazareth, that he would live in Egypt, that he would be crucified, the things the Roman soldiers said at the foot of the cross, all foretold many hundreds of years before he was born — that such prognostications could be made, did I not know it to be true, would offend my intellect. Yet it did all happen, and I have to accept that my intellect is an inadequate tool for the comprehension of some aspects of the things we are studying.

Of course, many theologians have found a comfortable half-way-house in spiritualising the 'second coming' of Jesus Christ. Reading the statements of Jesus, his disciples and his apostles, on the subject it seems he, and they, took great care to pre-empt any spiritualisation of his return to earth.

Since commencing this book I have studied, nay, agonised to see if, without violating the context, the coming again of Jesus could be 'explained away' — it cannot. I would have to accuse any theologian who attempted to teach any other than that Jesus taught he would return again in the same bodily form as he had when he lived on earth, of gross intellectual dishonesty.

# THE METHOD OF JESUS' COMING.

How did Jesus say he would come again? Directly after his prediction of "Men's hearts failing them for fear, and for looking after those things which are coming on the earth; for the powers of the heavens shall be shaken" he continued as follows:

*And then shall they see the Son of man coming in a cloud, with power and great glory. And when these things begin to come to pass, then LOOK UP, and lift up your heads; for your redemption draweth near.*

Another quotation from Jesus himself makes it quite plain that he predicted his own 'second coming':

*And then shall appear the sign of the Son of man in heaven; and then shall all the tribes of the earth mourn, and they shall see the Son of man coming in the clouds of heaven with power and great glory.*
*And he shall send his angels with a great sound of a trumpet, and they shall gather together his elect from the four winds, from one end of heaven to the other.*

Matthew 24: 30, 31

Yet another description of his 'second coming' is given by Jesus:

*When the Son of man shall come in his glory, and all the holy angels with him, then shall he sit upon the throne of his glory. And before him shall be gathered all the nations; and he shall separate them one from another, as a shepherd divideth his sheep from the goats ...*

Matthew 25: 31, 32

The story of the ascension, too, contains a reference to his 'second coming':

*And when he [Jesus] had spoken these things, while they beheld, he was taken up, and a cloud received him out of their sight. And while they looked steadfastly toward heaven as he went up, behold, two men stood by them in white apparel; Who also said, Ye men of Galilee, why stand ye gazing up into heaven? This same Jesus, who is taken up from you into heaven, SHALL SO COME IN LIKE MANNER AS YE HAVE SEEN HIM GO INTO HEAVEN.*

The Acts of the Apostles 1: 9-11

288

Paul the prophet apostle also foretells the 'second coming' of Jesus Christ in several passages:

> For this we say unto you by the word of the Lord, that we who are alive and remain unto the coming of the Lord shall not precede them who are asleep.
>
> For the LORD HIMSELF shall descend from heaven with a shout, with the voice of the archangel, and with the trump of God; and the dead in Christ shall rise first;
>
> Then we which are alive and remain shall be caught up together with them in the clouds, to meet the Lord in the air; and so shall we ever be with the Lord.

1. Thessalonians 4: 16, 17

It really is incredible stuff, isn't it, and yet, you know, you cannot be a member of most Christian denominations without believing things which are equally incredible. Is the virgin birth more credible, or the resurrection, or the miracles Jesus performed when he was on earth, or the existence of the soul of a dead person in a place called purgatory (as taught by the Roman Catholic Church) or the resurrection of the dead (taught by almost all churches) ? To be a Christian you either have to have a profound disregard for the meaning of words, have an absolute disrespect for logic or believe in the miraculous — there is no other way.

The prophet John, in the Apocalypse, confirms the statements of Jesus about the 'second coming' but lays considerable emphasis on the fact that the prophet of Nazareth returns to defeat the hoards invading Palestine. This view is in keeping with that of the more ancient prophets in which they saw the Messiah-God occupying the throne of David and ruling Israel.

## THE 'SECOND COMING' OF CHRIST FORETOLD IN THE APOCALYPSE.

Remember John wrote about 96 A.D. — after the FIRST coming of the Messiah:

> And I saw heaven opened and, behold, a white horse; and he that sat upon him was called Faithful and True, and in righteousness he doth judge and make war.
>
> His eyes were like a flame of fire, and on his head were many crowns; and he had a name written which no man knew, but he himself.
>
> And he was clothed with a vesture dipped in blood; and his name is called The Word of God. And the armies that were in heaven followed him upon white horses, clothed in fine linen, white and clean.

*And out of his mouth goeth a sharp sword, that with it he should smite the nations, and he shall rule them with a rod of iron; and he treadeth on the winepress of the fierceness and wrath of Almighty God.*
*And he hath on his vesture and on his thigh a name written, KING OF KINGS, AND LORD OF LORDS.*

Apocalypse Chapter 19: 11-16

The prophet Zechariah, writing six hundred years before Christ was born, foretold that the Messiah would return in the 'last days' at the time of the Battle of Armageddon:

*Behold, the day of the Lord cometh, and thy spoil shall be divided in the midst of thee.*
*For I will gather all nations against Jerusalem to battle; and the city shall be taken, and the houses rifled, and the women ravished; and half the city shall go forth into captivity, and the residue of the people shall not be cut off from the city. Then shall the Lord go forth, and fight against those nations, as when he fought in the day of battle.*
*And his feet shall stand in that day upon the Mount of Olives, which is before Jerusalem on the east, and the Mount of Olives shall cleave in it's midst toward the east and toward the west, and there shall be a very great valley;*

The Book of the prophet Zechariah 14: 1-4

This concept of God Himself coming to earth is to be found in one of the oldest prophetic books in existence, the Book of Job, for he says:

*For I know that my redeemer liveth, and that HE SHALL STAND AT THE LATTER DAY UPON THE EARTH and though after my skin worms destroy this body yet IN MY FLESH shall I see God:*

Job 19:25

## OUR FIRST SUMMARY.

Though the reader may well have heard mention of the 'second coming' of Jesus Christ, the chances are that few will have heard much more than a sketchy outline of what the 'second coming' is to entail. I think it prudent, therefore, to summarise what we have read from the writings of the ancient seers so far:

1  That the Messiah would return to earth in the 'last days'.
2  People who are referred to as 'the dead in Christ' it is said will be resurrected from their graves.

3    Living people will be 'caught up to meet the Lord in the air'.

4    The time this will take place is after the tribulation of the 'Times of the Gentiles' (after 1917).

5    It will also take place before or during the Battle of Armageddon.

6    At the time the 'second coming' takes place the greatest war in human history will be waging and the Messiah will lead a mighty army.

7    A select group of people will be 'taken' for Jesus said: "Two shall be sleeping in a bed, one shall be taken the other left ..."

8    Having subdued the warring nations, the Messiah will rule as King of Kings and Lord of Lords. Universal peace will exist.

9    The throne upon which the King will sit will be the throne of David and and his Kingdom will be the WHOLE of Israel both the House of Judah and the House of Israel.

You say it offends your sense of reason — I say to you that it offends mine too. It is such a persistent theme of the ancient seers, however, that it cannot be ignored.

I did say, didn't I, that this would 'out-science fiction' science fiction?

## THE SIGNS WHICH WERE TO PRECEDE THE 'SECOND COMING' OF THE MESSIAH.

The main 'sign' was, of course, to be the end of the times of the Gentiles, but there were other signs prophesied, too. Let us see if we can recognise any of these signs as happening in our world today.

In the very same Mount of Olives discourse in which Jesus predicted the destruction of the Temple and the duration and end of 'the Times of the Gentiles', he said something else very significant about the event immediately preceeding his second coming:

*...and they shall see the Son of man coming in the clouds of heaven with power and great glory ... But of that day and hour knoweth no man, no, not the angels of heaven, but my Father only.*
*BUT AS THE DAYS OF NOAH WERE, so shall also the coming of the Son of man be.*
*For as in the days that were before the flood they were eating and drinking, marrying and giving in marriage ...*
Matthew 24: Parts of 30, 36 and 38

The scene he sets is meaningful to those conversant with the narrative of the flood. There had been warning of a great world-wide catastrophe, but who took any notice? The world carried on as it had always carried on. Despite the signs, despite the warnings, people's lives went on normally. Is that not the story of every disaster the world has ever known?

Disaster has a habit of being sudden and people have a habit, as someone once said, of being like the ostrich — 'sticking his head in the sand hoping his bottom will be safe'. I'm told ostriches do not stick their heads in the sand — humans do! That's how Hitler crept up on us and how Russia is creeping up on us today.

There is, however, a far deeper meaning to Jesus' remark about the days of Noah. The reason the Genesis narrative gives for the destruction of the earth in those days is:

> *The earth was corrupt before God, and the earth was filled with violence.*
>
> Genesis 6:11

"As it was", said Jesus, "in the days of Noah". The earth was filled with violence.

## THE SOCIETY EXISTING IMMEDIATELY PRIOR TO THE SECOND COMING OF THE MESSIAH WAS TO BE A VIOLENT SOCIETY.

By sheer chance, as I typed the above words, I broke off to listen to the nine o'clock news on television and I heard that crimes of violence had increased by 40% in the last year.

It's about twelve years since American friends came to Britain and I took them around my home town. I do a lot of business with a firm of accountants who allow me to use their car park if I am ever in need of parking space. Though the offices are on the main street, the car park is down a dark, narrow lane at the back of the property.

"You're not going down there?" my American friends queried.

"Why?" I asked in some surprise.

"You'll get mugged!"

"Mugged", I said, "whatever is getting 'mugged'?"

As I say, that's just about twelve years ago — we all know what getting 'mugged' means now, don't we?

The prophet and apostle Paul foretold that in the days immediately preceding the coming of the Messiah the following would take place:

> *This know also, that in the last days perilous times shall come. For men shall be*
>
> *Lovers of their own selves,*
> *covetous,*
> *boasters,*
> *proud,*
> *blasphemers,*
> *disobedient to parents,*
> *unthankful,*

*unholy,*
*without natural affection,*
*trucebreakers,*
*false accusers,*
*incontinent,*
*fierce,*
*despisers of those that are good,*
*traitors,*
*heady,*
*highminded,*
*lovers of pleasure more than lovers of God;*
*having a form of Godliness, but denying the power thereof:*
*from such turn away.*

2. Timothy 3: 1-5

Yes, Paul really did say all that about the days immediately preceding the second coming of the Messiah. Do you recognise the society in which we live in those words?

There is little need for me to produce figures to prove to you how lawlessness has increased in the past few years. You KNOW it because it is no doubt happening where you live. Law and order continues to be the big issue in British and American elections but the more we talk about law and order the less law and order we seem to get — but then that's exactly what the prophet foretold would happen over nineteen hundred years ago.

## FAMINES, PESTILENCE AND EARTHQUAKES.

Jesus of Nazareth said that immediately prior to the coming for the second time of the Messiah there would be "Famines, pestilences and earthquakes in diverse places."

Once again I propose to let my reader judge whether we have seen such signs in this twentieth century. Here's a list of just SOME of the earthquakes which have taken place in the past eighty-five years:

1898 ...............Japan 22,000 killed

1906 ...............Chile 1,500 killed.

1906 ...............San Francisco 500 killed.

1907 ...............Jamaica 1400 killed.

1908 ...............Italy 160,000 killed.

1915 ...............Italy 30,000 killed.

1920 ...............China 180,000 killed.

1923 ...............Japan 143,000 killed

1930 ...............Italy 1,500 killed.

1932 ...............China 70,000 killed.

1935 ...............Baluchistan 60,000 killed.

1939 ...............Chile 30,000 killed.

1939 ...............Turkey 40,000 killed.

1946 ...............Hawaii 150 killed.

1948 ...............Japan 5,000 killed.

1949 ...............Ecquador 6,000 killed.

1950 ...............India 1,500 killed.

1953 ...............Turkey 1,200 killed.

1954 ...............Algeria 1,600 killed.

1956 ...............Afghanistan 2,000 killed.

1957 ...............Iran 2,500 killed.

1957 ...............Iran 1,400 killed.

1957 ...............Mongolia 1,200 killed.

1960 ...............Chile 5,700 killed.

1960 ...............Morocco 12,000 killed.

1962 ...............Iran 12,000 killed.

1963 ...............Libya 300 killed.

1963 ...............Taiwan 100 killed.

1963 ...............Yugoslavia 1,000 killed.

1964 ...............Alaska 100 killed.

1968 ...............Iran 11,600 killed.

1970 ...............Turkey 1,100 killed.

1970 ...............Peru 50,000 killed.

1971 ...............Los Angeles 64 killed.

1971 ...............Turkey 800 killed.

1972 ...............Iran 5,000 killed.

1972 ...............Nicaragua 10,000 killed.

1973 ...............Mexico 527 killed.

1976 ...............Guatemala 22,419 killed.

1976 ...............Italy 1,000 killed.

1976 ...............Indonesia 3,443 killed and missing.

1976 ...............Indonesia 600 killed.

1976 ...............China 700,000
(the second worst earthquake in history)

1976 ...............Philippines 8,000 killed and missing.

1976 ...............Turkey 4,000 killed.

1977 ...............Rumania 1,540 killed.

1977 ...............Iran 520 killed.

1978 ...............Iran 25,000 killed.

1979 ...............Iran 199 killed.

1979 ...............Yugoslavia 129 killed.

Probably the earthquake most vivid in the minds of most of us is that which we witnessed as it's results were beamed around the world via satellite onto our television screens — the Italian earthquake of 1980. I quote from the news coverage in the magazine "Now":

"The earthquake was massive and swift. In just 90 seconds of awesome power one tremor laid waste to 100 towns and villages in Italy's southern mountains. But the full scale of the horror took much longer to emerge.
First reports talked of 60 dead, then more than 100. As the authorities established contact with more and more remote mountain communities the toll, inexorable, went up. By the following morning it stood at 400. As further tremors shook the region the toll rose to 1,000 then 2,000, 3,000, 4,000 and more. Finally it was clear that this was Italy's worst earthquake for 65 years."

Of course, none of the numbers of killed I have quoted give any idea of the devastation of the earthquakes concerned. The Californian earthquake which hit San Francisco in 1906 whilst 'only' killing 500 people also devastated $400,000,000 worth of property.

In the Tokyo earthquake of 1923, in addition to the death toll of 74,000 over 700,000 houses were completely destroyed.

The 1972 Iranian earthquake, in addition to 5,000 killed, resulted in 45 complete villages being destroyed.

In Yugoslavia in 1979 the death toll was just 129 but 80,000 people were left homeless.

Would you consider that that is the fulfilment of the prediction of Jesus of Nazareth that there would be "earthquakes in diverse places"?

Though not wishing to be a prophet of doom, I must say that my reading of the ancient seers suggests to me that we shall experience an EARTHQUAKE AND PERHAPS TIDAL WAVE PHENOMENA IN THE NEXT FEW YEARS WHICH WILL BE ABSOLUTELY UNIQUE IN IT'S ORIGIN, POWER AND DESTRUCTIVE EFFECT IN DIVERSE PARTS OF THE EARTH. This will be no ordinary earthquake but a completely new kind of 'quake brought about by some cause outside of the world's ordinary earthquake experience.

Whether or not I am correct in my interpretation of the ancient seers in that matter, the fact remains that in the past 85 years more than 2,000,000 people have died as a result of earthquakes.

## "THERE SHALL BE FAMINES"

Jesus said "There shall be famines...."

This prediction should not really have come to pass, for as short a time as thirty years ago it was being confidently predicted that science would assure an adequate supply of food for all the inhabitants of the earth.

I well remember my teacher telling us that new methods of farming were being devised which, with the sophisticated farm machinery, chemical fertilisers and land reclamation schemes undertaken in a spirit of international co-operation, would ensure a surplus of food the world over. Once the profit motive had been removed from the production and distribution of food there would be plenty for all and equality of distribution — we'd see!

Of course, in those days college lecturers were not allowed to turn their lectures into party political 'broadcasts' on behalf of the Communist party though some teachers were already coming out of training college with a 'touch of the red brush'. 'Famines' indeed! Not for the first time was the Prophet of Nazareth laughed to scorn.

Just think for a moment — it does stand to reason, doesn't it, that if you removed the profit motive, remove the 'middle-man', irrigate deserts and reclaim non-agricultural land, increase the efficiency of harvesting methods, increase the efficiency of soil fertilisation, decrease the destruction of crops by pests by the use of highly sophisticated pesticides and harness the enthusiasm of the workers by turning them into collective farmers and letting them 'work for themselves' — you simply have to have an abundance of food.

Despite the theories, it is not the theorists but Jesus of Nazareth who was right. I know all common sense tells us that he should not have been right — BUT HE WAS!

1879 .... China. Thirteen million people died of FAMINE.

1894 .... China. One million people died of FAMINE.

1897 .... India. Five million people died of FAMINE.

1900 .... India. Three million two hundred and fifty thousand people died of FAMINE.

1921 .... China. Twenty million people affected by and half a million people died of FAMINE.

1922 .... U.S.S.R. Despite relief efforts of the UNITED STATES OF AMERICA twenty million people affected and five million people died of FAMINE.

1929 .... China. Three million people died of FAMINE.

1934 .... U.S.S.R. Soviet officials estimate that fifteen million Soviet citizens died of FAMINE.

So the list could go on. Time and time again the United States of America, Canada, and Australia have had to provide large scale international aid to prevent famines in the Soviet Union, India, China and African countries. It all rather stands the theory of a certain Mr. Karl Marx on it's head, doesn't it?

The extent of the Russian famine of 1947 has never been fully revealed but despite the usual aid from the United States of America the death toll was very high.

Even as I write, Russia faces another disastrous grain harvest and looks to the West — the wicked capitalist West — to provide food for them. If you ever hear anyone talking about Russia destroying America, don't believe it — they dare not — who'd grow their food for them?

## THE POPULATION EXPLOSION – FAMINE BREEDER OF THE FUTURE.

"If the 20th century ends with approximately double the population of the 1960's and with most of that population having diets no more adequate than those now existing, FAMINE WOULD BE A REAL AND CONSTANT DANGER."

So comments Encyclopaedia Britannica. Of course, the comment is valid but can we really envisage the vast masses of mankind who now live on a little fish and a few handfuls of rice continuing to be willing to do so?

We have not yet begun to appreciate the effect the population explosion will have on the ever increasing famine syndrome. Here are a few figures I read somewhere that illustrate the point:

"From the beginning of man's history it took until A.D.1850 for the population of the planet earth to reach 1 billion. It took only a further eighty years for the population of the earth to grow by a further 1 billion to 2 billion. It took only 30 years (1930-1960) for the next 1 billion to be added to the earth's population making 3 billion. Only 15 more years (1960-1975) were needed for the earth's population to increase by another billion to 4 billion. Most authorities agree that by the year 2000 there will be EIGHT BILLION people inhabiting our earth."

## HOW ARE WE GOING TO FEED EIGHT BILLION PEOPLE? 600 MILLION PEOPLE NOW LIVE IN A STATE OF FAMINE.

FAMINE! Inevitable, but we didn't recognise it even twenty years ago — the prophet Jesus foretold it nineteen hundred years ago. I don't know about you but, as I write, I am getting the awesome feeling that the Prophet of Nazareth knew far more about our generation than we do!

Of course, it would be wrong to judge the extent of famine only by the number of deaths it produces. Death is the ultimate effect of famine but there are other, and arguably, much more traumatic effects. Malnutrition when persistent can be even more punishing than the relatively quick death of actual starvation.

The United Nations Food and Agricultural Organisation estimates that in 1974 there were 460 million people in the world who could be described as living in a state of famine and, they say, the number is still RISING! It is possible that by now we are nearing the 600 million mark.

Who cares for the poor, the needy, the underdeveloped countries and the starving? Surely the Marxist countries for is that not their philosophy? Is not the Soviet Union the working man's hope, Marx the poor man's saviour and Communism the underdeveloped countries' lifeline?

Left-wing politicians, students, revolutionaries and Christian do-gooders please note that in 1963, 96% of food for the world's hungry was supplied and paid for by the United States of America and subsequently the capitalist countries of the E.E.C. have borne some of the burden. What does Communism contribute? Strife, criticism and guns!

## "THERE SHALL BE PESTILENCE".

Little did we think hunger would still be with us and to a greater degree than ever when, twenty years ago, we looked forward to the eighties. Less still did we think that pestilence would still stalk the earth to the degree it does.

Unlike earthquakes and famine, pestilence is not quite so easily written about. That pestilence does stalk the earth is undoubted, but I would not care to contend that it does so more now than it did, shall we say, two thousand years ago.

There is, of course, the oft-quoted incidence of 'Spanish flu' which is said to have killed as many people as died in battle in the First World War. I do not think that single incident ground enough to claim it as the fulfilment of the prophecy of Jesus. Of course, Jesus did qualify his prophecy of famines, pestilences and earthquakes with the words "in diverse places" — that is, they would not happen in every nation.

There is a great deal of pestilence in the world today, but I would not argue that there is enough to substantiate the belief that it is the fulfilment of prophecy.

My view is that the fulfilment of this prophecy is yet to come in it's full horror and there are signs that we may, those of us who subscribe to the belief that disease has been conquered, be in for a rude awakening.

There is, of course, the proliferation of establishments in which the most horrifying forms of germ warfare are being prepared which could plunge us into major pestilence.

Scientists, too, fear the 'super-germ'. A kind of 'rogue-evolution' seems to make it possible for bacteria and germs to develop their own resistance to our methods of destroying them. Diseases we thought had been conquered are making their reappearance, not alarmingly yet it is true, but significantly. Those valiant men who have fought back the ravages of disease are only too aware that there is the possibility that something unexpected may emerge.

Let us remember that it is the resistance we humans have built over the years which saves us from many killer diseases. There are still remote tribes in the world to whom the common cold is a killer disease — they have not been in contact with the germs enough to build up resistance to them. Should something appear to which we have lost our resistance or a mutation, perhaps, to which we have never been resistant, the speed of modern travel would ensure it's worldwide dissemination speedily.

Meanwhile, pestilence continues in those parts of the world where, because of administrative or political difficulties, drugs cannot be distributed. Some regard it as unfortunate that the production of drugs is still, to a great extent, dependent upon the 'profit motive'. In some ways it is, perhaps, regrettable, but I must return again to the theme that the record of the capitalist countries in supplying drugs and medical aid to underdeveloped peoples, though far too little, is so much better than the record of either the Communist countries — where drugs are allegedly produced not for profit but for people — and so much better than the efforts of the oil-rich Arab countries that the record of Britain, the United States of America, is eminently defensible.

"Famines, pestilences and earthquakes in diverse places...."

Surely a truly remarkable picture of our world in this end time.

# A RAPID GROWTH IN EDUCATION AND TRAVEL WAS TO PRECEDE THE COMING OF THE MESSIAH.

The prophet Daniel, writing 560B.C., foretold that the second coming of the Messiah to earth would be preceded by a rapid increase in knowledge and travel:

*But thou, O Daniel, shut up the words, and seal the book, EVEN TO THE TIME OF THE END; many shall run to and fro, and knowledge shall increase.*

Book of Daniel 12:4

It's as though the prophetic eye of Daniel was piercing 2500 years of time. "Many shall run to and fro", you can see it happening any day in the rush hour of our big cities, on our motorways, in our airports. Since 1917 not only the number of people who travel has increased but the speed at which they travel has increased.

Is it not true that little progress had really been made in travel from the invention of the wheel to the beginning of this century? Suddenly, at the very time in history the prophet foretold it would happen, 'the time of the end', a great leap forward in travel methods took place. Fast cars, fast planes and fast boats caused men to move about the earth's surface at ever greater speeds and in ever greater numbers.

Once again, I do not have to produce figures to show how many passenger hours are being flown today compared with, say, fifty years ago. I don't have to tell you how many more miles of road there are or how many more cars there are — you know it because the evidence is there for you to see every day of your life.

## "KNOWLEDGE SHALL INCREASE".

What comment need I make? Fifty years ago we had horse-drawn delivery carts, horse-drawn funeral corteges, horse-drawn ploughs. A hundred years ago we had horse-drawn fire engines and travel, unless by rail, was by horse-drawn carriage. Now we have the space-shuttle and aircraft capable of taking us around the world at supersonic speeds.

The advances in knowledge in the past hundred years have been so rapid and varied that it would take a library of books even to touch on the extent to which man has pushed the frontiers of knowledge either back or forward — according to the view you take.

Nothing to speak of happened for thousands of years and then, suddenly, at exactly the time the prophet foretold, all this has happened. Is it just chance or an indication that we really are living in the end time when the Messiah is about to return?

## THE RETURN OF THE JEWS TO PALESTINE TO PRECEDE THE MESSIAH'S SECOND COMING.

I have explained how the 'fig tree' is the symbol of the House of Judah (the Jews) whilst 'the vine' is the symbol of the House of Israel.

Having dwelt on this point at some length in another place I shall only mention the return of the Jews to Palestine as being one of the signs of the Messiah's imminent return briefly. Jesus said:

> ... and shall gather together his elect from the four winds, from one end of heaven to the other. Now learn a parable of the fig tree; When it's branch is yet tender, and putteth forth leaves, ye know that summer is near; So likewise ye, when ye shall see all these things, know that it is near, EVEN AT THE DOORS.
> Matthew 24: 31, 32

The 'fig tree' has put forth her leaves in our generation. The tree that was 'withered' when Christ was on earth has now sent forth it's shoots. At exactly the time the prophet said it would.

## POLITICAL TRENDS PRIOR TO THE SECOND COMING OF THE MESSIAH.

I have mentioned the prophecy of James in which he prophecies the difficulties which the rich will encounter before the second coming of the Messiah but I will repeat the quotation:

*Come now, ye rich men, weep and howl for your miseries that shall come upon you.*
*Your riches are corrupted and your garments are motheaten.*
*Your gold and silver cankered, and the rust of them shall be a witness against you, and shall eat your flesh as it were fire. YE HAVE HEAPED TREASURE TOGETHER FOR THE LAST DAYS. Behold the hire of the labourers who have reaped down your fields, which is of you kept back by fraud, crieth.*

The Book of the prophet James 5: 1, 2,3

Revolution after revolution has taken place which has not only caused the rich to be dispossessed of their riches but imprisoned, tortured and killed because of them. All over the world riches have brought upon their possessors a reason to 'weep and howl for the miseries which have come upon them'. The French Revolution, the Russian Revolution, the revolutions in African and Asian states have all brought retribution upon the rich of these countries.

Even in those countries where no such bloody revolutions have take place the bloodless revolutions in Britain and other European countries have caused the rich great concern.

Does not the prophecy of James foretell exactly what is happening in our generation? Can you not see the mass of industrial unrest which is taking place in almost every industrialised country in the world as 'the hire of the labourers crying'?

## THE GREAT SYMBOLIC SIGNS OF THE NEAR RETURN OF THE MESSIAH.

The signs given of the near return of the Messiah by the prophets I have so far mentioned have been the obvious and easily discernible ones. If you will re-read the chapter "Breaking the Code", however, you will sée that:

The Sun denotes main rulers.
The Moon denotes those who have power by consent of main rulers.
The Stars are the various smaller powers.
The powers of the heavens are the political systems of the world.

In the light of that read again the prophecy of Jesus which speaks of events in the political world prior to the second coming of the Messiah:

> Immediately after the tribulation of those days shall the sun be darkened, and the moon shall not give it's light, and the stars shall fall from heaven, and the powers of the heavens shall be shaken, and THEN shall appear the sign of the Son of man in heaven ...
>
> *Matthew 24:29*

"Immediately after the tribulation of those days.." The tribulation of what days? The context shows it means "Immediately after the times of the Gentiles have been fulfilled" there would be a great shaking in the traditional powers which had governed the world.

Is it by chance that we have seen the greatest social upheaval since the year 1917 that has taken place in the history of the world? Maps change so quickly these days that last year's Atlas of the World is out of date before the ink is dry.

We live in the age of revolution. It is worth obtaining a good history of the world and going through it carefully to see how the great ones in the firmament of government have been dislodged. Kings have departed, thrones tumbled and empires been forced to relinquish possession of their dominions. A British Prime Minister once coined the phrase "The wind of change is blowing through Africa". He was right, but not only Africa, that wind of change has blown through the world. Everywhere nations are emerging, people are casting off the chains of centuries, often unfortunately to be shackled by even heavier chains. The old order of government has passed away in many countries and will soon pass away in others as a tidal wave of revolution and anarchy sweeps the world.

## RELIGIOUS SIGNS OF THE MESSIAH'S SECOND COMING.

> *Now the Spirit speaketh expressly that, in the latter times, some shall depart from the faith, giving heed to seducing spirits, and doctrines of demons.*
>
> Timothy 4:1

The prophet and apostle Paul, looking down to our day, foresaw the time when there would be a great departure from the Christian faith and a great turning to satanism.

Since the First World War there has been a progressive 'departing' from the faith as Jesus Christ taught it and as his apostles taught it. All one needs, it seems, is a white robe and a considerable growth of greying whiskers and òne is in the "Messiah business".

Our newspapers are full of incidents of what they like to term 'religious brainwashing'. Is that really what it is, one wonders, or is it perhaps something more akin to what the ancient seers called 'devil possession'?

Perhaps the classic example of a counterfeit 'Messiah' wielding strange and almost superhuman powers over his followers was the Reverend Jim

Jones, an American 'evangelist' who was able to persuade over 900 men, women and children to partake of a strange communion service. It was a service in the jungle of Guyana, where Jones' followers had gone with him from America to set up a commune. Such was the supernatural, unnatural or supernormal power this demon of a man had over his 'disciples' that they partook of the final communion with him — a communion of death — they all with one consent joined him in drinking poison.

There seems to be a fascination today regarding satanism. Black Magic is experiencing a resurgence as is it's associate practice White Magic. The 90th Edition (1981) of Pears Cyclopaedia has the following comment:

"White magic has become fashionable with many young people, no doubt as a result of the almost total collapse of the authority of orthodox religion."

Those words in Pear's well respected publication unwittingly virtually repeat the words written by the ancient seer nineteen hundred years ago: "...in the latter times, some shall depart from the faith, giving heed to seducing spirits.."

Not only the United States of America, but the whole world was shocked by the Sharon Tate/Manson case in which devotion to satanism caused one of the most macabre bloodbaths of the century.

One does not have to be a prude to recognise that evil is in the ascendance in the days in which we live. Don Stanton tells us that in the United States alone five million people openly worship Satan and in one city there are six hundred 'churches' dedicated to devil worship. In Sydney, Australia, it is said that 50% of all high school students have experimented with satanism.

Anton Szandor La Vey founded the Church of Satan and published 'The Satanic Bible' — by 1975 it had sold more than a million copies.

## THE MESSIAH'S SECOND COMING – THE BIG LAUGH.

The prophet Peter foretold that the subject of the second coming of the Messiah would become a 'big laugh' before he actually returned. When you read the following prophecy, written nineteen hundred years ago, do you recognise the attitude of any of your friends? Do you, perhaps, recognise in it your own attitude as you have read this chapter?

*Knowing this first, that there shall come in the last days scoffers, walking after their own lusts, and saying, Where is the promise of his coming? For since the fathers fell asleep, all things continue as they were from the beginning of creation.*

2 Peter 3: 3, 4

Even the attitude of we who live in this, the twentieth century, was foreseen by the ancient seers.

## THE WARNINGS OF THE ANCIENT SEERS AGAINST PREDICTING THE DATE OF THE MESSIAH'S SECOND COMING.

The disciples of Jesus had no doubt about the fact that the second coming of the Messiah would result in the restoration of the kingdom to Israel. His return to earth would be at the time when the two parts of Israel, the House of Judah and the House of Israel, would be reunited. There was to be one King and one Kingdom.

When, therefore, the disciples of Jesus asked him the question: "Lord, wilt thou at this time restore again the kingdom to Israel " He replied, "It is not for you to know the times or the seasons, which the Father hath in his power." Acts 1: 6, 7.

He was equally emphatic on another occasion when he said:

> *Verily I say unto you, This generation shall not pass, till all these things be fulfilled ...But of that day and hour knoweth no man, no, not the angels of heaven, but my Father only.*
>
> Matthew 24: 34 & 36

There are two things said there with equal emphasis, the first is that we shall be able to know the 'generation' in which the Messiah is to return to earth for the second time but no-one should presume to fix the day, the hour or for that matter, the year.

The doctrine of the second coming of the Messiah has been brought into disrepute by 'date fixers' but it has also been brought into disrepute by the default of those who at the other extreme have neglected to teach this subject which is so emphatically taught by the ancient seers.

## THE MYSTERIOUS VISION OF GEORGE WASHINGTON.

George Washington told Anthony Sherman of a vivid vision he, Washington, had had one winter's afternoon. The vision was so vivid that Washington was unable to wipe it from his mind.

In the vision George Washington saw America facing three great perils before the 'second coming' of the Messiah — an event in which he firmly believed.

The first peril he saw was the War of Independence and what he saw gave him confidence even during the darkest days of that war. There were many dark hours for the American forces during that conflict, and Washington suffered severe defeats, but he was always confident because in his vision he had seen the dark cloud which enveloped America moving away eastward.

A second great peril was a spectre which approached from Africa. He saw this ominous cloud hanging over the towns and cities of America and he saw American at war with American. This vision was, of course, fulfilled in the Civil War of 1861-65. Though he foresaw this tragic Civil War, he died some seventy years before it happened.

The Civil War was, as we all know, brought about by the differing attitudes of the North and South of the United States of America to the question of slavery. It did, indeed, have it's origins in Africa just as Washington had foretold.

Perhaps the most horrifying part of Washington's vision was the last part. Washington describe the vision as "appalling". Thick, black clouds came over America from Europe, Asia and Africa. Separate at first, they ultimately joined together into one great threatening cloud. I quote Washington:

> "And throughout this mass there gleamed A DARK RED LIGHT by which I saw hordes of armed men who, moving with the cloud, marched by land and sailed by sea to America, which country was enveloped in the volume of the cloud. I dimly saw these vast armies devastating the whole country and burn the villages, towns and cities that I had beheld springing up."

It was at this point that Washington saw divine intervention saving the United States from destruction.

I include George Washington's prophecy here as a matter of interest and because it coincides with what is happening in our day and age. Hatred of the United States of America is rife in Europe, Asia and Africa — it is often said that people find it impossible to forgive their benefactors. The continent of America, apart from the United States itself, is in ferment and Communist armies are on the mainland. Cuba has for many years now, been a threat to United States security. There can be little doubt that the communised masses of the world will soon be prepared to hurl themselves at what the Iranians call "The Great Satan".

George Washington saw divine intervention saving America — in the personal return of the Messiah, one wonders? If I were an American I think I would ponder hard and long on the implications of Washington's vision.

That vision was in the 1700's — now let me refer you to the Daily Telegraph of December 4th 1979:

> "Col. Gaddafi, Libyan leader, spoke of signs of 'an international revolution against America' in an interview published just hours before the American Embassy in Tripoli was sacked. The seizure of hostages, occupation and mining of the U.S. Embassy in

Tehran and attacks against American diplomatic missions in Pakistan, India, Bangladesh, were all part of the same revolution, he told the Italian writer, Signora Oriana Fallaci.''

The West should not underestimate Col. Gaddafi. If Britain and America have a paramount failing it is that we always consider leaders of genius as being the inferiors of our own leaders. Gaddafi knows what he is doing and he knows where he is going and that's more than can be said for a succession of British, European and American governments.

## THE SECOND COMING OF THE MESSIAH – IS IT CREDIBLE?

Credibility is largely, like beauty, in the mind of the observer. I commenced this chapter by admitting freely that I find the concept intellectually unacceptable; my mind tells me that this is some kind of science fiction theory. The history of the 'second comers' and their past prognostications does nothing to assure me of the 'second coming' of the Messiah being a possibility and certainly not a probability.

There is, however, this large body of evidence that the ancient seers have never been wrong in their predictions and I must therefore ask myself why they should be wrong in this, their final great prediction. All the circumstances they foretold would take place prior to the second coming of the Messiah have taken place — it would be quite unreasonable to assume that on this one occasion they will be wrong.

The atheist, of course, is quite consistent if he says no such event as the second coming of the Messiah is possible. No-one else, however, can make such a statement and maintain any degree of intellectual honesty. Anyone who is prepared to accept that there is anything which may be described as an 'it' 'out there' must be prepared to admit the possibility that one day the 'it' will decide to visit this planet.

There is a great degree of dishonesty regarding this subject, for only a few weeks ago I spoke to a fairly high-ranking bank manager who was quite prepared to accept that one day 'people from other planets' would land on earth but could not accept the possibility of there being a second coming of the Messiah.

Let us recapitulate the things the ancient seers said would happen prior to the second coming of the Messiah:

Jerusalem was to be delivered from the hands of the Gentiles— this would usher in the final years of earth's history. That prophecy was fulfilled in 1917.

Against the predictions of the experts, the societies of the world were to become ever increasingly violent — they have.

Famines, pestilence and earthquakes were to take a high toll of life and property — they have.

There was to be a rapid growth in the level of education immediately before the Messiah came again — there has been.

A massive increase in travel was predicted — there has been a dramatic increase in both the speed of travel and the numbers of people travelling.

The Jews were to return to Palestine and Palestine was to flourish — that has happened.

The end time was to be heralded by an uprising of organised labour — we have seen that happen in every free country in the world.

Kingdoms were to vanish, kings be overthrown and the normally accepted methods of government dislocated — all that has happened.

There was to be a falling away from belief in the Christian faith — that has happened.

An increase in 'Devil Worship' and associate practices was to take place — that, too, has happened.

There was to be widespread cynicism about the possibility of the 'second coming' taking place — there is.

The ancient seers foretold that the Messiah would come to earth and intervene in earth's problems. One of the reasons for his coming was to be to save the human race from complete and utter extinction.
For the first time in the history of the world the complete and utter destruction of the human race and planet earth is within the capability of mankind. Never have the perils facing the human race been so many, so varied or so potentially catastrophic: As the prophet of Nazareth put it:

*For then shall be great tribulation, such as was not since the beginning of the world to this time, no, nor ever shall be. And except those days shall be shortened, THERE SHALL NO FLESH BE SAVED; but for the elects sake those days shall be shortened.*

Matthew 24: 21, 22

In the days when Jesus of Nazareth spoke those words there was no possibility of the human race destroying itself — wars were still fought with swords. Not until 1945 did the world have an inkling that man would have the capability of world destruction and until then the prediction of the Nazarene had sounded a gross exaggeration.

Two men, speaking almost two thousand years apart, one a wilderness preacher claiming to be the Messiah/God/King and the other a twentieth century scientist:

"I think human life is threatened as never before in the history of this planet. Not just by one peril, but by many perils that are all working together AND COMING TO A HEAD AT ABOUT THE SAME TIME. And that time lies very close to the year 2000. I am one of those scientists who finds it hard to see how the human race is to bring itself much past the year 2000."

Dr. George Wald of Harvard University
Nobel Prize Winner

What do I think in my humble opinion — well, I must admit to never having had a 'humble' opinion in my life! So, as the Americans say — "Here's sticking my neck out!" Having studied the predictions of the ancient seers — many more predictions than I have had space to deal with in this book — I am of the opinion that there is about to be an intervention in the affairs of this planet by that being the prophets called the 'Lord'.

Most of the other predictions have already come to pass, why should not this final prediction of the coming of the Messiah?

If I am wrong, then I am sure that Jesus Christ of Nazareth and Dr. George Wald of Harvard University will both be right.

# 19.
# 1992 –
# Year of
# Destiny?

"I am one of those scientists who finds it hard to see how the human race is to bring itself much past the year 2000."

Dr. George Wald of Harvard University
Nobel Prize Winner

"When shall these things be, and what will be the sign ... of the end of the world?"

Disciples of Jesus, speaking to Jesus when He was on earth.

From the dates given by the ancient seers it would appear that an event of world-shattering importance is to take place in the year 1992. Is it not indicative of the gravity of the days in which we live that as few as twenty years ago those men who walked the streets with placards proclaiming "The end of the world is nigh" were laughed to scorn, and yet now there is a large consensus of opinion in scientific circles that this may well be so. Such pessimistic prognostications are no longer the preserve of the eccentric, religious banner-carrier, they are the real fears of Nobel prize winners such as Dr. George Wald.

Nothing really changes, does it? Two thousand years ago, sitting on a mountain overlooking the city of Jerusalem, the disciples of Jesus were talking about the very thing that modern science fears, the very thing that modern politicians desperately try, through their international councils, to avoid — the end of the world.

There are those who firmly reject the fixing of dates for future events from the predictions of the prophets. It must be admitted that they have something of a case, for often the fate of the reckless projector of dates is to be proven wrong. The date passes without incident and the credibility of prophet, interpreter and prophecy alike, suffers.

Some past failures, however, should not blind us to the successes of the many who have correctly deduced from the writings of the prophets the time scale of future events. I have mentioned in previous chapters Dr. Grattan Guiness, for one. Just as it is wrong to recklessly give dates of future events, so it is altogether wrong to ignore the persistent exhortations of the prophets that we should study the times and the seasons. As we have seen, the prophecies of Daniel abound with the giving of time periods as does also the Book of Revelation. The giving of such time periods is invariably followed, or preceded, by exhortations to the reader to "understand". Can it be reasonable for us to accept, therefore, that the predictions were to remain forever obscure? If we are not to understand the meaning of the dates given by Daniel, then what can be made of his assertion that in the last days "The wise shall understand"?

Returning to our original hypothesis, if there is an 'It out there' and that 'It' has been attempting all these years, in diverse ways, through people spiritually attuned to hear his voice, to contact the human race, and if he has succeeded in contacting the human race through the ancient seers is it comprehensible that he would not comment upon these, the most traumatic days in human history?

We live in perilous times. That is not something we glean from Isaiah, or Ezekiel, or Daniel, or Jesus of Nazareth, that is something of which we are made aware constantly by the mass media, an opinion which is backed by the initiates of almost every science known to mankind.

We cannot but come to the conclusion from our reading of the ancient seers, especially Daniel, that the year 1992 will prove to be a year of destiny, a year which will have had no parallel in importance since that year nigh on two thousand years ago when, in the shepherd's fields of Bethlehem, angelic voices are said to have welcomed the first coming of Jesus Christ of Nazareth.

# THE OLIVET DISCOURSE.

I am sorry, but here I have to take you over old ground because we have discussed so much in this book that I am sure you will appreciate having your memory refreshed.

You will remember that in His reply to that memorable tripartite question, asked of Him by the disciples on the Mount of Olives, "When shall these things be? And what shall be the sign of thy coming and of the end of the age?", Jesus made reference to the writings of Daniel, the Old Testament prophet.

Jerusalem, He said, was to be trodden down of the gentiles until the 'times' of the gentiles were fulfilled. That was to be a continuation of the then existing state of things for, when He spoke, Jerusalem was already trodden down by the gentiles.

There was to be another happening, however, a happening which He put in the future, that is the future to His time.

*When, ye therefore, shall see the abomination of the desolation, spoken of by Daniel the prophet, stand in the holy place [whosoever readeth, let him understand], then let them who are in Judea flee into the mountains;*

Matthew 24:15

I do not want to dwell upon the facts which must now be well-known to you, facts which are accepted by most students of prophecy, that is that the 'times' of the gentiles represented the 'seven times' punishment period pronounced upon Judah. I will remind you, however, that the 'seven times' represents a period of 2520 years and that that period commenced with the Jewish captivity under Nebuchadnezzar and ended 2520 years later, precisely as predicted, in the momentous year 1917.

Please concentrate your mind on that year 1917, for it has a much deeper prophetic significance than one would at first think, a much deeper significance than we have yet dealt with elsewhere in this book.

## THE ABOMINATION SPOKEN OF BY DANIEL.

In the last chapter of his great prophetic book, Daniel is instructed to "shut up the words, and seal the book, even unto the time of the end;" Daniel 12:4. Note well that the instruction is not that the book should be sealed forever, but specifically "unto the time of the end". The plain corollary of the statement that the book should be sealed unto the time of the end is that at 'the time of the end' the book would be unsealed and therefore it's meaning made plain. I have tried to show you that we are living in what the prophets called the "time of the end", and perhaps you are, by now, convinced of that. If you are, then you must also believe that

313

now is the time when mankind will come to a knowledge of the writings of the ancient seers and a knowledge of the eternal purpose of whoever inspired their writings, such as has been denied to mankind throughout the ages until now. NOW, therefore, is the time we should be searching for the hidden meanings of those things that the great predictors of old foretold.

There has been much debate among students of prophecy about the identity of the 'abomination' that would make desolate. We have seen that the word 'abomination' in itself is not very significant despite the imaginative constructions which some have put upon it. We have seen that any non-Israelite standing in the Holy Place would have been an abomination to the Jews of Daniel's and Jesus' day.

We have seen that the abomination of the desolation spoken of by Jesus and Daniel was to stand in the Holy Place and we have identified that Holy Place as being a specific place on earth, the place where the Dome of the Rock now stands.

## THE THREE DATES OF DANIEL.

In his final chapter, Daniel gives us three dates which, he says, will bring us to the time of the end. One of these dates presents us with one of the most profound mysteries of ancient prediction.

Daniel tells us that after being instructed to close the book until 'the time of the end', he saw two other persons and he reports their conversation thus:

> *And one said to the man clothed in linen, who was above the waters of the river, How long shall it be to the end of these wonders?*

There are then three time periods given:

1. *"It shall be for time, times and an half;"*
   (Verse 7). That period is, of course, half of seven times of three and a half times. Seven times punishment therefore being 2520 years, this period must be 1260 years.

2. *"And from the time that the daily sacrifice shall be taken away, and the abomination that maketh desolate set up, there shall be a thousand two hundred and ninety days."* (Verse 11).
   The 'days' referred to are, of course, days of years. This time period, therefore, is 1290 years.

3. *"Blessed is he that waiteth, and cometh to the thousand three hundred and five and thirty days."* (Verse 12).
   This period represents 1335 years.

We have seen how the times of the gentiles ended in 1917, I have commented too, on the mysterious events which surrounded the deliverance of Jerusalem by the British troops. Dividing 2520 years, the times of the gentiles, by two we have, of course, 1260 years spoken of by Daniel. It was, in fact, 1260 years from the time of Nebuchadnezzar, who took Judah into captivity, to the capture of Jerusalem by the armies of Islam. It is 1260 years, too, from the time of Omar, who took the city of Jerusalem, to 1917. I would suggest to you that if that is a coincidence it is a very amazing coincidence indeed.

We have, in a past chapter, identified the end of Daniel's period of 1260 years as being the year A.D.1917. Two time periods were fulfilled in that year of 1917, the seven times, that is 2520 years from the date that Nebuchadnezzar took Judah into captivity, and the 1260 years from the date that the abomination, spoken of by Daniel the prophet, was set up and began to stand in the Holy Place.

Now let us refresh our memories as to the period of 1290 years given by Daniel. You will remember, and you won't need a calculator to work it out for yourself, that 1290 expires just 30 years after 1260. We have seen how in 1947/48 the Jewish State of Israel came into being. On 29th November, 1947, the United Nations adopted a resolution calling for a Jewish State in the land of Israel. On 14th May, 1948, the Jewish State of Israel was proclaimed and came into being. So we have the two dates, 1917/18 (remember A.D. years actually overlap A.M. years) in which Jerusalem was delivered and 1947/48 in which the Jewish State of Israel was set up.

There remains a mystery, however! What of the 1335 year period mentioned by Daniel? We have seen how if reckoned as being expressed in Moslem years it was, in fact, the year 1917. But why should two of Daniel's dates be in A.D. years and the third be Hegira (Moslem) dates? There seems to be no satisfactory explanation. Did Daniel insert the date 1335 to indicate the identity of the abomination? Was he, as so many believe, giving a Hegira date as a final gesture so that the abomination could be identified? There seems to be little reason for him to do that, for the abomination can be identified quite clearly, as I have said, by the fact it is standing, and has stood, since it was built, in the Holy Place. No other building stands in the Holy Place, no other person stands in the Holy Place. There can be no doubt that Daniel's prophecy is fulfilled in the Dome of the Rock.

## A FALSE PROPHECY – A FALSE PROPHET?

In the Book of Revelation, John writes of a person he calls "the False Prophet". He is quite distinct from the "many false prophets" which were to arise. The false prophet is of such importance that he is shown as being one of the three leading influences, together with the 'Beast' and the 'Dragon' who, at the end time, gather the world together to the Battle of

Armageddon which is described as the 'Battle of that great day of God Almighty'.

It seems ridiculous to contemplate a being which is singled out for the title of The False Prophet, a supreme false prophet, without him being associated with a very important false prophecy. Undoubtedly the deliverance of Jerusalem by the armies of Britain in 1917 ushered in the time of the end when the actors in the final act of the drama of the ages were to appear on the world stage. The establishment of the Jewish State in the land of Israel was a further fulfilment of the prognostications of the ancient seers.

Should it then not be so that the great false prophecy would be associated with the year 1917 and could it not be, also, that the year of the Hegira 1335 was, in fact, the great false prophecy of all times — a false prophecy which has misled a generation of prophetic students into believing that the 1260 date, which was fulfilled in 1917, and the 1335 date were one and the same year?

Despite their importance, the deliverance of Jerusalem in 1917 and the setting up of the Jewish State of Israel in 1948, are not the most important events in prophecy — the most important events are yet to come. I cannot believe, therefore, that Daniel's dates finish in 1948. Inevitably I am brought to the conclusion that the 1335 date is not a Hegira date, but was intended to follow on in chronological order from the 1260 and 1290 dates. The Hegira date, coinciding with 1917, is either a deliberate act of confusion by some sinister power to blind us to the relevance of the most important date in the prognostications of the ancient seers, or it is the supreme coincidence of the ages.

A quick calculation shows that if 1260 is 1917/18 then 1290 corresponds to 1947/48. We know that on the first date, 1917, Jerusalem was delivered by the British army. We know that on the second date, 1948, the Jewish State of Israel came into being. The year 1335, if it follows on to the 1260 and 1290 dates, in chronological order, will expire in 1992/3.

If that supposition is correct, then we live in a decade that is to be both traumatic and exciting, for spectacular, political and economic events are to take place.

Is Dr. George Wald of Harvard University correct? Can our civilisation not last to the year 2000? Are we about to see the final fulfilment of the predictions given by the Prophet of Nazareth in response to the question of His disciples, asked on that far away mountain those many years ago?

Whatever the answer to those questions, humanity can take heart from the words of the prophet:

*Blessed is he that cometh to the one thousand three hundred and thirty five days.*

Right now I think the world can use a little hope.